The summarie of Englishe chronicles (latelye collected and published) abridged and continued til this present moneth of Nouember in the yeare of our Lord God, 1567 / by J.S. (1567)

John Stow

The summarie of Englishe chronicles (latelye collected and published) abridged and continued til this present moneth of Nouember in the yeare of our Lord God, 1567 / by J.S.

Stow, John, 1525?-1605.
Date of publication suggested by STC (2nd ed.).
Signatures: [A]8 a4 B-2C8 2D2.
Marginal notes.
Numerous errors in paging.
Formerly STC 23321.
Imperfect: torn, with slight loss of print; signatures J1-P1 from defective Bodleian Library copy spliced at end.
[24], 100 [i.e. 400], [3] p.
[London] : Imprinted at London in Fletestrete nere to S. Dunstones church, by Tho[mas] Marshe, [1567]
STC (2nd ed.) / 23325.5
English
Reproduction of the original in the Harvard University Library

Early English Books Online (EEBO) Editions

Imagine holding history in your hands.

Now you can. Digitally preserved and previously accessible only through libraries as Early English Books Online, this rare material is now available in single print editions. Thousands of books written between 1475 and 1700 and ranging from religion to astronomy, medicine to music, can be delivered to your doorstep in individual volumes of high-quality historical reproductions.

We have been compiling these historic treasures for more than 70 years. Long before such a thing as "digital" even existed, ProQuest founder Eugene Power began the noble task of preserving the British Museum's collection on microfilm. He then sought out other rare and endangered titles, providing unparalleled access to these works and collaborating with the world's top academic institutions to make them widely available for the first time. This project furthers that original vision.

These texts have now made the full journey -- from their original printing-press versions available only in rare-book rooms to online library access to new single volumes made possible by the partnership between artifact preservation and modern printing technology. A portion of the proceeds from every book sold supports the libraries and institutions that made this collection possible, and that still work to preserve these invaluable treasures passed down through time.

This is history, traveling through time since the dawn of printing to your own personal library.

Initial Proquest EEBO Print Editions collections include:

Early Literature

This comprehensive collection begins with the famous Elizabethan Era that saw such literary giants as Chaucer, Shakespeare and Marlowe, as well as the introduction of the sonnet. Traveling through Jacobean and Restoration literature, the highlight of this series is the Pollard and Redgrave 1475-1640 selection of the rarest works from the English Renaissance.

Early Documents of World History

This collection combines early English perspectives on world history with documentation of Parliament records, royal decrees and military documents that reveal the delicate balance of Church and State in early English government. For social historians, almanacs and calendars offer insight into daily life of common citizens. This exhaustively complete series presents a thorough picture of history through the English Civil War.

Historical Almanacs

Historically, almanacs served a variety of purposes from the more practical, such as planting and harvesting crops and plotting nautical routes, to predicting the future through the movements of the stars. This collection provides a wide range of consecutive years of "almanacks" and calendars that depict a vast array of everyday life as it was several hundred years ago.

Early History of Astronomy & Space

Humankind has studied the skies for centuries, seeking to find our place in the universe. Some of the most important discoveries in the field of astronomy were made in these texts recorded by ancient stargazers, but almost as impactful were the perspectives of those who considered their discoveries to be heresy. Any independent astronomer will find this an invaluable collection of titles arguing the truth of the cosmic system.

Early History of Industry & Science

Acting as a kind of historical Wall Street, this collection of industry manuals and records explores the thriving industries of construction; textile, especially wool and linen; salt; livestock; and many more.

Early English Wit, Poetry & Satire

The power of literary device was never more in its prime than during this period of history, where a wide array of political and religious satire mocked the status quo and poetry called humankind to transcend the rigors of daily life through love, God or principle. This series comments on historical patterns of the human condition that are still visible today.

Early English Drama & Theatre

This collection needs no introduction, combining the works of some of the greatest canonical writers of all time, including many plays composed for royalty such as Queen Elizabeth I and King Edward VI. In addition, this series includes history and criticism of drama, as well as examinations of technique.

Early History of Travel & Geography

Offering a fascinating view into the perception of the world during the sixteenth and seventeenth centuries, this collection includes accounts of Columbus's discovery of the Americas and encompasses most of the Age of Discovery, during which Europeans and their descendants intensively explored and mapped the world. This series is a wealth of information from some the most groundbreaking explorers.

Early Fables & Fairy Tales

This series includes many translations, some illustrated, of some of the most well-known mythologies of today, including Aesop's Fables and English fairy tales, as well as many Greek, Latin and even Oriental parables and criticism and interpretation on the subject.

Early Documents of Language & Linguistics

The evolution of English and foreign languages is documented in these original texts studying and recording early philology from the study of a variety of languages including Greek, Latin and Chinese, as well as multilingual volumes, to current slang and obscure words. Translations from Latin, Hebrew and Aramaic, grammar treatises and even dictionaries and guides to translation make this collection rich in cultures from around the world.

Early History of the Law

With extensive collections of land tenure and business law "forms" in Great Britain, this is a comprehensive resource for all kinds of early English legal precedents from feudal to constitutional law, Jewish and Jesuit law, laws about public finance to food supply and forestry, and even "immoral conditions." An abundance of law dictionaries, philosophy and history and criticism completes this series.

Early History of Kings, Queens and Royalty

This collection includes debates on the divine right of kings, royal statutes and proclamations, and political ballads and songs as related to a number of English kings and queens, with notable concentrations on foreign rulers King Louis IX and King Louis XIV of France, and King Philip II of Spain. Writings on ancient rulers and royal tradition focus on Scottish and Roman kings, Cleopatra and the Biblical kings Nebuchadnezzar and Solomon.

Early History of Love, Marriage & Sex

Human relationships intrigued and baffled thinkers and writers well before the postmodern age of psychology and self-help. Now readers can access the insights and intricacies of Anglo-Saxon interactions in sex and love, marriage and politics, and the truth that lies somewhere in between action and thought.

Early History of Medicine, Health & Disease

This series includes fascinating studies on the human brain from as early as the 16th century, as well as early studies on the physiological effects of tobacco use. Anatomy texts, medical treatises and wound treatment are also discussed, revealing the exponential development of medical theory and practice over more than two hundred years.

Early History of Logic, Science and Math

The "hard sciences" developed exponentially during the 16th and 17th centuries, both relying upon centuries of tradition and adding to the foundation of modern application, as is evidenced by this extensive collection. This is a rich collection of practical mathematics as applied to business, carpentry and geography as well as explorations of mathematical instruments and arithmetic; logic and logicians such as Aristotle and Socrates; and a number of scientific disciplines from natural history to physics.

Early History of Military, War and Weaponry

Any professional or amateur student of war will thrill at the untold riches in this collection of war theory and practice in the early Western World. The Age of Discovery and Enlightenment was also a time of great political and religious unrest, revealed in accounts of conflicts such as the Wars of the Roses.

Early History of Food

This collection combines the commercial aspects of food handling, preservation and supply to the more specific aspects of canning and preserving, meat carving, brewing beer and even candy-making with fruits and flowers, with a large resource of cookery and recipe books. Not to be forgotten is a "the great eater of Kent," a study in food habits.

Early History of Religion

From the beginning of recorded history we have looked to the heavens for inspiration and guidance. In these early religious documents, sermons, and pamphlets, we see the spiritual impact on the lives of both royalty and the commoner. We also get insights into a clergy that was growing ever more powerful as a political force. This is one of the world's largest collections of religious works of this type, revealing much about our interpretation of the modern church and spirituality.

Early Social Customs

Social customs, human interaction and leisure are the driving force of any culture. These unique and quirky works give us a glimpse of interesting aspects of day-to-day life as it existed in an earlier time. With books on games, sports, traditions, festivals, and hobbies it is one of the most fascinating collections in the series.

The BiblioLife Network

This project was made possible in part by the BiblioLife Network (BLN), a project aimed at addressing some of the huge challenges facing book preservationists around the world. The BLN includes libraries, library networks, archives, subject matter experts, online communities and library service providers. We believe every book ever published should be available as a high-quality print reproduction; printed on-demand anywhere in the world. This insures the ongoing accessibility of the content and helps generate sustainable revenue for the libraries and organizations that work to preserve these important materials.
The following book is in the "public domain" and represents an authentic reproduction of the text as printed by the original publisher. While we have attempted to accurately maintain the integrity of the original work, there are sometimes problems with the original work or the micro-film from which the books were digitized. This can result in minor errors in reproduction. Possible imperfections include missing and blurred pages, poor pictures, markings and other reproduction issues beyond our control. Because this work is culturally important, we have made it available as part of our commitment to protecting, preserving, and promoting the world's literature.

GUIDE TO FOLD-OUTS MAPS and OVERSIZED IMAGES

The book you are reading was digitized from microfilm captured over the past thirty to forty years. Years after the creation of the original microfilm, the book was converted to digital files and made available in an online database.
In an online database, page images do not need to conform to the size restrictions found in a printed book. When converting these images back into a printed bound book, the page sizes are standardized in ways that maintain the detail of the original. For large images, such as fold-out maps, the original page image is split into two or more pages

Guidelines used to determine how to split the page image follows:

- Some images are split vertically; large images require vertical and horizontal splits.
- For horizontal splits, the content is split left to right.
- For vertical splits, the content is split from top to bottom.
- For both vertical and horizontal splits, the image is processed from top left to bottom right.

S. 2*

[illegible] Aug

[illegible]
[illegible]
[illegible] 1937

The Sum
marie of Englishe
Chronicles.

(Latelye collected and published) abridged and continued
til this present moneth
of Nouember in
the yeare of
our Lord
GOD.

1567.

By I. S.

Imprinted at London in Flete
strete nere to S. Dunstones
church, by Thomas
Marshe.

The principall Contentes of this booke, as foloweth.

1 First a Kalender at large.
A rule for the beginning and endynge of the Termes.

3 The Epistle dedicatorie.

4 The Description of Englande, Wales, and Cornewall.

5 The Kynges of Englande from Brute, who was the firste to this present, with the true accompte of yeares, howe longe they reigned, and what notable thinges wer don, durynge theyr Reignes.

6 The names and yeares of all the Bailiffes, Custos, Maiors, and Shereffes of the Citie of London since the Conquest.

7 The buildinge of the most auncient Cities, Townes, Castelles, with other Antiquities, and Monumentes within thys Realme.

8 Howe a man may iourney frome any notable towne in England, to the Citie of London: or from London to any notable towne in the same Realme.

KL. January hath xxxj. dayes

iii	A	Circumcision of Christ.	1
	b	Octa. of Sainct Stephen	2
xi	c	Octa. of Sainct John	3
	d	Octa. of Innocentes	4
xix	e	Deposition of sainct Edward	5
viii	f	[illegible]	6
	g	Translā. Wilhelmi	7
xvi		Lucian priest.	8
v	b	Lewes confessor	9
	c	Paule the first Heremite	10
xiii	d	[illegible]	11
ii	e	Richardus martir	12
	f	Hillarius	13
x	g	Felicis	14
xviii		Archadius martir	15
vii	b	S. Mauritius	16
	c	Saincte Anthonie.	17
xv	d	Prisce virgin	18
iiii	e	Wolstan bishoppe	19
	f	Fabian and Sebastian.	20
xii	g	Agnes virgin.	21
		Vincent martir.	22
i	b	Emerense	23
	c	Timothe bishop.	24
ix	d	Conuersion of S. Paule.	25
	e	Policarpe bishop	26
xvii	f	Julian confessor	27
vi	g	Valerii bishop	28
		Theodore priest	29
xiiii	b	Basilius bishop	30
ii	c	Saturne & victor.	31

KL.		February hath xxviii. dayes.	
	d	Brigide virgin. Fast.	1
xi	e	Purification of Mary	2
xix	f	Blase bishop	3
viii	g	Gilbert confessor.	4
	A	Agathe virgin	5
xvi	b	Amandus bishop & confes	6
v	c	Anguli bishop	7
	d	Paule bi[illegible].	8
xiii	e	Appolline virgin	9
ii	f	Scholastice vir Golden Pollice	10
	g	Desiderius bish.	11
x	A	Dorothe virgin.	12
	b	Wolstane bishop	13
xviii	c	Valentin martir	14
vii	d	Faustine Jouine	15
	e	Julian virgin	16
xv	f	Policronius bishop	17
iiii	g	Symon byshop	18
	A	Sabin and Julian mar.	19
xii	b	Mildred virgin	20
i	c	Lerie. martyrs.	21
	d	Cathedra Petri	22
ix	e	Fast. Locus bisexti	23
	f	Mathias Apostle.	24
xvii	g	Alexander bishop	25
vi	A	Eusebius priest	26
	b	Augustine	27
xiiii	c	Oswolde bishop	28

iii	d	Dauid bishop	1
	e	Chadde confessor	2
xi	f	Maurice confessor	3
	g	Adrian bishop	4
xix	A	Foce & Eusebei	5
viii	b	Victor & Victorin	6
	c	Perpetue & Felix	7
xvi	d	Deposit of Felix.	8
v	e	Quadraginta mar.	9
	f	Aggeus prophete	10
	g	Gorgonius mar.	11
xiii	A	Gregorius bishop	12
ii	b	Theodore martir	13
x	c	Longius mar.	14
	d	Cyriaci martir	15
xviii	e	Hilarius bishop.	16
vii	f	Patrick & Gertrudis	17
	g	Edward king and confessor	18
xv	A	Joseph the husbãd of Mary.	19
iiii	b	Cuthbert bishop	20
	c	Benedict abotte	21
xii	d	Aphrodosius bishop	22
i	e	Theodore virgin	23
	f	Pigmeni. Fast.	24
ix	g	Annunciation of Mary.	25
	A	Castor martir	26
xvii	b	Eulalie virgin	27
vi	c	Victor martir	28
	d	Augenci mar.	29
xiiii	e	Quirini mar.	30
iii	f	Adelmus bishop.	31

	g	Theodore virgin	1
xi	a	Mary Egiptiace	2
	b	Richard bishop	3
xix	c	Ambrosius	4
viii	d	Martianus mar	5
xvi	e	Sixtus bishop.	6
v	f	Egesippus	7
	g	Euphemii virgin	8
xiii	a	Perpetuus bishop	9
ii	b	vii virgyns	10
	c	Marcus martir	11
x	d	[illegible]	12
	e	Oswalde Archbyshop	13
xviii	f	Guthlacie	14
vii	g	Olive	15
	a	Isidore	16
xv	b	Aniceti	17
iiii	c	Eleutherius bishop	18
	d	Alphege	19
xii	e	Tyburtius	20
i	f	Sother virgin	21
	g	Simon bishop.	22
ix	a	S. George mar.	23
	b	Lucretia	24
xvii	c	[illegible]	25
vi	d	Anastasii	26
	e	Vitalis martir	27
xiiii	f	Petri Mediolanensis	28
iii	g	Clete byshop	29
	a	Depositio Erkenwald.	30

KL. Maye hath xxxj dayes

xi	b	[illegible] Jacob
	c	Athanasii bishop
xix	d	Inuen of the crosse
viii	e	Floriani mar.
	f	Godard
xvi	g	John port latin
v		John of Beuerley
	b	Apparitio Mich
xiii	c	Gengulfi martir
ii	d	Gordian and Epimachy
	e	Anthony mar.
•	f	[illegible]
	g	Boniface martyr
xvii		Sophia virgin
vii	b	Seru ciii confessor
	c	Transl.i.of S. Bernard
xv	d	Dioscoride martir
iiii	e	Dunston bishop
	f	Bernardine
xii	g	Helene Quene Fast.
i		Julyane vir
	b	Vrbane martir
ix	c	Translation Francisci.
	d	Desideri mar.
xvii	e	Adeline byshop
vi	f	Augustin of England
	g	Bede priest
xiiii		Germaine bish.
iii	b	Nicodeme
	c	Corona.mert.
xi	d	Marcell martyr

KL June hath.xxx.d[illegible]

	e	Nichomed
xix	f	Erasmus bishop.
viii	g	Basill
xvi	A	Petroce confessor.
v	b	Boniface bishop
	c	Melon byshop
xiii	d	Translatio. Wolstan
ii	e	Wilhelmi confessor
	f	Trans. Edmond
x	g	Iue confessor
	A	Barnabe Apostle
vii	b	Sol in Cancro
vii	c	Anthony
	d	Basill byshop & confessor
xv	e	Vite & Modeste
iiii	f	Trans. Richard
	g	Botulphe
xii	A	Marci & marcelliani
i	b	Geruasie
	c	Trans. Edward
ix	d	Walburge virgin
	e	Albon martyr
xvii	f	Etheldred Fast.
vi	g	Nati. John Baptiste
	A	Trans. Helene
xiiii	b	John & Paule
iii	c	Achasus confessor
	d	Leo byshop. Fast.
xi	e	Peter and Paule.
	f	Com me. of Paule.

KL. Iuly hath xxxi. dayes.

xix	g	Octa. John Baptiste	1
viii	a	Visitation of our Lady	2
	b	Transl. of S. Thomas.	3
xvi	c	Translation of S. Martin	4
v	d	Zoe virgin and martir	5
	e	Octa. Peter and Paule	6
xiii	f	Dog dayes begyn.	7
ii	g	Deposition of Grimbald	8
	a	Cirilli bishop	9
x	b	Seuen brethren	10
	c	Transl. of S. Benet	11
xviii	d	Nabor and Felix	12
vii	e	Priuate	13
	f	Translation of S. Thomas	14
xv	g	Transl. of S. Swythyn	15
iiii	a	Transl. of S. Osmund	16
	b	Kenelme king.	17
xii	c	Arnulphe bishop	18
i	d	Rufine and Iustine	19
	e	Margaret	20
ix	f	Praxede virgin	21
	g	Mary Magdalen	22
xvii	a	Appollinaris	23
vi	b	Christiane vir. Fast.	24
	c	James apostle	25
xiiii	d	Saint Anne	26
iii	e	vii. slepers	27
	f	Sampson byshop	28
xi	g	Martha	29
xix	a	Abdon & Sennes martirs	30
	b	Germain byshop	31

KL.		August hath xxxi. dayes.	
viii	c	Lammas day.	1
xvi	d	Sephen	2
v	e	Stephanus byshop	3
	f	Justini confessone	4
xiii	g	Affra virgin	5
ii	[illegible]	Transfiguratio u	6
	b	The feast of Jesu	7
x	c	Sixtake	8
	d	Romaine	9
xviii	e	S. Laurence day	10
vii	f	Tiburtius martir	11
	g	Clare virgin	12
xv		Rochus	13
iiii	b	Eusebii prest [illegible]	14
	c	Assumption Mary	15
xii	d		16
i	e	Oct. of S. Laurence	17
	f	Agapetke martir	18
ix	g	Magnus martir	19
	[illegible]	Lewes confessor	20
xvii	b	Bernarde	21
vi	c	Oct. assumptio Mary.	22
	d	Timothe Fast	23
xiiii	e	Bartholomew Apostle	24
iii	f	Ludouici king	25
	g	Seuerine bishop	26
xi	[illegible]	[illegible]	27
xix	b	Austin byshop	28
	c	Decolat. of S. John	29
viii	d	Felyx	30
	e	Cuthburge virgin	31

KL.

x	f	Egidius abbot	1
v	g	Anthonini mar.	2
		Gregory byshop	3
xiii	b	Transla. of Cuthbert	4
ii	c	Bartin abbot	5
	d	Eugenius	6
x	e	Gorgon	7
	f	Natiuitie of Marie	8
xviii	g	Prothus	9
vii		Siluius byshop	10
	b	Jacobus priest	11
xv	c	Maurelius bysh	12
iiii	d	Amantii martir	13
	e	Holy Roode day	14
xii	f		15
i	g	Edith virgin	16
		Diaozin byshop	17
ix	b	Januarie marter	18
	c	Lambart.	19
xvii	d	Eustace Fast.	20
vi	e		21
	f	Tecle virgin	22
xiiii	g	Mauritius confes.	23
iii		Indochi martir	24
	b	Firmin martir	25
xi	c	Cyprian and Justine	26
xix	d	Seuerine byshop	27
	e	Cosme and Damian	28
viii	f		29
	g	Hieromie prist.	30

xv	A	Remigius bishop
xiii	b	Leodegarii
xii	c	Candidi martir
i	d	Francis confesso
	e	S. Faith virgin
ix	f	Marci & Marcellian
	g	Pelagie virgin
xvii	A	Nicasius con.
vi	b	Dionise
	c	Wilfriede virgin
xv	d	Trans. of S. Edward
iiii	e	Calixtus byshop
	f	Wolfrane byshop
xii	g	Sol in Scorpio
i	A	Galli confessor
	b	Maximini martir
ix	c	Etheldred virgin
	d	S. Luke evangelist.
xvii	e	Quirini martir
vii	f	Austrebert martir
	g	xi. M. virgins.
xiiii	A	Mary Salome
iii	b	Romani archbysh.
	c	Chrispine
xi	d	Evaristus
xix	e	Ursula vir.
	f	Maglorius bishop
viii	g	Florence Fast.
	A	Simon & Jude apostle.
xvi	b	Abacuk prophete.
	c	Quirini martir

KL. [illegible] dayes

	d	[illegible]	1
xiii	e	All soules day	2
ii	f	Wenefrede virgin	3
	g	Amancius	4
x	[illegible]	Lete persb	5
	b	Leo[illegible]	6
xviii	c	Wi... ode byshop	7
vii	d	Quatuor coronato.	8
	e	Theodore martir	9
xv	f	Martin bishop	10
iiii	g	Martin	11
	[illegible]	Paternus [illegible]	12
xii	b	Bryce	13
i	c	Trans. of Erkenwald.	14
	d	Macute	15
ix	e	Depo[illegible]i. Edmond	16
	f	Hughe byshop	17
xvii	g	Octa. Martins	18
vi	[illegible]	Elizabeth	19
	b	Edmond king	20
xiiii	c	Present. of our Lady	21
iii	d	Cicilie virgin	22
	e	Clement bishop	23
xi	f	Grisogoni martir	24
xix	g	Katherine virgin	25
	[illegible]	Peter byshop.	26
viii	b	Vitalis & agricole.	27
	c	Ruffinus	28
xvi	d	Saturnine Fast	29
v	e	Andrew Apostle	30

December hath .xxxi. dayes.

xiii	f	Crescenti & Darie martir	1
ii	g	Libiani	2
	a	Depositi. Osmond.	
x	b	Barbara virgin	4
	c	Saba abbot	5
xviii	d	Nicolas bishop	6
vii	e	Octa. Andrew	7
	f	Concep. Mary	8
xv	g	Cyprian abbot	9
iiii	a	Eulalie	10
	b	Antippa	11
xii	c	Paule bishop	12
i	d	Lucy virgin	13
	e	Nicasii	14
ix	f	Valery	15
	g	O sapientia	16
xvii	a	Lazarus bishop	17
vi	b	Gracian byshop	18
	c	Venesy virgin	19
xiiii	d	July mart. Fast.	20
iii	e	S. Thomas apostle	21
	f	30. martirs	22
xi	g	Victor virgin	23
xix	a	40. virgyn Fast.	24
	b	Natiuite of Christ	25
viii	c	S. Steuen martir	26
	d	S. John Euangelist.	27
xvi	e	Innocentes daye	28
v	f	Thomas Becket.	29
	g	Transl. of S. James	3
xiii	a	Siluester bishop.	31

A rule to knowe when the Terme beginneth and endeth.

EIght dayes before any Terme be, the Exchequer openeth for certaintie, except trinitye terme, which is but iiii. dayes before.

beginneth the xxiii. daye of January, if it be not Sunday: then the next day after, & endeth the xii. day of February.

beginneth .xvii. dayes after Easter day and endeth foure dayes after Ascension day.

beginneth the next day after Corpus Christi day, and endeth the wednesday fortnight after.

beginneth the ix. daye of October, if it be not Sunday, and endeth the xxviii. of November.

In Easter terme on the Ascencion day. In Trinitye terme, on the Natiuitie of saynte John Baptist. In Michelmas terme on the feast of all saintes. In Hillary terme on the feast of the Purificatiō of our Lady. The quenes Judges of Westminster, do not vse to syt in iudgement, nor vpon any Sondayes.

A table for xxx. yeres to come.

The yeres of our Lord God.	Letter Dominical.	Leape yeares.	Easter daye.	Marche or April.	The yeres of our Lord God.	Letter Dominical.	Leape yeres.	Easter daye.	Marche or Aprill.
1564	a	b	2	A	1579	d		19	A
1565	g		22	A	1580	b	c	5	A
1566	f		14	A	1581	a		26	M
1567	e		30	M	1582	g		15	A
1568	d	e	18	A	1583	f		31	M
1569	b		20	A	1584	d	e	19	A
1570	a		29	M	1585	c		11	A
1571	g		15	A	1586	b		3	A
1572	e	f	6	A	1587	a		16	A
1573	d		22	M	1588	f	g	7	A
1574	c		12	A	1589	e		30	M
1575	b		3	A	1590	d		19	A
1576	g	a	22	A	1591	c		4	A
1577	f		7	A	1592	a	b	26	M
1578	e		30	M	1593	g		15	A

TO THE RIGHT HONORABLE, ROGER Martin lord Maior of the cite of *London*, the right *worshipful* Aldermen his brethern, and the cōmoners of the same citie, John Stowe. Citizen wyscheth long health and Felicitie

ALTHOUGHE (ryght honorable and worshipfull) I was my selfe verye redy to dedicate this my small trauayle of Englysh Chronicles vnto you, to thentent that through your protection it myght passe the snarlynges of the malicyous, whyche ar alwayes redy to hinder the good meanynges of laborious men

and studious writers: yet consyderynge thoccasyons necessaryly
unto me offered, and dutyfully to
be considered: I thought good to
begyn wyth the ryghte honorable
Therle of Leicester. For speakyng nothyng of my owne duetie,
the commoditie of my owne countreye men, moued mee hereunto,
who seynge they were deceyued
through hys authorytye by the fur
nyshynge of a friuolous abridgement in the fronture with his noble name, I thought good, (and
that after amendement promised,
but not performed) at vacante
tymes, to take me to my olde delectable studyes, and after a Summarie of Englishe Chronicles
faithfully collected, to requyre his
Lordshyps authoritye to the defence of that, wherin an other had
both abused hys Lordshyps name
and deceaued the expectaciō of ẏ cō
mon

In the seconde edition of thabridgement.

mon people. But nowe at the request of the Printer, and other of my louyng frẽds, hauyng brought the same into a newe forme, suche as maye bothe ease the purse and the caryage, and yet nothyng omitted conuenyent to be knowen: and besydes all thys, hauyng example before my face to chaunge my patrone (reseruynge styll my Printer, as carefull of hys aduantage rather thenne myne owne) I am bolde to submyt it vnto your honoure and worshyppes protectyons together, that thorough the thũdryng noyse of empty tonnes, & vnfruitfull graffes of Momus offsprynge, it be not (as it is pretended) defaced and ouerthrowne. Truthes quarell it is, I laye before you, the whyche hath bene (yf not hitherto wholy pretermitted) truelye myserable handled, mangled, I should, saye, and suche an hotchepotte made of truthe and

and studious writers: yet consy derynge thoccasyons necessaryly unto me offered, and dutyfully to be considered: I thought good to begyn wyth the ryghte honorable Therle of Leicester. For speakyng nothyng of my owne duetie, the commoditie of my owne countreye men, moued mee hereunto, who seynge they were deceyued through hys authorytye by the furnyshynge of a friuolous abridgement in the frontture with his noble name, I thought good, (and that after amendement promised, but not performed) at vacante tymes, to take me to my olde delectable studyes, and after a Summarie of Englishe Chronicles faithfully collected, to requyre his Lordshyps authorytye to the defence of that, wherein an other had both abused hys Lordshyps name and deceaued the expectaciō of ŷ cō mon

In the seconde edition of thabridgement.

mon people. But nowe at the request of the Printer, and other of my louyng frēds, hauyng brought the same into a newe forme, suche as maye bothe ease the purse and the caryage, and yet nothyng omitted conuenyent to be knowen: and besydes all thys, hauyng example before my face to chaunge my patrone (reseruynge styll my Printer, as carefull of hys aduantage rather thenne myne owne) I am bolde to submyt it vnto your honoure and worshyppes protectyons together, that thorough the thūdryng noyse of empty tonnes, & vnfruitfull graftes of Momus offsprynge, it be not (as it is pretended) defaced and ouerthrowne. Truthes quarell it is, I laye before you, the whyche hath bene (yf not hitherto wholy pretermitted) truelye myserable handled, mangled, I should saye, and suche an hotchepotte made of truthe and lyes together, that of thignorante in hystoryes, thone coulde not be discernde from thother. A strange case is it, and neglygence shall I call it, or ignorance, that hee that was moued to wryte euen for pyttyes sake, to restore the truthe to her integritye, shoulde commytte so great errors and so many, that he hymself had nede of a correcter, and the truthe of a newe laborer. For me a heape of old monumentes, wytnesses of tymes, & bright beames of the truth, can testyfye, that I haue not swarued from the truth: the whyche as I am redy at all tymes to shew for mine owne safe conducte agaynst thaduersaryes, So am I most certaine, that he that pretendeth most hath had very smale store of Authors for hym selfe before tyme, and now hath fraughte hys manerlye Manuell, wyth suche merchandyse (as to you it shall be moste

In the Epistle dedicatorie.

most manyfest at your conference) that by the bringe of my summarye, he scoured newlye, or rather cleanly altered his old abridgmēt, What preoccupacyon, or what insolence is it then, to transferre that unto mee, that am farthest frō such dealing. And yet hauing muche better presydentes before myne eyes, (euen that excellente learned Doctor Coeper, that I name no ancyenter, whose order and deuyse pryuatly he condemneth, and yet openly transformeth into hys owne Abridgement) hee accuseth me of counterfeatyng his volume and order: whereas it myght be wel sayde unto hym. What hast thou, ỹ thou hast not receaued of me? But ỹ I be not agaynst my nature angry wythe my undeserued aduersary, I will here surcease to trouble you anye farther at thys tyme, most earnestlye requyrynge youre honoure and worshyppes all ones againe, to take the tuityon of thys lyttle booke vppon you. The whych yf I may perceaue to be taken thankfullye, and fruitefullye vsed to the amendemente of suche grosse erroures as hytherto haue bene, in The great Abridgement, and presentely are in the Manuell of the Cronycles of Englande, in Thabridged Abridgemente, in The briefe collection of Histories, commytted: I shall be encouraged to perfecte that labour that I haue begon, and such worthye workes of auncyent Aucthours that I haue wyth greate peynes gathered together, and, partly performed in M. Chaucer & other I shal be much incensed by your gentlenes to publyshe, to the commoditye of all the Quenes maiesties louynge Subiectes,

To manye names for a tryfle.

Your moste humble
Iohn Stowe.

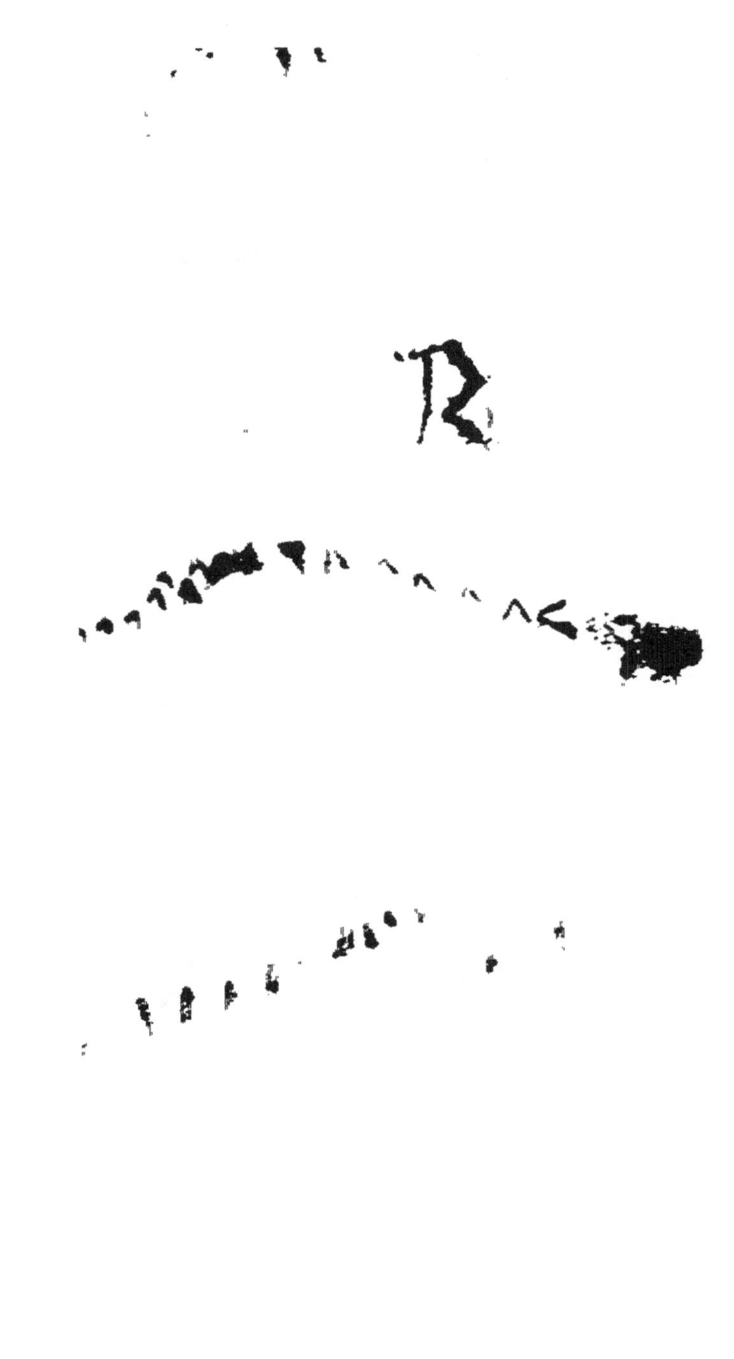

A briefe Description of Englande.

BEFORE I enter to bridge the factes and gestes of the Kyngs and other persons, within this Realme from Brutus ye first Kyng of the same: I purposed briefly to make Descriptiō of this noble Realme, gathered out of Polydore Vergil, reported in his worke of the English historie, who saieth: That all Britain, which by two names is called England & Scotland is an Iland in the Ocean sea, situate right ouer against the Region of Gallia: one parte of which Ile Englishmē do inhabite: an other part Scottes ye third part walshemen, and the fourth part Cornishmen. Al they either in languag, cōditions or lawes, do differ amongs them selues. England (so called of Englishmen, which did winne the same, is the greatest parte, which is deuided into xxxix. Counties, which we cal shires, wherof, ten (that is to say, Kent, Sussex, Surrey Southamptō, Barkeshire, wiltshyre, Dorsetshire, Somersetshire, Deuonshire & Cornwal) do contein ye first parte of that Iland:

whiche part bounding toward the South, standeth betwene the Thames and the Sea, From thence, to the ryuer of Trent, whiche passeth through the middes of Englande, be xvi. shires wherof ẏ fyrst vi. (standing east ward) are Essex, Middlesex, Hertforshire, Suffolk, Northfolk, and Cambrldgeshyre: the other ten which stand more in ẏ middle of the countrey, ar these: Bedford, Huntingdon, Buckyngham, Oxford, Northampton Rutland, Leicester, Notingham, warwike and Lincolne, After these, ther be vi. which border westward vpon wales, as Glocester Hereford, worcester, Salop Stafford, and Chester. Aboute the middle of the Region lye Darbyshyre, yorkeshyre, Lancashyre, & Cumberland, On the left hand toward the west is westmerland. Against the same is ẏ Bishoprike of Durham, and Northumberlande, which boundeth vpon the Northe, in ẏ marches of Scotlād. Those shires be diuided into. xvii Byshoprikes, whiche by a Greke word be called Dioceses. Of which Dioceses Cantorbury and Rochester, be in Kente.

Essex, Middlesex and parte of Hertforde, belongeth to the Bishoprike of London.

The Byshop of Chichester hath Sussex.

winchester hath Hampshyre, Surrey, & the Isle of wyght.

Salis-

Salisbury, hath Dorsetshire, Barkeshire and wylteshire.
Excetour, hath Devonshire and Cornwall,
Bathe, and welles, hath Somersetshire.
worcester, hath Glocestershire, worcestershyre, and part of warwikeshire,
Hereford, hath parte of Shropshyre, and Herefordshyre.

Coventree and Lichfelde, Staffordshyre and thother part of warwikeshyre

Chester, hath Cheshyre: Darbyshyre, and a piece of Lancashyre, nere ẏ ryuer of Repel
The Diocesse of Lincoln, which is ẏ greatest, hath eight shires, lying betwene ẏ Thames and Humber, as Lincolne, Northampton, Leicester, Rutland, Huntingdon, Bedford, Buckingham, Oxford, and the residue of Herfordshyre.

The Bishoprike of Ely hath Cantabrigshyre, and the Ile of Ely.
Suffolke and Norfolke, be in the circuite of Norwiche Diocesse. And this is the Province of the Archebishoppe of Cantorbury: which is the Primate of all England, with wales, which hath iiii. Diocesse, as hereafter shalbe declared.
The bishop of Yorke hath Yorkeshyre, Notynghamshyre, and a piece of Lancastshyre.
The bishop of Durham, hath the byshoprik so commonly called, & Northumberland

Carlille côteineth Cûbreland & westmerlâd And this is ŷ other prouince of tharchbishop of Yorke, which is an other Primate of England, and was of long time also primate of all Scotland. But these diocesses take their names of the Cities, where those seas be placed. The chiefe wherof is London: wherein the beginning was the Archbishops sea, but afterwardes transposed to Cantorbury, a citie in Kent, placed in a soyle amyable & plesant. London, standeth in Middlesex, on the northside of the Thamis. That most excellêt and goodly Riuer, beginneth a litle aboue a village called winchelcombe in Oxfordshire still increasyng: and passeth fyrste by the vniuersitie of Oxeford, and so with a meruaylous quyete course by London, and then breaketh into the french Ocean by main tydes, which twise in .xxiiii. houres space doth ebbe and flowe more then .lx. myles, to the great comoditie of trauailers: by whiche al kyndes of marchandise be easyly caryed to London, the principal store and staple for al cômodities within this realm. Vpô ŷ same riuer is placed a Stonebridge, a work very rare & meruaylous, which bridge hath .xx. Arches, made of .iiii. squared stone, of height .lx. fote, & of bredth .xxx. foot, distât one from an other .xx. foot, côpact & ioyned together with vaultes & sellars. Vpô both sides be houses

buil-

builded, that it semeth rather a continuall strete, then a Bridge. The Ocean sea doth bound England, the first part of Britayne east and South: wales, & Cornewall west. The riuer of twede deuideth England and Scotland north. The length of ẏ Island beginneth at Portsmouth in the south part & endeth at Twede in the North, conteinyng CCCxx. miles. This Realm aboue other is most fruitful on this sid Humbre: for beyō it is fuller of mountaines. And although to ẏ beholders of that conntrey a far of, it may seme plain, yet it is ful of many hils & those for the most part voyde of trees: the valleys wherof be very delectable, inhabited for the most part by noble men who accordinge to ancient and old order, desyre not to dwel in Cities, but nere vnto valleys and riuers in seueral villages: for aduoidyng of vehemēt winds because ẏ Iland naturally is stormy Humbre hath his beginnyng a little on this syde yorke, & by and by runneth southward & then holdeth his course eastward, and so into the main sea, greatly encreased by ẏ riuers of Dunne & Trent. Trent beginneth a little frō Stafford, running through Darbyshire, and Leicestershire, passyng by Lichfielde and Notyngham on the right hand, & Dune on ẏ left: so that both those riuers do make an Iland, which is called Auxolme, and then ioyning together on thisside king ston upon Hull, a goodly marchant town, they fall into Humbre: by whych riuer they may a ryue out of Fraunce, Germany, and Denmarke, England is fruitful of beasts, and aboundeth with cattel: wherby thinhabitauntes bee rather for the moste grasiers, then ploughmen, because they geue them selues more to feding, then to tillage, So that almost the third part of the countrey is unployed to cattel, dere redde and fallow, goates (wherof ther be store in the north parts, and conies) for euery wher ther is ioly maintenaunce of those kynds of beasts, because it is full of great woddes, wherof there riseth pastyme of huntyng greatly exercised, specially by the nobilitie and gentlemen.

Of Scotland, an other part of Britain, I purpose to say nothing, because I haue promised only and briefly to remembre thaffaires of myn own countrey, as best trauailed & acquainted with ỹ knowledge of ỹ same.

Wales, the third part of Britain lieth upõ the left hand: which like a Promontary or foreland, or an Isle (as it wer) on euery side it is compassed with the mayn sea: except it be on the east part with the riuer of Sabrin commonly called Seuern, which deuideth wales from England Although some late writers affirme Herford to be a bound be twene wales and Englande, and saye, that wales beginneth at Chepstol, where the riuer Weye augmented with an other ryuer called Lugg, passing by Hereford doth run into the sea: which riuer riseth in ẏ middle of wales out of that hil (but vncertein whether out of that springe that Sabrine dothe, which Corn. Tacitus calleth Antona. For euen to that place ther goeth a great arme of the sea which passeth through the land westward: on the right hand leaueth Cornwal, and on the left wales, which Topographye or description, althoughe it be newe, yet I thought good to follow. Therfore Wales is extended from the town of Chepstol, where it beginneth almost by a straight line a little aboue Shrowesburye, euen to westchester, northwarde. Into that part, so many of the Britaines as remained alyue after ẏ slaughter and losse of their countrey, at the length beyng dryuen to their shyfts, didde repaire as ancient writyngs report: where partly through refuge of the mountains and partly of ẏ woddes and marshes, they remained in safetie: which part they enioy euen to this day. That land afterwards the englishmen dyd cal wales: and the Britains the inhabitantes of the same walshmen: for amonges the Germains, walsman, signifieth a straunger, an alien, an outborn or strang man that is suche a one, as hath a contrary language frõ theirs (for wall, in their tonge is called a straunger borne as an Italian or Frencheman: whiche differ in speche from the Germaine. Man, signifieth Homo, whiche is a man in englishe. Therfore Englishemen, a people of Germanye, after they had wonne Britayne, called the Britains, whiche escaped after the destruction of theyr countrye, after theyr countrye maner, walshemen: because they had an other tongue or spech, besides theyrs, & the land which they inhabited, wales: whyche name afterwardes bothe to the people and countrey dyd remayn. By this meanes the Britaines with their kingdom lost theyr name. But they which affirm that name to be derived of theyr Kynge or quene, without doubt be deceived. The coũtrey soyle towardes the sea coast, and in other places in the valleys and playnes is moste fertile, which yeldeth both to man & beast, great plentie of fruit & grasse: but in other places for the most part it is bareyn, & lesse fruitful: because it lacketh tillage: for which cause husbandmen doo liue hardly, eatynge Oten cakes, and drinking milke myxt with water, and sowre whay. Ther be many townes and strong castels, and .xiii bishopri[c]es if ÿ bishopricke of Hereford bee counted in england, as ÿ late writers declare. The first

bisho-

bishoprick is Meneue, so called of Menenia, which at this day they cal Saint Dauids, a Citie very ancient, situated uppon the sea coast, and boundeth westward toward Irelande. An other is Landaffe, the third Bangor, and the fourth Saint Asaph. Al which be under Tharche bishop of Contorbury The walshemen haue a languag from thenglishemen, whiche as they say, that fetche their Petigree frome the Troians, dooth partely sound of the Troian antiquitie, and partlye of the Greeke. But howe soeuer it is, the walshmen do not pronounce their speache so pleasauntly and gentilly as thenglyshmen doo, because they speake more in the throte: and contrary wise, thenglyshmen rightly folowyng the Latines, doo expresse their voice somwhat within the lips, which to the hearers semeth pleasant & swete. And thus much of wales ye third part of Britain

Now foloweth the fourth and last part of Britayne named Cornewall. This part beginneth on that side, which standeth toward Spayne westward: Toward the East it is of bredth, iiii score and ten miles, extending a litle beyond saint Germains, which is a very famous village, situated on the ryght hand uppon the sea coast, where the greatest breadth of that countrey is but. xx miles: for this parcell of land on the right hand is cō-

 passed

passed with the coast of the mayn sea: and on the left hand with that arme of ŷ sea, which (as before is declared) parteth the land, and runneth vp to Chepstol, wher the countrey is in fourm of a horne: For at ŷ fyrst, it is narow, and then groweth broader, a little beyonde the said towne of saint Germayne, Eastward it bordreth vpon England: west, south, & North, the main sea is round about it: It is a very bareyn soyle, yelding fruite more through trauaile of the tyllers & husbandmen, then through the goodnes of the grounde: but ther is greate plentie of leade and tynne in the mynyng & diggyng wherof, doth specially consyst the liuyng and sustentation of the inhabitantes, In this only part of Britain, euen to this day continueth ŷ nation of the Britains, which in ŷ beginnyng brought out of Gallia occupied & inhabited that Ilãd (if credite may be geuen to them, which report the first inhabitants of Britayn to com out of the Cities of Armerica.) The argumẽt & profe wherof is because the Cornishmen doo speake that language, which ŷ Britains vse now in France, whõ the Britons do call Britonantes

This thing to be more true, an old ancient Chronicle doth declare, wherin I foũd writ ten, not Cornubia, but Cornugallia, compounded of Cornu, a horne, ŷ forme wher-

of that

of that countrey hath, and of Gallia, out of which countrey thinhabitants came first, ẏ maner of which name is not to be misliked. Their tongue is far dissonant from english but is much like to the walshe tongue, because they haue many wordes cōmon to both tonges: yet this difference there is betwen them, when a walshman speaketh, the Cornysheman rather vnderstandeth many wordes spoken by ẏ Walshman, then the whole tale he telleth. Wherby it is manyfeste, that those thre people do vnderstād one an other in lyke maner as the Southerne Scots do perceiue and vnderstand ẏ Northern. But it is a thing very rare and meruaillous, that in one Iland ther should be such varietie of speaches. Cornwall or Cornugall is in the Diocesse of Excetour, wich was ones worthy to be counted the fourth part of the Ilād as wel for ẏ contrariety of language, as for the fyrst inhabitants therof, as is beforesaid. Afterwardes, the Normains whiche constituted a kingdom of al those thre partes reckened Cornwall, to be one of the counties or shyres of the countrey, Thus much of ẏ particular description of Britayne, that the whole body of the Realm (by the membres may be the better knowen to som peraduenture that neuer heard the same before.

¶The forme of the Ilande is triquetra, ore thre

thre cornered, hauing thre corners, or thre sides: To wherd, that is to say: The corner toward theast and thother toward the west, (both extendyng northwardes) at the longest. The third syde which is þ southside, is far shorter then thother, for þ Iland is greater of length then of breadth. And as in the other two partes is conteyned the length, euen so in the last, the breadth. In which place, the breadth beginneth: and so continuyng from the south part to the North, it is but narow. The first and right corner of which Iland eastward, is in Kent, at Douer and Sandwiche. From whence to Caleys or Bologn in Fraunce, is the distaunce of xxx. myles. From this Angle which is agaynst France to the third Angle, which is in the Northe, in Scotland, the mayne wherof, boundeth vpon Germany, but no land seene: and ther the Iland is lyke vnto a wedge, euen at the very angle of þ lād in Scotlād. The lēgth wherof is viii. hundreth myles. Againe the length from this Corner at Douer in Kent, to the vttermost part of Cornewall, being saint Michaels mount (which is the west part or west angle) is supposed to be. CCC. myles. From this left angle, being the west part, & thuttermost part of Cornwal, which hath a prospect towards Spain, in whiche part also standeth Ireland, situated betwen twene Britaine and Spayne to the north angle in the further part of Scotlād: in which part the Iland doth ende, the length is. viii. hundred myles, in whiche part there be very good hauēs, and saufe harboroughs for shippes, and apt passage into Ireland, beyng not past one day saylinge: but the shorter passage is frō wales, to waterford, a towne in Irelande vppon the sea coaste much like to that passage betwene Douer and Calaice, or somwhat more: but the shortest passage of all, is out of Scotland. Frō this last angle to Hāpton: (which is a towne vpon the sea coast, with a hauen so called toward the south, and therfore called Southhampton) betwene the Angels of Kent and Cornewal, they do mesure by a straight lyne, the whole length of the Iland, and do say, that it conteineth viii. C. myles: as the breadth from Meneua, or Saint Dauids to Yarmouth, which is in the vttermost part of the Iland towards the east dothe conteyn. CC. myles, for the breadth of the Iland is in the south part, which part is the front and beginnyng of the Land, and endeth narowe, or as it were in a straight. So the circuite or compasse of the Iland is. xviii. C. myles, whiche is. CC. lesse, then Cesar doth recken or accompt.

Thus muche I haue thought good to take out of Polydore, touchynge the diuisyon of

A briefe Description of England with the fourme and situation of the same. Much other good matter that Authour doth alledge, which here for breuitie I do omitte, referryng those that desyre to know farther hereof, to that Boke: wher he shall fynde the style and story both pleasant and profytable.

Years of the world from Grafton (1563) pencilled in AM/BC & from Fabyan within [ ] (selected only, so far)

THE RACE OF THE KINGES OF ENgland, since Brute the first of this Realme: and in the margent are placed there yeres before Christ hys byrth, whē euery king began theyr reigns, til ye come to Cimbilinus, in whose time Christ ŷ Sauior of the world was borne, & then foloweth ŷ yeres from Christ hys byrth

AFTER THE commune and best allowed opinion of the most auncient and beste approued Authors, Brute the sonne of Syluius Posthumius, arriued in this Ilād, at a place now called Totnes in Deuonshyre: the yere of the worlde. 2855. the yere before Christes Natiuitie 1108. wherein he first began to reigne, & named it Brytayne which before was called Albion. And therin he buylded the noble citie of Lōdon, & named it new Troy, buildyng the 1108

2855/1108

London buylded

Hee stablished the Troyane lawes in this kyngdom.

there a Temple to Appolin, wherein he placed an Archflamyn. He deuided the same Iland among his thre sonnes vnto Locrine he gaue the middle part of Britayne, nowe called Englande, with the superioritie of all this Ile: Vnto Camber he gaue wales, and to Albanacte Scotlande: After whiche partition he decessed, when he had reigned xxiiii. yeares, and was buried at London, then called newe Troye, as is aforesayde.

1084. Locrine, the eldest sonne of Brute reigned xx. yeares: hee chased the Hũnes, which inuaded this Realm: & pursued them so sharpely, that many of them with their kyng, were drowned in a ryuer, whiche departed England and Scotland. And for so much as the king of Hũnes, named Humber, was there drowned, the Ryuer is tyll this daye named Humber.

Howe the Ryuer of Humber toke that name.

This king Locrine had to wyfe Guendolyn, daughter of Corineus, duke of Cornewall, by whome he had a sonne named Madan: he also kept a paramour, the beautifull lady Estrild, by whome hee had a daughter named Sabrine. And after the death of Corineus duke of Cornewal: he put from hym the sayd Guendolin

dolin

dolyn, & wedded Estryld, but Guendolyn repaired to Cornewall, where she gathered a greate power, & foughte with king Locrine, and slue hym: he was buried at Troinouant. She drowned the lady Estrylde with her daughter Sabrine in a ryuer, that after the yong maydẽs name, is called Seuern.

Howe the Ryuer of Seuerne tooke that name.

Gwendoleine, the daughter of Cori- 1063
neus, & wife to Locrin (for so much as Madan her sonne was to yonge to gouerne the land) was by common assent of all the Britains, made ruler of the whole Isle of Britayn, which she well and discretely ruled, to the comforte of her subiectes. xv. yeares, and than left the same to her sonne Madan.

The quene reigned during the minoritie of her son.

Madan, the sonne of Locrine and 1053
Guendolyne, was made ruler of Britain, he vsed great tiranny amõg his Britons: And beyng at his disport of hunting, he was deuoured by wylde wolues, when he had reigned. xl. yeres. He left after him. ii. sonnes, named Mempricius, and Manlius.

Kyng deuoured by wolues.

Mempricius, the sõne of Madã, be- 1009.
yng kyng, by treason slewe his brother Manlius, after whose death he liued in more tranquilitie, wherethorough he fel in slouth, and so to lechery

taking the wiues and daughters of his subiectes: and lastly, became so euyll that he forsoke his wife and concubines, and fell to the synne of Sodomye with beastes: wherby he becam odible to God and man. And goinge on hunting, lost his cōpany, & was destroied of wild wolues: wherof the land was then ful, whē he had reigned.xx.yeres.

Kinge deuoured of wolues.

989. EBrank, the sonne of Mempricius, was made ruler of Britain: he had .xxi. wiues, of whome he receiued.xx. sonnes, and.xxx. daughters, whiche he sent into Italie, there to be maried to the bloud of the Troianes. In Albany (now called Scotland) he edified the castel of Alclude, which is Dunbritain he made ỹ castell of Maidens, now called Edenbrough: he made also ỹ castell of Bamburgh: he builded Yorke citie: wherin he made a tēple to Diane, and set there an Archeflame: and there was buried, whā he had reigned.lx. yeares.

Dunbritain Edenbrugh Bāburgh, and Yorke builded.

929. BRute Grienshielde, the sonne of Ebranke, ruled this lande.xij.yeres, and was buried at Yorke, leauyng after hym a sonne named Leill.

917. LEill the son of Brute Greneshielde beeing a iust mā, & louer of peace in his time builded Carleil, & made ther a

temple

téple, placing therin a Flamin, to rule yͤ same, according to yͤ lawes of their goddes at that tyme: & there was buried, when he had ruled Britain.xxv.yeres.

LUd Rudibras, the son of Leil, builded Cãtorbury, Wichester, & Shaftesbury, wherin he builded.iii.téples, & placed in yͤ same.iii. Flamins, like as bishops now be, he reigned xxix.yeres & left a son after him named Bladud. 892.

Catorbury winchester & Shaftesbury builded.

BLadud, son of Lud Rudibras, who had lõg studied at Athens, brought with him.iiii.philosophers, to kepe scole in Britain: for yͤ which he builded Stamford, & made it an vniuersitie: wherin he had greate nũbre of scolers, studying in all yͤ seuen liberal sciẽces: which vniuersitie dured to yͤ cõmig of S.August. At which time yͤ bishop. of Rome interdited it, for heresies yͤ fel amõg yͤ Saxõs & britõs together mixt. he builded Bath, & made ther a téple to Apollo, & placed there a Flaming: he made there the hot bathes, & practised his necromãcy: he decked himselfe in fethers, & ꝑsumed to flie in yͤ aire, & falling on his téple of Apollo, brake his neck when he had reigned.xx.yeres. 863.

Stamforde buylded.

Bath with yͤ hot baths builded.

The kinge atẽpting to flye, brake his necke.

Leire, yͤ son of Bladud succeded his father, he builded Cair Leir, now called 844.

Leicester, and made there a temple of of Janus: placyng a Flamyne there to governe the same, he had .iii. daughters Gonorell, Ragan, and Cordell, which Cordelle for her wisedom & vertue towards her father, succeded hym in the kingdom: whē he had reigned xl. yere, he decessed, & was buried at Leycester.

3158/805 805. Cordyla, the youngest daughter of Leire, succeding her father, was sorowed by her two nephues, Morgan of Albanie, and Conedagus of Camber and Cornewall, who at the length toke and caste her in prison: where she beyng in dispaire of recoueryng her estate, slewe her selfe, when she had reigned .v. yeares, and was buried at Leicester in Janus temple by her father.

3162/801 803. Morgan, the eldest sonne of Dame Gonorel claimed Britayn, & warred on his nephue Conedagus, ꝧ was kyng of Camber (that now is wales) and of Cornwall: but Conedagus met with Morgan in wales, and there slue him: which place is called Glamorgan tyll this daye. And then Conedagus was kyng of all Britayn: he builded a temple of Mars at Perch, that now is S. Johns towne in Scotland, & placed there a Flamyne: he builded an o-

How Glamorganshire toke that name.

S. Johns towne in Scotland builded.

ther

her of Minerue in wales, which nowe is named Bangor. The third he made of Mercurie in Cornewall, where he was borne: he reigned. xxiiii. yeares, and was buried at London.

Bangor in wales builded.

RIuallo, sonne of Conedagus succeded his father, in whose time it ray- 766.
ned bloud.iii.dayes: after the whiche
tẽpest, ensued a great multitude of venemous flies, which slew much people And then a great mortalitie thoroughout this land, which caused almost desolation of the same. This Riuallo reigned ouer this whole Ilãd xlvi. yeres and then deceased, and was buried at Caire branke, that nowe is Yorke.

It rayned bloud.

GUrgustius, sonne of Riuallo, succe- 721.
ded in the kingdom of Britain, who reigned quietly: but was a cõmon drõkard, wherof folowed all other vices. when he had reigned.xxxviii.yeres, he deceased, and was buried at Yorke.

CIcilius, the brother of Gurgustius 684.
succeded in the kyngdom: of whõ is left but litle memory: but that he reigned lix.yeres, & was buried at Bathe

IAgo or Lago cousin of Gurgustius, 636.
reigned. xxv.yeres: for his euill gouernement, he died of a litargie, and was buried at Yorke.

612. KYnimacus succeded Jago in this realme of Britain, wherein he reigned liiii. yeres, and was buried at Yorke.

559. GOrbodug succeded his father Kynemacus in this realm of britain, as our Chronicles write: he reigned lxiii. yeres, and was buried at London.

496. FErrex with his brother Porrex, ruled this lād of Britaine. v. yeres but it was not lōg ere they fel at ciuil discorde for the soueraigne dominion, in whiche Ferrex was slain. And Porrex afterwardes by his mother was killed in his bedde. Thus cruelly was the bloud & house of Brute destroyd, when ẏ this realme by the space of vi C.xvi. yeres had ben gouerned by ẏ lynage.

Porrex slue his brother Ferrex, & Porrex was afterward slain by his mother.

Brutus blud extinguished.

After the death of the two brethren, Ferrex and Porrex, this Realme was deuided with ciuile warres, for lacke of one soueraigne gouernor, which cōtinued by the space of. li. yeres, untyll that noble Dunwallo reduced ẏ same into one Monarchy.

441. MOlmutius Dunwallo, the sonne of Cloten, duke of Cornwal reduced this realme into one Monarchie, being before by ciuile warres and discention, seuered and brought into diuers dominiōs, & he was the first that

wais

ware a crowne of golde: he cōstituted good lawes: whiche longe after were called Mulmutius lawes: he gaue priuileges vnto Temples, & ploughes and began to make the foure notable wayes in Britayne. In London, called then Troy Nouant, he builded a great temple: which some suppose to be Saynte Paules, some Blackwell hall, which was called Templum pacis. Finally when he had brought this Realme to welthe and quietnes, reignyng herein xl. yeares: he died honourably, leauyng after hym two sonnes, Belinus and Brennus. He builded the towne of Walmesbury & of Vies. He was buryed at London in the temple of Peace.

First king that ware a crowne of gold, who buylded Blackwel hall in Lōdon.

The second lawes were Mulmuti9 lawes.

The towne of Walmisbury built.

Belinus and Brennus, sonnes of Mulmutius deuided this whole Ile of Britayne betwene them. Unto Beline the elder brother was appointed England, Wales, and Cornewall. Unto the other the North part beyond Humber. But Brennus a yonge man, desirous of glory and dominion, thinkynge hym self equal with his brother in marcial prowes, was not therwith content: Wherfore he raised warre agaynst Beline, But in conclusion by

401. 3562/400

the meanes of their mother, they were accorded: and Brennus beyng geuen wholly to the study of warres, left his countrey to the gouernance of his brother, and went into Fraunce amongest the Galles: where in the prouince of Aliōs, for his excellēt qualites, he was greatly estemed of Siguenus Kyng of the countrey, whose daughter he maried: And of the Galles was made soueraín captain whē they made their voiage to Rome. Beline in the mean time both in ciuil Justice and also religion such as at that time was vsed, greatly increased his realme. Hee made three Archflames, whose seas were at London, Yorke, and Carlion. He finished the fowre great wayes begon by his father: He subdued and made tributarie vnto hym, Denmarke. In London he made the hauen, which at this day, reteineth the name of him, called Belins gate: and buylded the tower of London. He maried his daughter Cambria vnto a prince of Almayn called Antenor, of whom these people wer called Cymbri, and Sycambri Finally, after he had reigned with his brother and alone. xxvi. yeres, he died: and after the pagan maner, with great pompe was

Thre arch flames.

Foure notable wais

Tower of Lōdō first buildid.

burned

[bu]ried: and his ashes in a vessell of [b]rasse, set on a high Pinacle ouer Belyns gate: he builded Carlion and also the temple of Concord: whiche after the opinion of many, is now the parish church of the Temple.

Carlyon builded. The olde tēple nere to temple bar built.

GOrgunstus, sonne of Beline, succeded his father: he subdued Dēmark compelling them to continue their tribute. He reigned .xix. yeares, and was buried at Carlion, in his time Cambridge was first builded. 375.

GWinthelinus, sonne of Gurgunstus was crowned kyng of Britayn. A prince sober & quiet, who had to wife a noble womā named Marcia, of excellēt learning & knowledge. She deuised certaine lawes, which lōg time amōg the Britains were greatly estemed, and named Marcian lawes. Finally, whē this vertuous prīce had reigned. xxvi. yeres: he dyed, & was buried at Londō. 356.

Thies lawes were Marcian lawes.

CEcilius, the sonne of Guintheline & Marcia, reigned vii. yeres: of him ther remaineth nothing notable: But ỷ in the first yere of his reigne, a people of Almaine called Picts, arriued here in Britayn, and possessed those parties whiche nowe be the marches of bothe realmes, England and Scotland. Ce- 330.

Picts first ēhabited ỷ marches of Scotlād & Englād

cilius was buried at Carlyon.

3640/323 323. Kymarus succeded Cecilius & reigned thre yeres in Britaine, he was slayne as he was huntyng.

3643/326 322. Elanius, called also Danius, was kyng of Britayn. ix. yeares.

3652/311 311. Morindus, the bastard son of Danius began to reigne in Britayne: he fought with a kyng, who came out of Germany, & arriued here & slewe him withal his power. Moreouer, out of the Irish seas in his time came forth a wonderfull monster: which destroied muche people. wherof the kyng hearing wold of his valiaunt courage, nedes fyghte with it: by whom he was cleane deuoured, when he had reigned. viii. yeares.

Kynge deuoured.

3660/303 303. Gorbomannus eldest sonne of Morindus, reigned. xj. yeres. A prince iust and religious: he renued the temples of his gods, and gouerned his people in peace and wealth. He builded Grantham, in Linconshere.

Graunthã built.

3671/291 293. Archigallo, brother of Gorbomannus, was crowned king of britain. he was in conditiõs vnlike to his brother: for he deposed the noble men, and exalted the vnnoble. He extorted from men their goodes to enrich his treasurie: for which cause by ye estates of the realme,

realme, he was depriued of his royall
dignitie, when he had reigned v. yeres. Kyng depriued.

Elidurus the third sonne of Morindus, and brother to Archigallo, 286.
was elected Kyng of Britayne: a vertuous & gentyl prince who gouerned
his people iustly: As he was in huntyng in a forest by chance he met with
his brother Archigallo, whome moste
louyngly he imbraced: and found the
meanes to reconcile him to his lordes:
and than resigned to him his royal dig
nitie: when he had reigned. v. yeres.

Archigallo thus restored to his roy- 281.
all estate: ruled the people quietly
and iustly. x. yeares, and lyeth buryed
at Yorke.

Elidurus aforenamed: after the deth 272.
of his brother Archigallo, for hys
pity and Justice, by the generall consent of the Britains was again chosen
Kynge. But he reigned not passynge
two yeres, but that his yõger brethren
Vigenius and Peredurus raised war
againste hym, toke him prisoner: and
caste hym into the Tower of London:
Where he remayned durynge theyr
Reygne.

Vigenius & Peredurus after the takyng 270.
of theyr brother reigned together
vii.

Pickering buylded. vii. yeres. Vigenius thā died, & Peredurus reigned after alone. ii. yeres. He builded the towne of Pickering after the opinion of dyuers writers.

261. ELidurus, the third time was made king of Britayne, who cōtinued his latter reigne honorably and iustly: but beyng sore bruised with age and troubles he finished his lyfe, when he had nowe lastly reigned. iiii. yeres, and was buried at Carlile.

258. GOrbonian reigned in Britayne. x. yeres.

248. MOrgan was crowned kyng of britayn, who guyded the realme peaceibly. xiiii. yearis.

324. EMerianus brother to Morgan succeded in the realme of Britaine. And when he had tirannously reigned. vii. yeares, he was deposed.

225. IVall was chosen King of Britaine for his iustice & temperance, which gouerned peacibly. xx. yeres.

RYmo gouerned this realme of Bri-
107. tayne. xvi. yeares. In his time was great plentie and peace.

GEruncius reigned here in Britayne
161. xx. yeres.

CAtillus reigned peacibly in britayne
173. x. yeres: he houg vp al oppressours of the

the poore people: to geue ensample unto other.

Coilus succeded Catellus in the re- 163.
alme of Britayn, who quietly reig-
ned.xx.yeares.

Porer, a vertuous and gentill prince 143.
reigned in Britain.v.yeares.

Chirinus king of Britain, through 138.
his drōkēnesse reigned but one yere.

Fulgen his sonne reigned two yeres 137.
in Britayne.

Eldred, reigned in Britayn one yere. 135.

Androgeus, likewise reigned one yere 134.
in Britaine.

Varianus, the sonne of Androgius, 133.
succeded his father in this realm of bri
tayne. He wholly gaue himselfe to the
lustes of the flesh, & reigned.iiii. yeres.

Eliud, kyng of Britayne reigned. v. 130.
yeares: who was a great Astronomer.

Dedantius king of Britayn reigned 124.
v. yeares.

Detonus reigned in this land of Bri 120.
taine.ii.yeres.

Gurgincus reygned. iii. yeares in 118.
Britaine.

Merianus was Kynge of Britayne 115.
ii. yeares.

Bladunus gouerned Britain ii.yers 113.

Capenus reigned kyng of Britayne 111.
iii.

iii.yeares.

108. Quinus ruled Britain.ij.yeares.

106. Cecilus reigned in Britain.ij.yeres.

104. Bledgabredus was.x.yeres kyng of Britaine. He delited muche in Musyke: and gaue hymselfe to the studye thereof.

94. Archemalus was kynge of britayn ij.yeares.

92. Eldelus reigned kynge of Britayne iiij.yeares.

Signes in the ayre. In this tyme diuers prodigies wer sene, as globes of fyre, burstyng out of the ayre with great noyse.

88. Rodianus was kynge of Britayne two.yeares.

86. Redargius reigned kynge of britaine iij.yeares.

83. Samulius reigned in britain.ij.yeres

81. Penisellus was made kynge of britayne: who gouerned it.iii.yeres.

78. Pirrhus ruled britain.ii.yeares.

76. Caporus: was kyng of britayne.ii.yeares.

74. Dinellus the sonne of Caporus, a iust and vertuous prince, gouerned this realme of britain.iiij.yeares.

70. Helius the sonne of Dinellus, reigned not fully one yere kig of britain.

Howe the Isle of Ely. Of this prince the Isle of Ely toke this name.

name, for that he there buylded a goodly palace wherein was his most delight to lyue: and also was there buried. toke fyrst ẏ name,

LVd the eldest son of Hely succeded his father, and reigned. xi. yeares in britayne. As sonne as he was made kyng, he reformed the state of his common weale: for he amended his lawes, and tooke awaye all vsages that were naught: Morouer, he repaired the Citie of Lōdon then called Troynouant, with fayre buyldings and walles: and buylded on the West parte therof, a stronge gate: whiche vnto this tyme retaineth the name of hym, and is called Ludgate. Finally he dyed, leauyng after him two sonnes Androgeus and Theomantius: who beynge not of age to gouerne, their vncle Cassiuelane obteyned the Crowne. London tooke the name of this Lud, & was called Ludston. He was buryed nere to the same Ludgate, in a Temple whiche he there buylden. 69. Lud buylded London from London ston to Ludgat. 3894/69

CAssiuelana, the son of Hely, after the deth of his brother Lud was made gouerner of britaine, whiche he ruled. xix. yeares. 58. 3905/58

In ẏ. viij. yere of his reign, Julius Cesar; who warred long in France, made

the

Julius Cesar his first voyage in to Englãd.

the first voyage of any straunger into this Realme, and afterwarde subdued it. When C. Julius Cesar had warred seuen yeres in France and Germany, comyng vnto that part where Calaice and Boloigne nowe stande, he determined to make warre into Britayne, whiche vntill that time remained vnfrequented and vnknowen of the Romains. His quarell was, because that in the warres of France, he perceiued the Frenchemen to haue much succour and aide from thens. Wherfore hauing prepared .lxxx. shippes, he sailed into Britaine: where at the first, being wearied with an hard and sharpe battaile. And after with sodain tempest, his nauie almoste destroied: he retourned agayne into France, there to wynter his men.

The secõd voyage of Julius Cesar.

The next Spring whiche was the yeare before Christ .li. His nauy being newe rigged and encreased, he passed the seas againe with a greater armye. But whiles he went towardes his enemies on land, his shippes lying at anker, were again by tempest almost lost. For either they were driuen on the sãdes where they stacke fast: or els through beatyng one an other, with force of the tempest, they were destroyde, So that

all,

lx. were lost, the other with much labour were saued. Vpon lande also his horsemen at the fyrste encountre were vanquished, & Labienus the Tribune slayn. At the second conflict, not without great danger of his men, he put the Britains to flyght, and pursued them to the riuer of Thamis: on the further side wherof, Cassiuelan, with a greate multitude of people, was kepinge the bankis, but they not able to resist ye violēce & force of the Romains, hyd them selues in woddes, and with sodayn irruptions oftētimes inuaded them: but in the mean times their strongest citie, Troynouant submitted it selfe to Cesar, deliuerynge vnto hym hostages: whiche exaumple also the other cities folowed: Whereby Cassiuelane after many losses was constreigned to geue pledges, and to agree that Britayne shoulde become Tributarie to the Romaynes. Then Cesar lyke a Conqueroure with a greate nombre of prysoners sayled into Fraunce, and soo to Rome, where shortely after he was slayne with bodkyns. John Lydgate in his booke named the Serpente of deuision, wryteth, that Julius Cesar buylded in this Lande dyuers Ca-

Lōdon submitted to Julius Cesar.

Englande first tributarie to the Romains.

stelles and cities for a perpetuall me-
moire: That is to saye, The castell
of Douer, of Cantorbury, Rochester,
and the Tower of London, the Castel
and townes of Cesars burye: takynge
his name after Cesar, the whiche is
nowe called Salisbury. He also edi-
fyed Cesars Chester, that nowe is
called Chichester, and the castelle of
Excester. &c.

The castels of Douer, Cantorb. Rochest. & the Tower of London built. Salisbury. Chich. and Excetor buylded.

3921/42

42. Theomantius, the sonne of Lud, & nephue to Cassiuelane succeded in the realme of Britayne, and reygned quietlye xxii. yeres: and was buried at London.

3944/19

19. Cymbalinus, the sonne of Theomantius reigned king of Britayn. xxxv. yeares, and was buried at London.

When Cesar Augustus the second Emperour by the wyll of God hadde stablyshed moste sure peace thorough the worlde, oure Redemer Jesu Chryste, very God and man, vpon whom peace wayted, was borne in the. xii. yeare of the reigne of Augustus.

The birth of Christe.

From this place folowing, the yeres sens Chrístes birthe are placed in the margent, &

th

Grafton 1561, states this new form of chronology

the begynnyng of euery Kynges Reygne.

GUiderius, the fyrst sonne of Cym- 17.
beline beganne his reigne ouer the
Britaines, in the. xvij. yeare after the
byrth of Christe our Sauiour. This
man was valiant, hardy, welthy, and
trustyng much in his strength, denyed
to paye tribute to the Romains. For
which cause Claudius the. v. Emperor
came into Britain with a great power,
to clayme agayne the payment therof: &
lastly slewe the sayde Guiderius, when
he had reigned. xxviii. yeres.

ARuiragus, the youngest sonne of 45.
Cymbaline, and brother of Gui- Southāpton, how it
derius, was ordeyned Kyng of Bri- tooke that
tayn: he reigned. xxvij. yeres. He slue name.
Hamon nere to a hauen of the sea, and
threw hym gobbet meale therin: wherfore it is now called Southampton.

Claudius the Emperour (after diuers
happes of battaile toke kynge Aruiragus to his grace. And for so much as he
perceiued hym to be a valiant prince in
token of frendship, gaue to hym his

Gloucester buylded. daughter in mariage, named Genissa. This Claudius buylded Gloucester: and was there buried.

Firs[t] chri-steans in England Some wryters affirme that in the yere after Christs incarnasion. lxiij. came into britaine sent be S. Phelippe the Apostle, Josephe of Aramathe and .xj. other Christians who buylded them a chapel in the Isle of Aualon, sens named Glastonberie.

S. Peter crucified, & S. Paule beheaded, S. Peter by the tyrannye of Nero, was crucified at Rome, after ÿ birthe of our Sauiour Jesus Christe. lxviij. yeares: and S. Paul was there beheaded with the sworde.

73. Marius, the sonne of Aruiragus, an excellent wyse man was ordeyned kyng of Britayne. He reigned. liij. yeres. In his time Lodrike kynge of the Pictes accompanied with the Scots, inuaded brytayn, and spoiled the countrey with sword and fyre: against whō Marius with his knightes assembled in all haste, and gaue them sharpe battaile. Wherin Lodrike captayne of the Pictes was slayne, with a great numbre of his souldiors: to them which remained, Marius gaue inhabitaunce in the further parte of Scotlande. And forasmuch as the Britains disdained to

geue

geue theyr daughters to thē in mariage
they acquainted them with ẏ Irish mē,
and maried their daughters, & grewe
in proces of tyme to a great people.
This Marius buylded the towne of Chester
Chester, and is buried at Carlyon. town builded.

COilus, the son of Marius, was ordeyned Kynge of the brytaines. He 126.
was brought vp euen from his young
age in Italy among the Romains, and
therfore fauoured them greatly, & payd
the tribute truly. Some wryte, that he
builded the town of Colchester, he rei- Colchester
gned .liiij. yeres, & was buried at York. buylded.

LUcie, the son of Coilus was ordeined kyng of britain, who in al hys 180.
acts and dedes folowed the steppes of The Chri-
his forefathers, in such wise ẏ he was sten faith
of al men loued and dread. This Lucie receiued.
in the .viij. yere of his reigne aboute
the yere of our Lorde. 187. sent letters
to Eleutherius byshop of Rome, desy-
rynge hym to sende some deuout and
learned men, by whose instructiō both
he and his people might be taught the
faith and religion of Christ: wherof
Eleutherius beyng glad sent into britain .ii. famous clerkes. Faganus and
Dunianus. By whose diligence Lu-

cie and his people of Britayne were instructed and baptised in the faythe of Christ, 1294. yeares, after the arriuall of Brute: The yere of Christe. 189. Lucius kyng of Britain, when he had reigned .xii. yeares deceased, and was buried at Gloucester: after whose death, for so muche as of hym remayned no heire, the Britaines betwene them selues fell at greate discorde and warre, whiche continued to the great disturbance of the realme about. xv. yeares. By meane of this foresayde discorde amonge the Britons, Seuerus was moued to make haste into this Countreye, as well to quiete the realme, as to kepe back the Pictes and Scots, which vexed them with warre: he caused a walle of turues and greate stakes to be made of the length of. 112. myles (or after some) repaired the wall of Adrian: It began at Tyne, & reached to the Scottishe sea. This Seuerus gouerned Britaine. v. yeares, and was buried at Yorke.

Adrians wall, whiche is called Scottish banke.

219. BAssianus Caracalla succeded hys father in the Empire, and reygned vi. yeares. Of nature he was cruell and fierce, able to endure al payns and labors, & especially in warfare, wherto he

to he semed to be framed of nature.

IN Britayn was yet no Kynge: but the Emperor was accopted as king, wherfore Carassus, a Britayn of lowe byrthe (but valiant and, hardy in marciall dedes) purchased of the Emperour, the kepyng of the coastes of Britayne. By meanes where of he drue to hym many knightes of his countreye, and addressed deadly warre against the Romains, hauing the better hope, for that he heard of the deathe of Bassianus the emperor, who about this time was slain by one of his own seruants. 256

Alectus, a Duke of Rome was sente to subdue Carassus, whiche vnlefully vsurped the Crowne of Britayn: whiche Alectus vanquished Carassus: and lastely slue hym, whan he had reigned vij. yeares.

ALectus, the Romayn gouerned the Britayns after hee had subdued the land agayne to the Romains: and vsed among them much crueltie & tyranny. Wherfore they intēdyng vtterly to expel þ Romains, moued a noble mā called Asclepiodatus, to take on hym the kingdom: who gathered a great power and made sharpe warre vpon the Romains, and chased them from countrey 22[illegible].

to countrey, untyll at lenghte Alectus kept hym at London for his most suretie: whither Asclepiodat⁹ pursued hym
Alectus slain. and nere to that citie gaue him bataile: in whiche Alectus was slain when he had gouerned britaine, vi. yeares,

232. ASclepiodatus, after Alectus was thus slain, belaied the citie of Lōdō with a strong siege, wherin was Linius Gallus the Romain capitain, & ere it were long, by knightly force and violence, entred the citie, and slue the fornamed Gallus, nere unto a broke there at that day runnyng, into which broke
Walbroke in London he threw him: by reasō wherof, it was called Gallus or Wallus brooke: and this day, the strete where somtyme the broke ranne, is called Walbroke. After which victory Asclepiodatus gouerned Britayn. xxv.

262. AT this time hapened a great discention in Britain betwene Asclepiodatus their king, & one Coill duke of Colchester: wherby was raised a greuous warre, in whiche Asclepiodatus was slain. And Coill toke on hym the
Asclepiodatus slaine kyngdome of Britayne, and gouerned the realme the space of. xxvii. yeares.

CОnstantius, a duke of Rome was
289. sent into Britayn to recouer the tribute:

duke: shortely after whose arriual, Coill which then was king, dyed: wherfore the britains to haue more suertie of peace, willed this duke to take to wife Helena, the daughter of Coill, which was a wonderfull faire mayden, and therwith well learned. This Constantius when he had recouered the tribute, returned with his wife Helena to Rome as chief ruler in Britaine, who gouerned the same. xxj. yeares: he was buried at Yorke.

In this Constantius time, was S. Albon prothomartir of England, martyred at Werolan.

Constantine, the sonne of Constantius, succeded as well in the kyngdome of Britayne, as in the gouernāce of other realmes, that were subiect afore to his father. This Constantine was a ryght noble and valyant prince and sonne of Helena, a womā of great sanctimonie, and borne in Britayn. He was so myghty in marciall prowesse, that he was surnamed the great Constantine: and had the Fayth of Christe in suche reuerence, that alwaye moste studiously he endeuoured to augmente the same. In wytnesse of his beleke, he caused a Booke of the Gospell to bee 310.

caried

caryed before hym, and made the Bible to be copied out, and sent into all partes of the Empyre. Of this man the kynges of Britayne had fyrste the priuilege to weare close crownes or Diademes: he reigned. xviij. yeares.

Close crownes in Englād.

Octauius came into Britain, (who is called in ÿ English Chronicles Octauian) reigned in this lande at the lest 54. yeres. In which tyme he was troubled with oftē warres by ÿ Romains.

Maximus, sonne of Leonine, and cousyn Germayne to Constantine the great, was made kyng of Britain, This man was mighty of his handes: but for that he was cruell, and pursued somedeale the Christians, he was called Maximus the tyraunt. Betwene him, and one Conon Meridoke a Britain, was strife and debate, in which they both sped diuersly: but at length they were made frendes. Maximus reygned. viij. yeares. He made warre vpon the Galles, and sayled into Armerica, now called little Britain: and subduyng the countrey, gaue it to Conon Meridoke, to hold for euer of the kynges of great Britayn.

383.

Little Britaine conquered.

Saint Ursula, with the. 11000. virgins, which were sent into litle Britayne

S. Ursula Englād.

tayne to be maried to the forelayd Conon and his knyghtes: were slaine of ÿ barbarous people beyng on the sea.

GRatian that was sent into Britayn of Maximus to defende the lande from Barbarians, toke on hym the kyngdome of Britayn and exercised al tyranny and exaction upon the people: for which cause he was abhorred of all the Britains: and by them was slaine: when he hadde reygned fower yeres. Then was the realme a good space without heade or governoure: In the whiche tyme they were nowe and then very muche vexed wyth the foresayd Barbarous people, and other foreyn enemyes. 384

Here about the yere of Christ. 427. the Britayns were invaded agayne by the Picts and Scots: which not withstandyng the foresayde walle that was made by the Romains, spoiled the coūtrey very sore, so that they were driven to seke newe helpe of the Romaines: who sent to them a company of souldiors: which again chased the Picts, and made a wall of stone of the thickenes of viii. foot, & in heyght 12. foot. Which thing when they had done comforting the Britains, and admonishynge theym

The scots and Pictes invade England.

A walle of stone betwene England and Scotland.

heres

hereafter to trust to their own mãhod & strength, they returned again to Rome.

The scots & Picts inaded this Realme, ẏ Romains efuse to defende: but ther lose he tribute.

The Scottes and Pictes yet once agayne entred the lande of Britayne, spoylynge the countreye, and chasyng the commons so cruelly, that they were altogether comfortlesse, and broughte to suche myserie, that eche robbed and spoyled other, and ouer this, ẏ groũde was vntilled whereof ensued greate scarcitie and hunger, and after hunger death. In this necessitie they sent for ayde to Aetius, thē Romaine capitaine beynge then occupyed in warres in a part of France: but they had no comfort at his hande. And therfore were forced to send ambassade to Aldroenus kyng of lytle britayne, to desyre ayde and comforte: whiche they obteyned, in condition, that yf they atchieued the victory, Constantine his brother shold be made kyng of britayn: for to that day they had no gouernour. Whiche thyng of the ambassadours beynge graunted, the sayd Constantine gathered a company of souldiors, and wēt forth wyth them. And when he had manfully vanquesshed their enemies, obteined the victory: accordyng to the promise made, he was ordeined their kyng, and guyded this

this lande.x.yeres.

Here endeth finally the dominion & tribute of the Romains ouer this lãd, whiche had continued by the space of 483. yeres, from the tyme that Brute began to rule this land.1541. After the city of Rome was builded.1585.yeres 433.

Then it folowed, that when Constantine brother of Aldroenus, had chased and ouercome the Picts and Scotes (as is beforesaid) he was crowned kyng of greate Britayne, and guyded the lande the space of.x.yeares in quietnesse.

In the court of Constantine Kinge of Britayne was a certaine Pict, in so greate fauour and authoritie wyth the kyng, that he mighte at all times come to his presence, who watchynge hys tyme, by secrete meanes trayterouslye slue the king in his chamber. The kynge slayne by a Picte.

Then Constantius his eldest sonne, which for his soft spirit was made a monke at saincte Swithens in Winchester, by ỹ means of Wortiger, duke of Cornewal, was taken out of ỹ cloister, & made kinge: vnder whose name the forsaid Wortiger ruled all the lande and vsed great tirannie, the which Constancius was slaine of certaine Pictes whome A Monke made king of Englãd.

The kynge slayne by Pictes. whome Vortiger had ordeined for a gard to the kynges bodie. Wherof whē Vortiger had knowledge, he wept and makynge semblaunt of greate sorowe caused the said Picts to be put to death, thoughe he in dede were the chiefe causer of their treason and murder. So this Constantius reigned but. v. yeares: And Aurelius and Uther, the kynges yonger brethren, fled into Britayne.

448. VOrtiger was by force ordeined kig of Britain, & gouerned the realme xxi. yeres, not without trouble. For the nobles of Britaine suspected, that Constantius was not murthered without his consent: and therfore alienated their myndes from hym.

Plentie of corne. In Britayn was so greate plentye of corne and fruite, that the lyke had not bene sene many yeares. Which plenty was cause of idelnes, glutony, lechery, and other vices: so that through their incontinent and riotous lyuyng, ensued so great pestilence & mortalitie that the lyuing scantly sufficed to bury the dead. Pestilence.

The Pictes and Scots also, hauing knowledge of the deth of their knightes, les, whiche were slayne by Vortiger, for murderyng of the kynge: inuaded, and in moste cruell wyse spoyled the lande of Britayne.

The Scots and Pictes spoiled this lande.

Vortiger beynge sore abashed, for so much as he knewe the myndes of his people to be alienated from hym: sent for the Saxons, named Angli, whiche had no place to dwell in: and gaue to the inhabitance in Kent. By their help and manhode in many batails he vanquished and droue back the Picts and other enemies: and therfore had them euer after in great loue and fauour.

Saxons entryng this realme.

Hengist, one of the captaynes of the Saxons, found meanes that Vortiger maried his daughter Rowan, a mayde of wonderfull beautie and pleasauntnesse, but a myscreant and Pagane. For her sake, the kynge was deuorced from his lawfull wyfe: by whom he had. iij. sonnes. For whiche dede welnere all the Britaines forsoke him: and the Saxons dayly encreased both in fauour, multitude and auctoritee: and from this time sought alwaye occasion to extinguishe vtterlye the power of the britains, and subdue the lād to them selfe, couenauntynge wyth the Britains, that they shuld attēd to their

Vortiger diuorce & maried Rowan.

wor[illegible]

worldly busynes: and the Saxons (as their souldiours) would defend yͤ land from the incursions of all enemies: for which seruice the Britains shuld geue to them competent meate and wages. And vnder this pretence caused more Saxons to be sent for, entendyng at conuenient tyme, by force to haue the lande in their subiection.

Pelagius heresye. Sainct Germain came into britayn to reduce them from the heresy of Pelagius, to the faith of Christ.

The Britaines consideringe yͤ dayly repaire of the Saxons into this realm shewed their kyng, the ieopardie that might therof ensue, and aduertised him to auoyde the danger, and expell them out of the realm: but all was in vaine. For Vortiger, by reason of his wife,

Vortiger depriued. bore suche fauor towardes the Saxons that he would in no wise heare the coūcell of his subiectes. Wherefore they with one wylle and mynde depriued hym of his royall dignitie, and ordeyned to theyr Kynge, his eldest sonne Vortimerus.

464. Vortymer beynge made Kynge, in

Kyng poysoned. all haste pursued the Saxons: And by hys marciall knyghthode, vanquished theym in .iiij. greate batailles, great battailes, besydes conflyctes and skyrmyshes. Untyll at length he was poisoned by meane of Rowen his step=mother, after he had reigned vii. yeres.

Vortiger obteined againe the kyng=dom of great Britayn, and reigned 374
after this time ix. yeares

The Saxons in Britayne, by priuy guyle and treason, got the king Vorti=ger into their handes, and kept him as prisoner: and by that meanes constrey=ned the Kynge to graunte vnto theym: thre countreys in the land of britaine (that is to say) Kent, Sussex, Suffolk and Norfolke. Then Hengist begann his dominon ouer Kent: and sendynge for moo Saxons, to inhabite the other prouinces: shortly after made war vp=pon the britayns and soo chased theym, that hee kept his kingdome of Kent in peace and war. xxiiii. yeres.

Vortiger fled into Wales, and there buylded a Castell. Of which buildyng and longe lette of the same, and of his prophet Merline the common voice of the people speketh many thynges.

Aurelie surnamed Ambrose, and Vther, the brethren of Constantius kyng of britayne: whyche was slayne by the treasõ of Vortiger, landed with a Na=

nye of shyppes att Totnes: and by the healpe of britaynes, which gathered to thē in al hast made war vpon Vortiger & burned him in his castell in wales,

Vortiger burned.

481 Aurelius Ambrose, was ordeyned kyng of Britayn, which immediatlye hasted hym with an army towards Yorke, against Octa sonne of hengiste, who with hys saxons kepte the Citie where he dyscomfited, and tooke prisoner the sayd Octa

The secōd kingdome of the saxons

A Saxon named Hella, with hys iiii sonnes and a company of Saxons landed in the south part of Britayne, slue the britons & chased manye of thē into desertes & wods, and subdued the countreis of Southery, Somerset, Deuonshyre and Cornewall, which after was called the kingdome of southe Saxons

A Saxon named Porthe, lāded with his ii sonnes, at an hauen in southhamton shire, After whom, the hauen is named Portsmouth,

How portsmouth came by that name

The kingdome of the East Saxons began in britayne vnder a duke named Offa: The kingdome whereof conteyned Norffolk and Suffolke: the kings of that lordshipp were called Offinges: gret murder & vexation of the britains was at the entryng of those Saxons.

The third kingdome of the Saxons,

In

In the ende of Aurelie, hys reigne, Pascentius, the yongest sonne of Vortiger: who for feare of Aurelius fled in to Irelande, inuaded this lande with a great army. Aurelius died being poisoned when he had reigned xix yeares,

Uther, surnamed Pendragon, was crowned kynge of Britayne, and reigned.xvi.yeares. Hee was enamored vpon the dukes wife of Cornwall, and to obteyne his vnlefull lust, made warre vppon her husbande Garlus, and slewe hym in battayle hee was buryed at Stonehing. 500

Arthur, the sonne of Uther Pendragon, a striplinge of xv.yeares of age began his reigne ouer Britayne, and gouerned the land.xxvi.yeares hauyng continual warr and mortal battayle wyth the saxons. 517

John Frosarde affirmeth, that kyng Arthure builded the castell of Wyndesoure: and there founded the order of the rounde Table.

Windesor castel builded

The fourth kyngdome of the weste Saxons beganne in Britayn, vnder a Saxon called Cerdicus. They landed first at an hauē in Norfolk called Yarmouth Wyth this Saxon Cerdicus, & hys people, Arthur hadd much trouble

The fourth kingdome of the saxons

and war. This lordship, conteined the west parte of Englande, as Wilshyre, Somersetshyre, Barkeshyre, Dorsetshyre, and other.

Arthure, when after many and dyuers battayls, he hadde sette hys land, in some quietnes: hee betoke the rule thereof to hys nephewe Mordred, and with a chosen army sayled into Fraunce where he did meruailous thynges, and vanquished Lucius Hibertus, the Romaine Captayne, whiche thyng semeth not to agree with other hystoryes.

Mordred usurpeth

Mordred, whyche hadde the gouernaunce of Britayne in the absence of Arthure, by treason was crowned kyng through the healpe of Cerdicus kyng of west Saxons. Of whiche treason when relation came to Arthur beyng then in Fraunce, with all haste he made backe to Britayne: where hee was mette of Mordred, whiche gaue to hym thre strong battayls, In ye whiche manye noble and valiaunt knightes perysshed. And lastely, in a battayle foughten besydes Glassenbury, Mordred was slayne. And Arthure wounded vnto the death. He was buryed in the valley of Aualon, and afterwardes at Glassenbury.

Mordred ...yne ...thur ...unded

Con-

COnstantine, kinsman to Arthure 548
by assent of the Britons was ordeyned kynge of Britayne, and reigned
thr yeres. Thys man was by the two
sonnes of Mordred greuouslye vexed.
For they claimed the land by the ryght
of theyr father: soo that betwene theym
was foughten sundrye battayls: In the
whyche lastelye the two brethren were
vanquished and slayne. Gildas the wyse

Holy Gildas our countriman flou-
ryshed in thys tyme, he was called Gil
das the wise.

Aurelius Conanus a britayne raysed
mortall war, agaynste Constantine the
kyng: and after sore fyght, slew hym in
the field, when he had reigned. iii. yeares, and was buryed at Stonehing.

AUrelius Conanus, was crowned 546
kyng of britayne: he was noble, har
dy, and therwyth very liberal, but hee
cheryshed such as loued strife and discention wythin hys Realme: and gaue
lyght credence to theym, whyche accused other, wer it ryght or wrõg. He im-
prisoned by strength hys vncle, whych
was ryght heyre to the crowne: & died
when he had reigned .iij yeares.

The kingdome of Northumberland The b an vi. kyng
began first in britayn vnder a Saxon

[...]m of the [...]cons named Ida. Thys prouince was first deuided into two kingedomes: The one was called Deyra, which conteyned the land frō Humber to Tine: the other Brenitia, whyche included the countrey from Tyne to the Scottishe sea. After this day ẏ britaynes decresed dayly in lordship and rule, and drewe them towards Wales, so that the countrey about Chester was the chiefe of their lordshypp.

[...]548 Vortiporus, the sonne of Codanus: was ordeyned kyng of Britayne: of whom is little memory left: sauinge ẏ Guido testifieth, that he was a victorious prince: and that he in diuers battayles discomfited the Saxons: he reigned. iiij yeares

[...]52 Malgo, a duke of Britayn, beganne his reygne ouer the britayns, and gouerned theim. xxxv. yeares, he was the most personable man of all the britans then liuing, and therewyth indued wyth knightly manhode: but he delited in the foule syn of Sodomye: and therfore was greately spoyled by hys enemies the Saxons.

[...]he fyrste [...]atte be[...] [...]ene the [...]cons Ethelbert, kynge of the Saxons in Kent, gaue battaile to Ceaulinus king of the west Saxons: in whyche fyghte were

were slayne. ii dukes of Ethelberts, & him selfe wyth his people chased. This was the fyrst warre betwene the Saxons after they had land and dwelling within thys realme,

Careticus began to rule the britons: this man loued ciuile warre, & was odible both to god and to hys subiects they moued the Saxons to warre vpon hym: who toke from hym a great part of hys lande. 586

The Saxons hearing of the discention betwen Careticus & his britons, beynge accompanied wyth Gurmundus kynge of Ireland, made war vpon Careticus, in suche wyse that he was fayne too take the towne of Cicester, wher they assaulted him so sore that he wyth hys men fledde from thence into Wales: by whyche meanes hee lefte a greate part of his dominion: and shortly after ended hys lyfe when he hadde reigned iii yeres. Gurmundus buylded Gurmend chester

The Britaynes whiche were chased by their enemies into Wales (as is before sayd) held them in those parties, and assaulted the Saxons some whyle in one coaste and somtime in an other vnder sundry dukes, and so continued the space of xxiiii yeares 589.

A Summerie

In Britayne Ethelfridus gouerned the Northsaxons, who made such continuall warre vpon the Britons, and chased them so sore, that it is thoughte he slew mo of them, then all the other Saxons kynges. By this crueltie, the fayth of Christe was almost vtterly extinguished amõg the Britains, whych hadde continued sence the tyme of Lucius aboute 400. yeares, and many of the Britaynes were chased oute of the Ilande, the reste remayned in Wales: who there kepte the Christen Faythe, which they had receiued.

...xons ...de the ...ole pos ...ion of ...s realm

The britains being chased out of theyr countrey into Wales, the Saxons obteined the whole dominion of this Ilãd: Sauing a part of Scotlãd which was subiecte to ÿ Pictes and Scots: & the britons kept thẽ selues in Wales.

Augus. ...e into ...glande Austẽs Cãtorb Pauls ...rche in ...ndon & ...drews Roches.

In Anno dñi. 596, S. Gregorie sente S Augustin Millitus Iustus, & John, with other lerned men to preach the christen fayth to the Angels: which were fyrst receiued of Ethelberte kynge of Kente, whom they cõuerted to the fayth, with diuers of hys people. Thys Ethelbert (as some wryte) firste began to buylde: S. Austins in cantorbury S. Poules church in London & S. Andrews in Rochester

chester

chester: he also excited a citiſē of Lōdon to buyld the Abbey of Westmynster. 613

Adwan duke of Northwales, was made soueraigne of the Brytaynes, who commyuge oute of Wales gaue strong battaile to Ethelfride kynge of Northumberlande theyr moste deadly enemye: and in dyuers encountres soo discomfited the sayd Ethelfride, that he was forced to intreate for peace: After whych concord made betwene those ii. princes they continued all theyr lyfe tyme, as two speciall and louyng frendes, he reigned xxii. yeares.

Also about this tyme began ỷ kyngdom of Mercia or middle England vnder the strong painim & Saxon called Penda: whych lordship conteined Hūtingtonshire, Herefordshyre, Glocestershire, and other, and was greatest of all other kyngdomes. Att that tyme reigned in dyuers parts of thys lande vii. kynges.

The .vii. kyngdom

Edwyn kyng of Northumberlande was baptised of ỷ holy bishoppe Paulinus: and after hym, many of hys people: he for the refreshyng of wayfaring menne, ordayned cuppes and dyshes of yron to be fastned by such clere welles and fountains as did runne by the

Paulinus builded the great churche at Lincolne

Iron cups fastned by welles & fountaines

was es

ways syde.

635 Cadwallyn the son of Cadwane be-
gan his reigne ouer the Britayns. He was valiaunte and myghtie, and warred strongely vppon the Saxons: and made Penda kyng of Mercia tributarie to him: he reigned.xlviii.yeres and was buried at London in S. Martins church by Ludgate.

Fyrste Schole in Cambridg

Segeberte, kinge of East Angles or Northfolke, ordeyned good learning to be taught, and erected Schooles in dyuers partes of hys dominion, as hee sometyme hadde seene in Fraunce, By hym was the first common Schole founded at Cambridge.

Penda kyng of Mercia warred vppon Oswalde the good and holy kynge of Northumberland: and slue hym in battayle with many of his knights

Oswye, the brother of Oswald obteyned the kyngdome of Northumberlande: who slue Oswyne his brothers sonne: and made Oilwaldus partaker of his kingdome.

The bishops of Winchester

Kenwalcus kyng of West Saxons was restored to his kingdome by the helpe of Anna, king of east angles. He builded the byshops see of Winchester, and made Agelbert the first bishopp of that see. And after him was one named Wyne, of whome the citie tooke the name of Wynchester.

Benet the monke, and maister of the reuerend Beda, was famous in Britayn. This Benet brought fyrst the craft of glasyng into this lande.

Glasyng brought Englande

Cissa begun to builde thee abbey of Abingdon, and Erkenwalde bishop of London builded the abbeys of Chertsey, and of Barking in Essex. Chertsey in Southery was afterward destroied by the Danes.

The abbes of Abingtō Chertsey & Barkinge builded

681

CAdwallader was ordeyned Kynge of Britons, and ruled onely .iii. yeares, hee vanquished and slewe Lothayre kyng of Kent, and Athelwolde kyng of South saxons, and then forsakyng hys kingly authoritie, he went to Rome, and there became a religious man, and was buried at saint Peters church at Rom. He was at the last king of Britayne. And this lande after this tyme was called Anglia, and ye enhabitantes therof Angles or Englishmen, and the Britaynes were called Walshe men. This happened .1791. yeares, or as sayeth Fabian .1812. after that Brute fyrste arriued in this lande: After the conquest of Cesar 735. yeres:

The kinge became a monke

The Iland called vniuersally England

From

From the entryng of the Saxons vnder there leaders Hengist and Horsus in the tyme of Vortiger. 2 3 6. or nere there about.

Thus endeth the reigne of the Britons: and now foloweth the reigne of the Saxons. And althoughe the Saxōs hadd deuides this realme into seuen seuerall kyngdomes: yet I wyll nowe speake chiefely of the west Saxons in order, because that (in proces of tyme) they subdued the other Kynges, and broughte it agayn ento one monarchie.

Ine reyned amonge the weste Saxons a noble manne of greate po-
99 wer and wisedome, and therwith va-
liant and hardy: in feates of armes very expert, he mainteyned such war agaynst the Kentyshe Saxons, that hee constrayned theym to seke and intreate meanes of peace, geuyng to hym for the same great gyftes. This man builded first the college of Welles, & the abbey of Glastenbury: he payd ŷ Peter pens first to Rome, when he hadd gouerned the west Saxōs by the space of xxxviii. yeres, by the earnest labour of his wife Etheldreda, which was an holy womā and abbesse of Barking in Esser, gaue vp his royal power, and became a pore

[Margin:] The colleg of Wels, & the abbei of Glastēburi newly builded.

[Margin:] The quene west sax- as abbesse Barking e kynge r husband religious

man

man, & went to Rome on pilgremaige

After hym Ethelarde was kynge of west Saxons, in whose tyme the reuerēd Beda was famous, and wrote hys boke called Anglica historia, to Offrick king of Northumberland. Ethelarde reigned .v. yeares.

S. Beda

726

Cuthred was kinge of west Saxons This man made warre vpon Ethelwald of Mercia, and sped therin diuersly. In hys tyme appeared two blasing sterres, castynge as it were burnynge brandes towards the north. Hee reigned .xvi. yeres. Ethelwalde before named builded the abbey of Crowlande,

two comets

Crowlande abbey builded

The holy man Beda, which for hys learnyng & godly life, was renoumed in al ẏ world, ended his last day about the yere of Christe. 734. he in his lyfe compiled lxxviij, bookes

Beda deceased

Sigeberte was made kynge of Weste Saxons: he was cruel & tirannous towards his subiectes & chaunged auncient lawes and customes, After hys owne will and pleasure. And because a certain noble man, somedeale sharpely aduertised him to change hys maners, he maliciously caused the same person to be put cruelly to death: And for so much as he continued in his malice, & 745

woulde

From the entryng of the Saxons vnder there leaders Hengist and Horsus
in the tyme of Vortiger. 2 3 6. or nere
there about.

Thus endeth the reigne of the Britons: and now foloweth the reigne of
the Saxons. And althoughe the Saxōs
hadd deuided this realme into seuen seuerall kyngdomes: yet I wyll nowe
speake chiefely of the west Saxons in
order, because that (in proces of tyme)
they subdued the other Kynges, and
broughte it agayn into one monarchie.

Ine reyned amonge the weste Saxons a noble manne of greate po-
99 wer and wisedome, and therwith valiant and hardy: in feates of armes very expert, he mainteyned such war a-
gaynst the Kentyshe Saxons, that hee
constrayned theym to seke and intreate
meanes of peace, geuyng to hym for the
same great gyftes. This man builded
first the college of Welles, & the abbey
of Glastenbury: he payd ye Peter pens
first to Rome, when he hadd gouerned
the west Saxōs by the space of xxxviii.
yeres, by the earnest labour of his wife
Etheldreda, which was an holy womā
and abbesse of Barking in Essex, gaue
by his royal power, and becam a pore
man

he colleg
Wels, &
e abbei of
lastēburi
wly buil
d.

he quene
west sax-
s abbesse
Barking
e kynge
r husband
religious
man

man, & went to Rome on pilgremaige

After hym Ethelarde was kynge of west Saxons, in whose tyme the reuerẽd Beda was famous, and wrote hys boke called Anglica historia, to Offrick king of Northumberland. Ethelarde reigned. v yeares. S. Beda 726

Cuthred was kinge of west Saxons. This man made warre vpon Ethelwald of Mercia, and sped therin diuersly. In hys tyme appeared two blasing sterres, castynge as it were burnynge brandes towards the north. Hee reigned. xvi. yeres. Ethelwalde before named builded the abbey of Crowlande, two comets Crowlande abbey builded

The holy man Beda, which for hys learnyng & godly life, was renoumed in al ẏ world, ended his last day about the yere of Christe. 734. he in his lyfe compiled lxxviij, bookes Beda deceased

Sigeberte was made kynge of Weste Saxons: he was cruel & tirannous towards his subiectes & chaunged auncient lawes and customes, after hys owne will and pleasure. And because a certain noble man, somedeale sharpely aduertised him to change hys maners, he maliciously caused the same person to be put cruelly to death: And for so much as he continued in his malice, & 745

woulde

ynge depri- would not amend: he was depriued of all kyngly authoritie: and lastelye as a
ued, & person desolate and forlorn, wandring
slayne by a alone in a wood, was slayn by a swine-
swineherd herde, whose lord and mayster (when he had reigned as king) he was wrong fully put to death, whenne he had reigned, iii, yeares.

748 Kenulphus, of the linage & bloud of
Winchomb Cerdicus fyrst kyng of west saxons
abbey buil- reigned in the kingdom xxxi. yeares
ded Kenulfe king of Mercia builded the
The abbey abbey of Wynchcombe,
S. Albons Offa, kynge of Mercia builded the ab-
builded bey of saint Albons, hee chased the britons or walshemenne into Wales, and made a famous dike betwene Wales and the vtterbondes of Mercia, which is now called Offa dike.

Kenulphus as hee haunted to a woman, which he kept at Merton, was
Kynge slayne by treason of one Clio, the kins-
Kenulphus man of Sigebert, late kyng. Hee was
slayne buried at Winchester.

Brithricus, of the bloude of Cer-
778 dicus, was made kinge of weste
It raynede saxons: and knyghtly ruled his lande
bloud y space of xvii yeares: he maried one of the daughters of Offa, king of Mercia In his tyme it reigned bloude frome

heauen

heauen, whych fallynge on mens clothes appeared lyke crosses. The danes first entred this land

The Danes fyrst entred this land of Britayne, but by the strength and puissance of Brithricus, and other kynges of the saxons they were driuen backe, and compelled to voyde the land. Brithricus was poisoned by his wyfe Ethelburga. For whiche dede the nobles ordeined, that frome thence foorth thee kinges wyues shoulde not bee called Quenes, nor suffred to syt with theim in places of estate. kyng poysoned.

Egbert the Saxon whych by Brithricus was chased oute of the Realme, hauing knowledge of the deathe of Buthricus, returned oute of Fraunce and in so knightly wyse demayned him selfe, that he obteined the gouernmente of weste saxons, hee tamed the welshe men, vanquished, Berthulphus kynge of myddle Englande, and reigned as kyng ouer the more part of Englande, the space of xxxvii yeres, and was buried at Wynchester, in hys tyme The Danes wyth a great hoste, entred thys land the second tyme, and spoiled the Isle, of Shepey in Kent, agaynst whō Egbect the kyng addressed hym 796

The danes seconde entring thys land

wyth

with his power: whō the Danes forste to flee the fielde. After which time, som of the Danes continually abode in one place or other of this lande.

832 Ethelwolphus, the son of Egberte began his reign ouer the more part of England. He went to Rome, where he repaired the englishe schole, whiche was first foūded by Offa king of Mercia. This schole was after tourned to an hospitall for englyshemen, whiche cam to Rome, he first founded the vniuersitie of Oxenford, which some writers attribute to Offa, kinge of Mercia He reigned. xxiii yeares, and was buried at Winchester.

An hospital for english mē builded at Rome

Onforde buylded.

855 Ethelwaldus, after the death of his father, began his reign in England he maried a woman, which his father had kept before as his concubene: and dyed when he hadde not reygned fully one yeare.

856. Ethelbert, the brother of Ethelwold was made kyng ouer the more part of Englande, In the beginnyng of his reigne, the Danes entred the west part of the realm, and spoyled the countreye afore theym, til they came to Winchester and by stregth toke it. But by the kyng and his dukes, they were forced

The Danes thirde entrynge this land

to leaue Wynchester, and in retyryng towards the shyps, they lost a greate number of their men. He reigned vij. yeares, and was buried at Sherborn.

Etheldred the third sonne of Ethelwolphus, toke on him ỹ gouernãce of Weste saxons, and other prouinces of England. He was a man framed of nature aswell to peace as warre. Amõg his subiectes, he was myld, gentil, louing and pleasant: against his aduersaries, seuere, fierce, valiant, and hardye. He lyued in continuall war with the Danes: whiche all the tyme of his reign, vexed this land with most deadly warres: he deuided the day in three parts. viij. houres to serue god. viij. to here suites of his people, and. viij. to take his slepe and rest. 893.

This king deuided the day & night in. 3. parts 8. houres to serue god 8 to here suites of his people. and 8. to take his slepe & rest.

A company of Danes landed in Northumberlande: and after many battailes, possessed and held that countreye, the space of. lx. yeares, and got also the Citie of Yorke. An other company of Danes entred the coūtrey of Norfolke where they slue ỹ holy king Edmond, which gouerned that prouince: because he wolde not forsake ỹ faith of Christ.

The danes landed in Northumberland.

Kyng Edmund slain

At Colyngham abbey saint Ebbe abbesse cut of her nose & ouerlip, & per-

Women to kepe their

Chastitye. suaded al her sisters to do the lyke that they beyng odible to ŷ Danes, mought the better kepe their virginitie: in despite wherof, the Danes burned the abbey, and the Nunnes therin.

Also those Danes landed in Southrey, and went forward til they came to Readyng, and toke that towne and castel: at which tyme, whyle Etheldred was busied against them, he had worde

Kyng slain of the landynge of Offrike Kynge of Denmarke with an other company, to whome the kynge gaue many stronge battayles. But in the ende he was put to the worse, and receyued a wounde, wherof he died, when he had reigned. ix. yeares was buried at Winborne.

872. Alured, the fourth sonne of Ethelwolphus began his reigne ouer the more parte of Englande, and reigned xxviii. yeares. He was wyse, discrete, and lerned, and fauoured good letters excellently wel. He buylded the house

Shaftsbury & Ethelingsei builded. of Nunnes at Shaftisburye, and an other at Ethelyngsey.

First schole in Oxeford. By the counsayle of Nottus, Alured ordeined the first Grammer schole in Oxenford, and franchesed the towne with many great liberties. He buylded

ded the newe minster in Wynchester, and there lyeth buried. New abbey in Winch.

Edward, the elder sonne of Alured, began his reigne ouer the most part of England, and gouerned this lande well and nobly .xxiiij. yeres. He buylded Hereford castell, and adioyned to his lordshyp all this Ilande, sauynge onely Northumberlande, which was possessed of the Danes. He lyeth buried at Wynchester by his father, in the newe minster. he builded the monastery of S. Peter in Gloucester. 901. Kyng Edward the senior. Herford castel built. S. Peter in Gloucester buylded.

Adelstane, the sonne of Edwarde senior began hys reygne in Englande. He was a prince of worthy memorye, valyant and wise in all hys actes: and broughte thys lande to one Monarchye: for he expelled vtterlye the Danes, subdued the Scottes, and quieted the Welshemen. He reigned .xv. yeares, and lyeth at Malmesbury. 925. King crouned at kingston.

Edmunde, the brother of Adelstane tooke on hym the gouernaunce of this Realme: whose shorte reygne tooke from hym the renoume of most hyghe prayses that shoulde haue redounded to his posteritie: for he was a man disposed of nature to noblenes 940.

and iustice: he reigned v. yeares and was buried at Glastenbury.

946. Eldred succeded Edmunde his brother: for his sonnes Edwine and Edgar, were thoughte to young to take on them so great a charge. This Eldred hadde the earnest fauoure of the commons, because he was a greate mainteyner of honestye, and also moste abhorred naughty and unruly persons for his expertnes in feates of armes, he was much commended. Whereby he quieted and kept in due obeisance, the Northumbers & Scotes, and exiled the Danes. He reigned. ix yeares, and was buried in the cathedrall churche of Wynchester.

Crowned at Kyngstō.

955. Edwine succeded his uncle Eldred in the kyngdome: of whome is left no honeste memorye, for one heynous acte by hym commytted in the begynnynge of his reigne. In the selfe daye of his Coronation, he sodaynlye withdrewe him selfe from his Lordes, and in the sighte of certaine persons, rauished his own kynswoman, the wife of a noble man of his Realme: and afterwarde slewe her husband, that he myght haue the unlawfull use of her beauty: Whiche acte, and for banishinge Dunstane

Crouned at Kingstone.
[V]icious [K]yng.

stane, he becam odible to his subiectes and of the Northumbers, a people of middle Englande, that rose agaynste hym was depriued, when he had reigned .iii. yeres, he was buried in the cathedrall churche of Winchester.

The kynge depriued.

Edgar, brother to Edwine, began his reigne in Englande. He was a prince of worthye memorye, for hys manifolde vertues greatly renoumed: so excellent in iustice, and sharp in correction of vices, aswel in his magistrates, as other subiectes: that neuer before his dais was vsed lesse felonye by robbers, or extortion & bribery by fals officers. He chastised also the gret negligēce, couetousnes, & vicious liuyng of the clergy, he refourmed, & brought them to a better order: of stature he was but litle, but of mynd valiaunt & hardy, and very expert in martial policie, he prepared a great nauye of shyppes, which he disposed in .iiij. partes of hys realm, and had souldiours alway readye againste the inoursions of forein enemies, he reigned .xvi. yeares. He builded Peters Bury, Thorney, Ramsey, and manye other, and was buried at Glastenbury.

959.

Crouned at Bath: some say at Kingston.

This king builded & repaired Wiltō, Peterborowe, Thorney, Ramsei, &c.

675. EDward the sonne of Edgar by hys fyrst wyfe, beganne his reigne ouer this realme, contrary to the mynd and pleasure of Elfrede hys stepmother, and other of her alliance. In all kinds of honest vertue, this man myght well be compared to his father: and began his Reygne wyth suche modestie and myldenesse, that he was worthylye fauoured of all men: Excepte onelye Elfride, whiche euer bare a grudge againste hym: for so muche as she desyred to haue the gouernaunce of the Realme, for her owne soonne Egel-
The kyng murdered. red. And whyle he was huntynge in a forest (by chaunce) he lost his company, and rode alone to refreshe hym at the castell of Corffe: where by the counsayle of his stepmother he was traiterouslye murthered, as he satte on his horse: When he had reigned. iij. yeares. He was buryed at Shaftsburye. The foresayde Elphred after-
Almesbury & Warwel buylded. warde takynge greate penance, buylded Almesbury and Warwel: In whiche Warwell she after lyued a solitarie lyfe tyll she dyed.

EThelrede or Etheldrede, the sonne of kyng Edgar and Elphrede, was ordeyordeined Kyng of England, and crowned at Kyngston. In his tyme the Danes arrued in sundry places of Englande: as in the Ile of Thenet, in Cornewalle, and Sussex. In conclusion, for aduoidyng of further daunger, he was compelled to appeace them with greate summes of money: but when the money was spent, they fell to newe robbynge. And to augmente the kynges sorowe, Elphricus that then was admirall of Englande, traiterously fled to the Danes. And after, beyng reconciled, fledde to them the seconde tyme.

The kyng crowned at Kyngston.

The blondy flixe, the burnyng feuer with diuers other maladies vexed the people throughout all Englande.

Swaine Kinge of Denmarke repented of the former couenauntes, made with the Englishe men, with a stronge armye entred Northumberlande, and so wente foorthe tyll he came to London, which he besieged: and destroyed the countrey of Kent. Egelred dispairynge of all recouerye, fled to Richard duke of Normandy: and then possessed Swayn the hole kyngdome of this realme: who spoiled the landes of S. Edmunds. But after

London besieged.

his death succeded Canutus his sonne who inclosed the same wyth a depe diche, and graunted to thinhabitants therof, great freedome. And after builded a churche ouer the place of his sepulture, and ordeined there an house of monkes enduyng them with fayre possessions.

S. Edmundes bury buylded.

The Englyshmen sent agayn for Etheldred out of Normandy, who by the helpe of the Normãs, and present assistauce of his commons expelled Canutus, but shortly Canutus retourned again into Englande, where he spared nothing that myght be destroyde wyth sword and fyre. In whiche tyme king Etheldred ended his life, when he had reigned .xxxviii. yeares, and was buried in the north Ile of Paules church in London, aboue the altar. In the seconde yeare of this Kynges reigne a greate parte of the city of London was wasted with fyre: But ye shall understand, that the citie of Lõdon had most housyng and buyldyng from. Ludgate toward Westminster: & littel or none where the chiefe or hart of the Citie is now, excepte in diuers places was housing. But they stode without order. So that many townes and cities, as

A great fire in London.

Cantor-

Cãtorbury, Yorke, and diuers other in England, passed London in buildyng. But after the conqueste it increased, and shortely after passed and excelled all the other in the. xvj. yere of his reigne he erected a Byshoprike in Cornwall, placyng the bys hops see in the citie of Exceter.

Bishops see at Exceter.

Edmunde the son of Etheldred, a yong man of lusty and valiant courage in martiall aduentures, both hardy and wyse, and one that coulde very well endure all paynes: Wherfore he was surnamed Ironside was by the citysens of London chosen to be kynge: but the more part fauored Canutus the Dane. By meanes wherof, betwene those two princes were foughten many great battails: in the whiche eyther party sped diuersly to the great slaughter of them that toke their parts. But lastly it was agreed, that the two captains should trie their quarell betwen them selues only. In whiche fight, although Edmond semed to haue the vpper hand: yet he cõdescended to deuide the realme, and make Canutus felowe with him in the kingdome.

1016.

Edmond. Ironsyde.

An Englishe Earle called Edricus, which by his falshode wrought muche

hurte

harte to his naturall countreye, lastly was auctor of the death of the noble Edmunde. And therof hym selfe brought first knowledge to Canutus, saying in this wise: Thus haue I done Canutus, for loue of thee. To whome he aunswered, sayinge: For my loue thou haste murdered thyn owne soueraigne Lorde, whome I loued moste entierly: I shall in rewarde therof, exalte thy head aboue all the Lordes of

A iust rewarde.

Englande. And forthwith commaunded hym to be beheaded, and his heade to be set on the hyghest gate of London. These princes reigned together. ii. yeres. This Edmund was buried at Glastenbury.

1018. Canutus beynge stablished in the kyngdome, he had knowlege howe Olanus kynge of Norway in his absence inuaded the countrey of Denmarke: wherfore in all hast he sped him thitherward: & by the manhod of the englishe souldiours, obteined of them a noble victory, and recouered Norway to his seignorie. Wherfore when he retorned into Englande, he demeaned hym toward all men as a sage gentyll and moderate prince, and so continued xx. yeares, he subdued the Scotes, wher-

whereby he was kinge of. iiij. kyngdoms, that is to saye, of Englande, Scotland, Denmarke, and Norwaye. And after his death was buried at Saincte Swithins in Winchester.

1038 Harold, the sonne of Canutus, by his wife Elgina, for his swyftnes surnamed Harefoote, began his reigne ouer this realme of Englande. In the begynnynge he shewed some token of crueltie, in that he banyshed his stepmother Emma, and toke from her suche iewels and treasure as she hadde. He reigned. iii. yeares. He was buried at Westmynster, and after at S. Clementes without Temple barre.

1748 Hardikenitus, kyng of Denmarke, after the death of Harolde, was ordeyned Kynge of Englande. He for the iniurie done to his mother Emma, caused the corps of Harolde to bee taken out of the sepulchre: and smytynge of the head, caste it with the body into the riuer of Thames: where by a fysher it was taken vp, and vnreuerently buried at S. Clementes) as afore is sayd. He burdeined his subiectes with exactions and tribute: and in meat and drinke was soo prodigalle, that hys

tables

tables were spreade. iiij. tymes in the day, and the people serued with greate excesse: when he had reigned. iij. yeres, he died sodeinly at Lambeth, not without suspection of poysonyng, and was buried at Winchester: After whose death the Danes were beaten, slaine, and driuen out of this land, into theyr owne coūtrey. xxviij. yeares after that Swayn began to reigne.

1043. Edwarde, the sonne of Egelrede or Etheldred, by the aduice of Godwyne and Leofricus Erle of Chester, after the death of Hardikenitus, was sēt for out of Normādy to take on him the gouernance of this realme, whiche he guided with muche wisedome and Justice, from whome issued as out of a foūtaine, very godlinesse, mercy, pitie, and liberalitie toward the poore, & gentilnes and iustice towards al men: and in all honest lyfe, gaue most godly exaumple to his people. He discharged the Englishmen of the great tribute called the Dane gelt, which was often before tyme leuied to the empouerishynge of the people. He subdued the Welshmen, whiche rebelled.

William bastarde. William bastard duke of Normandie, about this tyme came with a goodly comly company into Englande: and was honorably receiued, to whom the king made great chere. And at his retourne enriched him with great giftes & pleasures: and (as some write) made promise to him, that if he died without issue, the same William shoulde succede hym in the kyngdom of England.

Harold the sonne of the Erle Godwin, went to Normandy: wher he made faithful promise to duke William, that after the death of Edward, he woulde kepe the kyngdome to his behalfe: on which condicion, he brought with him at his retourne his brother Tosto.

Kyng Edward finished his last daye when he had reigned foure and twenty yeares. vii. monethes and odde dais. He purged the olde and corrupt lawes and picked oute of theym a certayne, whiche were moste profytable for the commons. And therfore were they called the common Lawes. For restitution wherof, happened diuers commotions and insurrections in this Land. He was buried at Westminster. The lawes of S. Edwarde.

Harolde, the eldest sonne of Earle Godwyne, beynge of greate power in Englande, and therwith valyaunt and hardye, tooke on hym the gouernaunte 1066.

uernaunce of this lande, nothynge regardyng the promyse that he made to Wyllyam, duke of Normandye. Wherfore whenne Wyllyam sente to hym Ambassades, admonyshynge hym of the couenauntes that were agreed betwene them. Harolde would in no wyse surrendre to hym the kyngdome, whiche Wyllyam claymed, not onlye for the promise that was made to him: but also bycause he was the nexte of kyng Edwards bloud.

Whenne Wyllyam Duke of Normandye perceiued, that he coulde not by any meanes bryng Harolde to fulfylle hys promyse, nor by treatie to yelde vnto hym the kyngedome: By force he entred the lande, to whome Harolde gaue stronge and sharpe battayle. In the ende whereof, Willyam chased the Englishemen, slewe Harolde, and obtayned the gouernance of this lande, when Harolde had reigned but.ix.monethes He was buryed at Waltham abbey, whiche he hym selfe had buylded, and was the laste that reigned of the bloude of the Saxons in this Realme.

Waltam abbey.

Kynge

Kyng William Conqueror.

Anno Regni. i.

WIllyam Duke of Normandy, surnamed Conquerour, Bastarde sonne of Roberte the syxte Duke of ye duchye, and nephew vnto kynge Edward the Confessour, beganne his dominion ouer this Realme of England, the. xxiii. daye of October, in the yeare of oure Lorde. 1067. and deceased in the yeare 1087. The nynth daye of September, and reigned xix. yeares. xi. monethes, lackyng fyue dayes. He vsed greate crueltie towarde the Englyshemenne, burdenynge them with greuous exactions: By meane whereof he caused diuers to flee the lande into other countreyes. And lyke as hee obteyned the kyngdome by force and dent of swearde so he chaunged the whole state of this cōmon weal, and ordeined new lawes at his pleasure, profitable to himselfe: but greuous and hurtfull to the people This William was wyse and polétike riche and couetous, and loued well to 1067.

be magbe magnified. He was a fayre speaker and a great dissembler. A man of comly stature, but somdeale grosse bealied: sterne of countenaunce, and stronge in armes, and had great pleasure in huntynge, and makinge of sumptuous feastes.

Anno.2.

1068. The towne of Excetour, and the Northumbers rebelled, whiche were both subdued, and greuously punished.

Tho castels buylded at yorke one other at Notingham, an other at Lincolne.

This kynge William buylded foure stronge castels: Twayne at Yorke, one at Notyngham, an other at Lincolne. whiche he furnished with garrisons of Normaynes..

Anno.3.

1069. Canutus kyng of Denmarke beynge encouraged therto by certayne Englishe outlawes, inuaded the Northe partes of Englande, and passed thorough to Yorke: from whens he was driuen backe by Wylliam, and forced to flee into his owne countrey.

Anno.4

1070. The Scots with their kynge Walcolyne, inuaded Northumberland, and spoyled the countrey.

Anno. 6

Kynge William by the counselle of the Erle of Hertford caused the money and ryches of the abbeys to be brought into his treasorye: he made also the new Forest in the countreye of Southampto, for ỹ atcheiuing of which enterprise he was forst to cast downe diuers townes & churches. xxx myles of lengthe, and replenished thee same wyth wylde beastes, and made sharpe lawes for the maintenaunce & increase of the same, — 1072 — The newe forest

Anno. 10

Roger erle of Hertford & Ranulphe earle of Norffolke conspired agaynste Kinge William beyng in Normandye, bothe whiche were by him outlawed, and chased oute of thee Realme. And Waldiffe that was duke of Northumberlande, & Earle of Huntingdon and Northampton (who vttered the conspiracie) was beheaded at Winchester, and buried at Crowland — 1076 — Execution

Anno. 13

At this time Oswalde Byshoppe of Salisbury was famous in Englande. The kyng gaue the Elrcdome of Northumberlande to Walter byshoppe of — 1079

Ducham, who was after slayne by the men of Northumberland

Anno.15

1081 Roberte the eldest sonne of William inuaded his fathers Duchye of Normandye, where wyth William beynge gretly displeased: gaue his son a strong battayle, in which it fortuned Roberte to mete vnwares in the field with his father, and bere him to the earthe. But perceiuynge by the voyce who it was forthwith hee lepte from hys horse, and saued his father. By whiche deede hee was reconciled, and peace betwene them was a greed

Anno.16

1082 Aboute this.xvi. yere, earle Maryn
Shrewes, & Welok abbeis built. erle of Shrewsbury, made two abbeis wherof the one was in the suburbes of Shrewsbury, & the other of Wenloke.

Anno 19

1085 The number of men cattell and hids of lād noted in england. Kynge William caused a newe maner of tribute to be leuied throughe oute thys realme, for euerye hyde of lande (that is twentye acres) vi.s. And not longe after, commaunded a valuation to be taken of all landes, fees, and possessions, and diligent search also to

be

be made, what number of men and cattell were within this lande. And accordyng to the quantitie & number therof, gathered an other payment

A greivous exaction

Anno, 20

Englande was vexed wyth manye plagues, For greate moraine fell emonge cattell, brennynge feuers, and honger amonge people, greate bareynnesse vpon the earth, and muche hurt was done in manye places, by the misfortune of fyre: & specially in London For a part of Poules was brente ye vii. of July. Kinge Willia͂ builded the abbei of Battell in Sussex: he ended his lyfe the ix, day of September, and was buried at Caue in Normandy, he had. v children, Roberte, to whome he gaue Normandy Richard, who dyed in hys youthe. William Rufus, and Henrye, whiche were kynges after hym, And one daughter, named Adela, who hee gaue in, mariage too Stephen Erle of Bloys, who got on her Stephen that after was kyng of England

1 0 8 6

gret plags

A parte of Paules church brēt

Battel abbey

William Rufus or William the red kynge.

Anno regni.1.

1087 William Rufus, the seconde sonne of William conqueroure beganne hys reygne the ninth daye of September in the yere of our Lord 1087, and deceased in the yere of our LORDE 1100. the first daye of August he reygned xii. yere xi. monethes lacking. viii. dayes. He was variable and inconstant very couetous and therwithall cruel. He pilled the ryche, and oppressed the poore, And caused manye to lose theyr landes for small causes. And what he thus gott by pillynge he prodigally spente in greate bankettyng and sumpteous apparell.

Roberte Curthoise hys elder brother came wyth an armie into England, agaynst William, wherof when the sayd William had knowledge, he entreated peace.

1088 Anno.2

Diuers Lordes of this realme conspired agaynste William, and assaulted

saulted diuers townes wythin Englād they stirred agaynst hym Robert Curthoyse duke of Normandy, the seconde time. But William vanquished thee traitours, chased theym oute of thys realme, and made peace wyth his brother Robert. Thys yeare was a greate earthquake, the 3. Idus of Auguste, that ouertorned manye houses and churches in Englande A gret erthquake

Anno. 3

The Scottes spoyled Northumberland, Wherfore williā Rufus prouided a nauy and sayled thither: wherafter diuers skirmishes a peace was concluded. 1089

Anno, 4

A Great tempest fell on saynct Lukes day in sundry places of England, & speciallye in Winchecombe: where a great parte of the steple was ouerthrowen with thundring & lightning: and in London the wynd ouer tourned. vi. hundred houses, and the roofe of Bow church in Cheape. 1090 The roofe of Bowchurch & sixe hundred houses blowen down

Anno. 5

In thys yere William Rufus wente into Northūberlād, & repaired such holdes & castels, as the Scots by their 1091 warres had impayred: & builded other there besydes, as the newe castell on Tyne. &c. This. v yere the roofe of Salisbury Church was cleane consumed with lightnyng

Newcastel vpon Tine builded

Salis. church brent

Anno 6.

1092 In England fell wonderfull aboundance of raine: and after ensued so gret frost, that horses and cartes passed commonly ouer great riuers: when it thawed, the gret cakes of yce brake down many great brydges

greate frost

Normandy morgaged.

Robert Curthose duke of Normãdy layd his dukedome to pawne to his brother William of Englande for tenne thousande poundes

Huge Lupus Earle of Chester sente to Normandye for Anceline, to builde an abbey of Chester, whyche after builded, and then was made archebishoppe of Cantorbury: and after was exiled by William Rufus

Chester abbey builte

Anno. 7.

1093 Malcoline kynge of Scottes for displeasure taken with William Rufus inuaded the marches of England: & in Northumberland was slayne wyth hys eldest sonne Edwarde, by Roberte Mowbray Erle of that prouince

The kinge of Scottes slayne

This

Anno.8

England and Normandye were greued with exactiõs, and murreyn of men so sharply, that tillage of the earth was layed asyde for x.yere, wherby ensued great hunger and scarsity the yeres folowing, 1094

Gret morreine of mē

Anno.10

The x.yere was sene a blasing sterre o. great brightnes. 1096

Anno. 11,

ABoute this time William Rufus builded westminster hal, who misliking the same, for that it was so smal was determined to make a bigger, and that it shoulde serue for a chamber. 1097

Anno.12

This yere the ryuer of Thames rose so hye that it drowned many townes in Englande, and at Finchauster in Barkeshire a wel cast oute bloud as before it had done water, and after by the space of xv. dayes greate flames of fyre was sene in the elemente. 1098

gret flouds

A wel caste out bloude & flames of fyre sene in the elemēt.

Anno,13

WIlliã Rufus being at his desporte of hũting by glaũsing of an arrowe that Walter Tyrell a french knight did shotte was wounded to deathe in the 1099

newe

newe forest in Hampshire, on a Lammas day: and buried at Winchester

King Henry the first called Beauclerke

Anno. Reg. 1

1100 HEnry, the brother of William Rufus, and the firste of that name, for hys learninge called Beauclerke, began his dominion ouer this realme, the first daye of August, in the yeare of our Lord .1100. and reigned xxxv. yeares iiii monethes and one day, he toke to wyfe mauld the doughter of margaret quene of Scots the doughter of S. Edwardes nephewe.

Anno. ii

1101 RAnulphe bishopp of Durham procured Robert Curthoise duke of Normandye, to warre vppon hys brother Henry for the crown of England, who assembled a strong army, and landed at Portsmouth. But by meditation peace was made on this condition, that Henry should pay three thousande markes yerely to duke Robert.

Tribute to duke of Normandy

Anno. 3 This

This yere the churche & hospitall of saint Bartholomew in Smithfield was begon to be founded by a minstrel of the kynges named Rayere And after finished by good and well disposed citizēs of the citie of London, and especially by Richarde Whittington This place of Smithfielde was att that daye a laystowe of al ordure of fylth: and the place where felons and other transgressours of the Kynges lawes were putt to execution. 1102.

The priory & hospitall of S. Bartholomewe in Smithfield begon to be bulded

Anno. 4

Robert Duke of Normandye commyng into England by the entreatie of kynge Henry & his wife. released to hym the tribute of three thousande markes. 1103.

Anno. 5

But it was not long ere that by meanes of yll reporte great malice was kindled betwene the two brethren: And deadly warre sprange, in the ende whereof, Robert was taken and kepte in perpetuall prison in Cardiffe, by his brother, who immediatly seised the duchye of Normandy, and held it in hys possession. 1104.

Syr Robert le Fitzhā builded Teukesbury, and there was buried

Teukesbury abbey builded

Anno. 6

Anno.6

1105 Rebellion ROBert Earle of Shrewesburye, and William of Cornewall, rebelled agaynste kynge Henry, and were taken and condemned to perpetuall imprisonment.

Anno.7

1106 IN England appered a blasinge starre betwene the south and the weste, and agaynst that in the east apered a greate beame (as it were) stretching towarde ꝧ sterre, and shortly after were sene two moones, the one in the easte, and the other in ꝧ west. This yere prior norman founded the priorie of the holy trinitie called christs church in lōdō next unto algat

A blasynge sterre

Christes churche in londō builded

Anno.9.

1108 HEnry the emperor desyred to wife Maude, ꝧ eldest daughter of king Henry of England, being then but .v. yeres of age

Anno.10

1109 IN the.10.yere of his reigne, the king maryed Roberte hys basterde sonne, of Mabel daughter ꝧ heyre of Robert Fitzham, and made hym the fyrste earle of Gloucester who after buylded the strong castel of Brystowe, and the priorie of saint James in the northsyde of ꝧ same citie, wher his body was buried

The strong castel of bristow builte

Anno

Anno.13

AT Shrewesbury was a great earth quake, and the ryuer of Trente was so dried that the space of one day menne went ouer dryshod. And this yeare the kyng builded the abbey of Hyde without the wales of Winchester that of old time was within the wales. 1116 A gret erth quake Hide ab[bey] builded

A blasing sterre appeared sone after and thereupon folowed a hard winter, death of men, scarsitie of victuals, and morayne of beystis. A blasin sterre

Anno,15

King Henry gaue his daughter in mariage to the Emperour wyth greate dower and made William his sonne Duke of Normandy, wherof began the vsage and custome that the Kinges of England made theyr eldest sons dukes of Normandy 1114?

Anno.18

LEwes inuaded Normandye wyth muche cruelty, and toke the city of Lignes in Cauise. wherfore king Henri assembled a strong armye, mette wyth Lewis in plaine field, and fought with him a cruell and deadly battell: in the ende wherof Lewes was ouercome, & constreined to flee. Henry recouered þe towne of Lignes 1117.

Anno

Anno 20.

1119. William Duke of Normandye and Richard the sones of king Henry of England and Mary his doughter, Rychard earle of Chester, with hys wyfe, the kinges nece, and other to the noumber of 160 persons passyng from Normandie into England, by oversighte of the shyppe mayster were drowned, savynge one butcher, whyche escaped the danger.

The Kings children drowned

Anno. 24

1123 In this yeare the abbey of Readynge was begunne to be builded by kinge Henry the first: he also builded Cicester Wyndesore: and Woodstoke wyth the parke.

Readinge, Cicester Windsor & Woodstock builded.

Anno. 17

The graye friers came nowe first into Englande, and hadde their fyrste house at Contorbury.

1126. Maude the daughter of kynge Henrye after the deathe of her husbande the Emperoure, came into England to her father

Graye friers

Anno. 28

1127 The order of saincte Johns Hospitals Templers, and other lyke began first at this tyme

Anno. 32.

IN this yeare began Foūtains abbey. .1131.

Geffreye Plantagenet Erle of Angew maried Maude ye empresse, daughter of kynge Henry: of whiche, ii. descended Henry the seconde whiche reigned after Stephen.

Fonntains abbey builded

Aboute this tyme was builded the priorye of Norton in thee prouince of Chester, by one William, the sonne of Nichole. Also the abbeye of Combremore in thee same prouince was builded aboute the same time

The priory of Norton & the abbey of Combermore built

Robert Curthois dyed in prison, & was buried at Glocester.

33.

HEnry kynge of Englande because he hadde none issue male, ordeyned that his daughter Maude, whiche had ben Empresse shoulde succede hym in the kyngdome. 1132.

Anno.36

KYng Henry of Englande beynge in Normandy, wyth a fall of his hors tooke his death, and was buried at Reading: when he had reigned. 35 yeares. iiii. monethes, and one day 1135

Kynge Stephen

Anno Regni. i.

Stephen

Kyng Stephen

Tephen Earle of Bolloyne, yͤ son of the erle of Bloys and Adela, William Conquerours daughter, and nephewe to Kinge Henry yͤ fyrst toke on him the gouernaunce of thys realme of England the second daye of December, in the yere of our lorde .1135, and left the same yͤ xxv day of October, in yͤ yere of our lord.1154 so that he reigned xviii.yeres, x.monthes, & xxiiii, days, Although he had contenuall warre, yet dyd he neuer burden his cõmons with exactions. He semed in this blame worthy, that contrarye to hys othe made to Maude the daughter of Henry, he was thoughte vniustlye to take on him the Croun. For which cause he was vexed with warres all the tyme of his reigne

At this tyme was great trouble and slaughter in England: for somuche as diuers of yͤ nobles maintayned Maude the empresse agaynst Stephen, which was in possession of the croune.

Kinge Stephen made warres agaynst Dauid of Scotlande, because hee refused to do hym his homage, for Northumberland, & huntingdon, which he held

by

by his wyfe. In this warre the Earle of Gloucester was taken. But att the lengthe Stephen made peace, and agreed with Dauid king of Scots, and receiued of him homage, after that hee had wonne from him certaine townes and castelles, and gaue to Henry the sonne of Dauid, the erledom of of Huntingdon. Anno. 2

STephen passed ouer into Normandy agaynst Geffrey erle of Augewe the husband of Maude the empresse, which was right heire to the crowne, & when he had quieted the prouince hee made Eustace his sonne duke of Normandy, and ioyned frendship and league wyth Lewes king of France. Anno. 4. 1136

DAuid kyng of Scots in moste cruell wise inuaded Northumberland wher by meane of Thurston byshop of Yorke, the Scots had an ouerthrowe & slayne in greet number, and Dauid was constrayned to geue his sonne Henrye in hostage for suertie of peace, 1138

Anno. 6

MAude the Empresse came into this lande out of Normandy, by ayde of Robert erle of Glocester, & Ranulphe of Chester, made strong war vpõ kyng Stephen. In thend wherof the Kinges 1140

King Stephen taken prisoner.

partie had the worse, and him self takē prisoner, and sent to Bristow. But the kentishemen and Londoners, fauoureyng the kyng, warred vpon the rebelles, and toke Robert erle of Gloucester But shortlye after, bothe the kynge and the duke were deliuered out of prison by exchaunge. And Stephen assemblynge a stronge armye, in suche wyse pursued hys enemies, that hee forced Maude to forsake the Realme.

Stratford abbey builded

Aboute thys tyme was founded the abbey of Stratforde Langthorn within iiii. myles, of London, by a Knight called sir William de mount Fichet.

Anno.10

1144 ABoute thys tyme the Jewes crucified a chylde vppon Easter daye att Norwyche en derision of Christe and his religion.

Anno 11.

1149 GEffreye Plantagenet, the husbande of Maude the Empresse (who hadde longe continued the warres egaynste kynge Stephen(wanne frome hym the Duchye of Normandye: and streight there vppon dyed: and hys sonne Henry

Henry succeded in the dukedome.

Anno. 12.

STephen after long warre and much 1146.
trouble, was agayn crouned at Lincolne, but Robert Earle of Glocester
made new warre vpon him: in whiche
he had the vpper hande of the kynge at
Wilton, so that the kynge was lyke to
haue fallen into Roberts danger: and
escaped with much paine.

Anno. 15.

THis yere the riuer of Thames was 1149.
so strongly frosen, that horse and
cart passed ouer vpon the yce. A greate frost.

Anno. 16.

THis yere kinge Stephen brent the 1150.
citie of Norwiche. Anno. 17.

HEnry duke of Normandye in the 1151.
quarel of his mother Maude, with
a great puisance arriued in Englande,
and won the castell of Malmesbury,
the tower of London, and the towne of
Notingham, with other holdes and castels, betwene him and king Stephen
were foughten many battails, wherby
this realme was sore troubled.

Anno. 18.

BVt at the last peace was agreed be- 1152.
twene Maude the empresse, her son
Henry, and king Stephen: vpon this

condition that Stephē duryng his life should holde the Kingdom of England, and Henry to be heire apparent.

Anno.19.

1153 King Stephen builded the abbey of Coggeshal in Essex another at Furneis in Lancashere, and the third at Feuersham in Kent, where now his body resteth, and deceassed the.xxv. daye of October: in the yere of our Lord.1154. when he had reigned.xviij.yeres.x.monethes and.xxiiij.dayes.

The Abbeis of Cogshal Fourneys, and Feuersham builded.

Kyng Henry the second.

Anno regni.1.

1154 Henry the seconde of that name the son of Geffrey Plantagenet, and Maude the Empresse daughter of king Henry the first, began his reigne ouer this realm of England, the.xxv. day of October in the yere of our Lord.1154.and deceassed in the yere of our Lord.1189. the.vj.day of July, so that he reigned xxxiiij.yeres.ix.monthes, & .xii. daies.

Anno

Anno.2.

King Henry cast down diuers castels 1155.
which wer erected in the time of Stephen: He went into the north partes, and got from the Scots Cumberlande and Northumberland, which they said were geuen to thẽ by Maude his mother, and set an order in that countrey.

Anno.3.

In Englande were sene.ii.sunnes in 1156
the firmamẽt: and in the Moone appeared a redde crosse.

Castell of Rutland & abbey of Basingwerk built

Kyng Henry went into Wales, and quieted that countrey, and after builded the strong castell of Rutlande, and founded the abbey of Basyngwerke.

Anno.4.

About this tyme came into Englãd 1157
certain Germaines, to the number of xxx. which taught ỹ abrogatiõ of the Sacramentes of the alter, Baptisme, and Wedlocke. Anno.6.

Lewes kynge of Fraunce gaue his 1159
daughter Margaret in mariage to Henry the sonne of kynge Henry of England. By reason wherof, was pacifyed the warre betwene Englande and Fraunce, for the landes of Poytoue, and others.

Anno.7.

1160 KIng Henry went into Scotlande, and made war upon king William so that he toke him, and made him yeld the castel of Carlile, the castel of Camburgh, with diuers other, and receiued of him fealtie and homage.

Anno.8.

1161 THis yere the citie of Cantorburye was fiered by negligence, & a great part therof brent.

Great fiere at Cantorbury.

Anno.10.

1163 Thomas Becket byshop of Cantorbury fled to Rome to complain upon the king to the byshop.

Anno.14.

1167 KIng Henry caused Henry his eldest sō to be crouned king as he thought to the great quietnes aswell of himselfe as of the realm: but as it proued, to the utter disturbation of them both.

K. Henris sō crouned his father being aliue

Anno.17.

1170 Thomas Becket by the mediation of Alexander bishop of Rome, and Lewes the Frenche king, was restored to his bishopricke: and not longe after by certayne gentilmen, he was slayne at Cantorbury. Anno.18.

1171. KIng Henry sent Ambassade to Alexander bishop of Rome to purge him selfe of the deth of Thomas Becket. Among monge other thinges it was enioyned him in his penaunce, that it should be lawful to his subiectes as often as they listed to appeale to the see of Rome, & that no man shoulde be accompted as king untill such tyme as he were confirmed by the Romaine bishop.

Anno.19.

Thomas becket was canonised by the byshop of Rome. 1172

Anno.21.

Henry the sonne of kinge Henry of England was crouned the second time with his wife Margaret, ye french kinges daughter. 1174

The kings son ye the second time crowned.

Anno.22.

King Henry the sonne by the settyng on of the king of France, Elanour his mother, and certaine other nobles, toke armes, & raised dedly war against his naturall father. Diuers strong battels were foughten as well in England by the deputies & frendes of both parties, as also in Normãdy, Poytow Guyen, & Britain: wher they wer corporally present: but ye victory fel alway to the father. There toke party against king Henry the father, Lewes king of France. William kyng of Scotlande, Henry, Geffrey, & John, his own sons: 1175

Henry the son of king Henry rebelled.

Robert Earle of Leicester, Hughe of Chester, and other. But in the ende the sonnes with their alies were constreined to yelde to their father, and desyre peace, which he gentilly graunted and forgaue their trespace.

Anno.24.

1177 IN Englande fell great wetherynge and tempest of thunder & lightenyng in the middes of winter: and in Sommer folowyng fell hayle of such greatnes that it slew both man and beast.

Anno.26.

1179 AT this tyme Jewes in Englande, against the feast of Easter did sacrifice yong children in despite of Christen religion.

Anno.28

1182 Henry the eldest sonne of Henry of England ended his lyfe. Shortly after began the warre betwene king Henry and Philip of France for homage that the Frenche kinge required to be done for the landes of Poytow, and other, for the castel of Gysours.

Anno.29.

1182. S. Austis at bristowe builded. ROBert Harding a burges of Bristow to whō kyng Henry gaue the Baronye of Berkleye, builded the abbey of S. Austen at Bristowe.

Anno.31.

HEraclius Patriarke of Jerusalē which had bene in diuers partes of Europe came to king Henry, desyring him of ayde agaynste the Turkes, but was denied therof. 1184

Anno.32

At Bury the Jewes crucified a child in despite of Christes passion. 1189

Anno.34.

Rycharde Earle of Poytowe made warre against kyng Henry his father, and takyng part with the French king in proces of tyme wan from him diuers cities, tounes, and castels, and namely the citie of Cenomannia. For sorow wherof at the lengthe, that is to say, on the.vi.day of July, in the yeare of our Lord.1189. king Henry ended his life, when he had reigned.34.yeres 9.monethes, and.12.days: he was buryed at Founteuerard. 1187

King Richard the first. called Cueur de Lion.

Anno regni.1.

Richarde the fyrste.

1189 RIchardes the fyrste of that name, for his valiantnesse surnamed Cucurdelion, beyng the second son of Henry the seconde, was crowned King of England. He began his reigne the .vi. daye of July, in the yere of our Lorde. 1189. and he deceased, the yere of our Lord. 1199. the vi. day of April: so that he reigned. ix. yeres and .ix monethes.

The fyrste bailiffes in London. This yere, the citisens of London obteined two officers to guide theyr Citie, whiche were called Bayliffes: whose names were as foloweth.

1189	Henry Cornhyll	Anno regni. i.
	Richard Reinery	Baylyffes.

Jewes ... This yere the Jewes were very brag here in this realm, for that their number was so great. But the commō people, especially about London, fel vpon them, and despoyled them without pitye or mercy, they so hated them for theyr vsury.

Elianor released. This yere the kyng set at libertie Elianor his mother, which lōg before at the cōmaundement of his father her hasbande, had ben kept close prisoner. But after her enlargement, the realme was much gouerned by her.

Kynge

Kynge Richard gaue ouer the Castelles of Barwike and Rokesburg to the Scottishe Kynge, for the summe of x. M. li. He also solde to the bishoppe of Durham his own prouince, for a great piece of money, and created him erle of the same Wherfore the kyng saide after in game: I am a wonderous craftsman, I haue made a newe earle of an olde bishoppe. He gaue his brother John many dignities, as the prouinces of Notingham, Deuonshyre and Cornwall, and created hym earle of Lancaster.

Jhon Herlyon   Anno reg. 2.   1190.
Roger Duke.   Bailiffes

THis yeare kyng Richarde be tooke the guiding of this lād to ŷ bishop of Ely then beyng Chancelour of England, and sayled into Normandy: and when he had appointed good gouernoures ouer that countrey, he went to mete the Frenche kynge: and hauynge made sure league one with an other, went eyther of them onwarde of theyr iorney toward Jerusalem.

The Jewes in diuers places of this Realme, as at Lincolne, Stamforde: and Lynne, were robbed and spoyled. And at Yorke to the number of foure hundred

Jewes robbed & many slew themselues,

hundred and more, had their maister vaines cut, and so bled to death.

William Hauershall } Anno reg. 3.
1191. John Bukmotte } Baylyffes.

King Richard went to Jerusalē and his brother rebelled.

King Richard in his iourney to wardes Jerusalem, subdued the Ecle of Cipres, and then ioyning his puisance with the Frenche kinges in Asia, conquered Acon, wher ther grew betwen King Richard and Philip the Frenche kynge a greuous displeasure. John the brother of kyng Richarde toke on him the kingdome of Englande in his brothers absence.

King Richard restored to the Christians the citie of Joppa, and in many battels put the Turke to great sorow.

Anno. 4.

1192 Nicolas Duke } Baliffes
Peter Newlay }

Kyng Richard exchaunged Cypres, with Guye of Lesyngham for the kingdom of Jerusalem, Wherfore the kings of England a long time after was called king of Jerusalem.

1193 Roger Duke } An. reg. 5.
Richard Fitz Alyn } Baliffes.

King Richarde hauinge knowledge that Philip of Fraunce innaded Normandy, and that John his brother had

made

made himselfe king of Englande, made peace with the Turkes for .iii. yeares, and with small company returnynge homeward by Thrace, was taken prisoner by the Duke of Ostriches men, an brought to Henry the Emperour, and there kept in streite prison, a yere and .v. monethes. Where it is sayd that he slewe a Lyon.

King Richard take prisoner.

Anno reg. 6.

William Fitz Isabell } Bailiffes 1194
William Fitz Arnold. }

John the kinges brother by the settyng on of the Frenche king made gret warre within the land, & toke by strengthe the castelles of Windsore, of Notingham, & others. And the French king made strong warre in Normandy.

Robert Beysant } Anno. reg. 7. 1195
John le Josue } Bailiffes.

Hubert bishop of Salisbury was by king Richard sent into England to haue the guiding thereof, and also to treate with the lords & comons for the kings deliuerance. The sayd Hubert was by the monkes of Christs church in Canterbury chosen archebishop.

Gerrad de Anteloche } Anno. reg. 8 1196
Robert durant. } Bailiffes.

This yere king Richarde was deliuered out of prison for the summe of

one

great rans- sume payde for ÿ kyng.

one C.M. pounds of sterlynge money, for paiment of whiche ransom all the wole of white monkes and chanons was sold and rings and crosses of prelates, with vessels and chalices of all churches through the land.

Richard again crouned.

Kyng Richard beyng thus deliuered shortly after landed at Sandwich, & so came to London: where when he had arested hym: with a certayne number of knightes: he rode to notinghã, and wan the castell: and after that the castell of Tikhill, he deposed his brother John, & crouned himselfe agayne King of Englande in the citie of Winchester, and then called a parliament, where he called again into his handes all suchthinges as he hadde eyther geuen or sold by patentes, or other wyse: by whiche meanes he gathered a summe of money and sailed into Fraunce, wher shortlye a peace was concluded betwene the two kinges for one yeare. Then John whiche had taken part against his brother, made meanes to Elianor his mother, by whose mediation he was reconciled.

William with the long beard

In this time one William with the longe bearde, moued the common people to seke libertie and fredome, & not

to be

to be subiect to the riche and mightye. By which meanes he drew to him many great companies, and with all hys power defended theyr cause against the riche. The king beyng warned of thys tumult, commanded hym to cease from those attemptes. But the people stil folowed him as they before had done: and he made to them certaine orations openly, lastly he was taken in Bowe churche in Cheape, but not without sheddynge of bloude for he was forced by fyre and smoke to forsake the churche. And wyth nyne of his adherentes wer hanged.

Roger Blunt Anno reg. 9. 1197
Nicholas Ducket Bailiffes.

This yere the warre was renued betwene Kyng Richarde of Englande, and Philip of Fraunce, in which eyther of them sped diuersly.

Constantine Fitz Arnold } An. reg. 10 1198
Robert le Beau. } Bailiffes.

Kyng Richard of England besieged the castel of Galiarde, and was wounded with a quarell that was shot from the wal, and therof died the. vi. daye of Aprill, in the yere of our Lord. 1199. when he had reigned. ix. yeres, and. ix. monethes, His bodye was buried at Foun-

King Richard, wounded to death.

Founteuerard, his bowels at Carlile, his hart at Roan.

Kyng John.

Anno Regni. i.

John, brother to Richarde
afore named, began his
1199 reigne ouer this realm of
England the .vi. day of Aprill, in the yeare of oure lord. 1199. and decesed in the yere. 1216. the. xix. day of October: He reigned. xvii. yeres. vi. monethes, and. xiiii. dais. Of person he was indifferent. But of melancolye and angrey complection.

1199 Arnold Fitz Arnold } An. reg. i
Richard Fits bartilmewe } bailiffes.

Philip king of France (in the quarell of Arthur duke of Britain, whome certayn of the Lordes had named king of England) made warre vpon kynge John, inuaded Normandy, and tooke from him diuers castels and townes.

iii.s. of euery plough land.

Kyng John hearyng therof, assembled a counsayle, wherin was graunted to him iii.s. of euery plough lande through England, beside the subsidy of

the

the spirituall landes: he sayled into Normandy, where he spent the time to his losse and dishonour. But aboute Michelmas a truce was concluded.

This yere was a deuorce betwene king John & his wife, the erle of Glocesters daughter, because of nerenesse of bloude: and after he was maried to Isabel, the daughter of the Erle of Engolesym in Fraunce: by whom he had .ii. sonnes, Henry and Richard, and .iii. daughters, Isabel, Elianor, and Jane. — king John deuorced.

Roger Dorset } An. re. 2. 1200
James bar'elmew a'dermã } bailifes.

This yeare Raynulphe Earle of Chester, by thexample aforeshewed by kynge John, lefte his owne wife named Constance, which he before had maried, & wedded one Clemens some saith, he did so to haue issue: but he therwith displesed God so muche, that he would suffer him to haue none issue. 1201

Walter Fitz Ales } An. re. 3
Simon de Aldermanbury. } bailifes.

This yere in Yorkshyre were sene .v. Moones, one in the east, an other in the Weste, the thirde in the northe, the fourth in the southe, and the fyfthe in the myddes of the other: and went compassing the other .vi. times, as it were — Fiue mones in the firmamente

the

the space of an houre, and banished awaye.

xxv. gouernours of the citie. In this yere were chosen .xxv. of the most substantial and wysest men of the Citie of Londō, to maintayn and kepe the assises of the same Citie, of the whiche yerely the bailiffs were chosen: and after the Maior and Sheriffes were taken of the same number.

1202 Normand Blundell An. reg. 4.
John de Ely Bailiffes.

Great tempest. This yere fel excedyng lightnynge, thunders, & other stormes of wynd and rayn with hayl of ỹ bignes of hennes egges: which perished fruit & corn houses, and yong cattell. Also spirites were sene in the ayre, in likenes of foules bearyng fire in their byles, which set fyre on dyuers houses.

Philip of France cōtinually made warre vpon the Duchy of Normandy, tyl at the last he subdued the same with the prouinces of Guyen, Poytiers, and Britaine, whiche before pertayned to the crowne of Englande.

Kyng John saylyng into Normandy warred on the borders of Frannce, but of his victories is litle written.

Anno. 5.

Walter

Walt. Iohn Iwn } Bailiffes. 1203
Willia. Chāberlain

This yere by meanes of euyll weather, in the yeare passed, wheate was solde for xx. s. a quarter, Dearth of wheate

Kyng Iohn maried his bastarde daughter to Lewlyn prince of wales, and gaue with her the castel and lordshyppe of Elyngsmore, being in the marches of Southwales.

The byshop of Rome wrate to kynge Iohn, gentilly requiryng hym to admytte Stephen Langton into the byshoprike of Cantorbury, and the monkes by hym expelled frome theyr owne abbeye, to restore theym agayne to the same: but the more hys lordes aduised hym so to do, the more was hee bente to to the contrary. So that they retourned wythout obteynynge their request.

Thomas Hauerill } } Anno Reg. 6 1204
Hamond Bronde } } Baylyffes.

The bishop of Rome denoūced king Iohn with hys whole realme accursed because he woulde not admit Stephen Langton to thee bishoprike of Cantorbury: but he little regarded hys threatnyngs, and would not obbey hym Englonde interdited

At this time in Suffolke a fish was takē like to a man, & was kept lyuynge vi. moneths vpon the lande wyth rawe A monstreus fish

great ranson one C.M. pounds of sterlynge money, for paiment of whiche ransom all the wole of white monkes and chanons was sold and rings and crosses of prelates, with vessels and chalices of all churches through the land.

sume payde for ÿ kyng.

Kyng Richard beyng thus deliuered shortly after landed at Sandwich, & so came to London: where when he had arested hem: with a certayne number of knightes: he rode to notinghã, and wan the castell: and after that the castell of Tikhill, he deposed his brother John, & crouned himselfe agayne King of Englande in the citie of Winchester, and then called a parliament, where he called again into his handes all suchthinges as he hadde eyther geuen or sold by patentes, or otherwyse: by whiche meanes he gathered a summe of money and sailed into Fraunce, wher shortlye a peace was concluded betwene the two kinges for one yeare. Then John whiche had taken part against his brother, made meanes to Elianor his mother, by whose mediation he was reconciled.

Richard again crouned.

In this time one William with the longe bearde, moued the common people to seke libertie and fredome, & not to be

William with the long beard

to be subiect to the riche and mightye. By which meanes he drew to him many great companies, and with all hys power defended theyr cause against the riche. The king beyng warned of thys tumult, commanded hym to cease from those attemptes. But the people stil folowed him as they before had done: and he made to them certaine orations openly, lastly he was taken in Bowe churche in Cheape, but not without sheddynge of bloude for he was forced by fyre and smoke to forsake the churche. And wyth nyne of his adherentes wer hanged.

Roger Blunt Anno reg. 9. 1197
Nicholas Ducket Bailiffes.

This yere the warre was renued betwene kyng Richarde of Englande, and Philip of France, in which eyther of them sped diuersly.

Constantine Fitz Arnold } An. reg. 10 1198
Robert le Beau. } Bailiffes.

Kyng Richard of England besieged the castel of Galiarde, and was wounded with a quarell that was shot from the wal, and therof died the .vi. daye of April, in the yere of our Lord. 1199. when he had reigned .ix. yeres, and .ix. monethes. His bodye was buried at Foun-

King Richard, wounded to death.

Founteuerard, his bowels at Carlile, his hart at Roan.

Kyng John.

Anno Regni. i.

1199 John, brother to Richarde afore named, began the his reigne ouer this realm of England the vi. day of Apriil, in the yeare of oure lord. 1199. and deceased in the yere. 1216. the. xix. day of October: He reigned. xvii. yeres. vi. monethes, and. xiii. dais. Of person he was indifferent. But of melancolye and angrey complection.

1199 Arnold Fitz Arnold } An. reg. i
Richard Fetz bartilmewes } bailiffes.

Philip king of France (in the quarell of Arthur duke of Britain, whome certayn of the Lordes had named king of England) made warre vpon kynge John, inuaded Normandy, and tooke from him diuers castels and tounes.

iii. s. of euery ploughland. Kyng John hearyng therof, assembled a counsayle, wherin was graunted to him iii. s. of euery plough lande through England, beside the subsedy of the

the spirituall landes: he sayled into Normandy, where he spent the time to his losse and dishonour. But aboute Michelmas a truce was concluded.

This yere was a deuorce betwene king John & his wife, the erle of Glocesters daughter, because of nerenesse of bloude: and after he was maried to Isabel, the daughter of the Erle of Engolesym in Fraunce: by whom he had .ii. sonnes, Henry and Richard, and .iii. daughters, Isabel, Elianor, and Jane. — King John deuorced.

Roger Dorset } An. re. 2. — 1200
James bartilmew aldermā } bailifes.

This yeare Raynulphe Earle of Chester, by thexample aforeshewed by kynge John, lefte his owne wife named Constance, which he before had maried, & wedded one Clemens some saith, he did so to haue issue: but he therwith displesed God so muche, that he would suffer him to haue none issue. — 1201

Walter Fitz Ales } An. re. 3
Simon de Aldermābury. } bailifes.

This yere in Yorkshyre were sene .v. Moones, one in the east, an other in the Weste, the thirde in the northe, the fourth in the southe, and the fyfthe in the myddes of the other: and went compassing the other .vi. times, as it were — Fiue mones in the firmamente

the

the space of an houre, and banished awaye.

xxv. gouernours of the citie.

In this yere were chosen.xxv.of the most substantial and wysest men of the Citie of Londō, to maintayn and kepe the assises of the same Citie, of the whiche yerely the bailiffs were chosen: and after the Maior and Sheriffes were taken of the same number.

1202 Normand Blundeil An.reg. 4.
John de Ely Bailiffes.

Great tempest.

This yere fel excedyng lightnynge, thunders, & other stormes of wynd and rayn with hayl of ye bignes of hennes egges: which perished fruit & corn houses, and yong cattell. Also spirites were sene in the ayre, in likenes of foules bearyng fire in their bylles, which set fyre on dyuers houses.

Philip of France cōtinually made warre vpon the Duchy of Normandy, tyl at the last he subdued the same with the prouinces of Guyen, Poytiers, and Britaine, which before pertayned to the crowne of Englande.

Kyng John saylyng into Normandy warred on the borders of Fraunce, but of his victories is litle written.

Anno.5.

Walter

Walt[illegible]wn } Bailiffes. 1203
Willi[illegible]abrlain }

This yere by meanes of euyll weather, in the yeare passed, wheate was solde for xx.s.a quarter, Dearth of wheate

Kyng John maried his bastarde daughter to Lewlyn prince of wales, and gaue with her the castel and lordshyppe of Elyngsmore, beyng in the marches of Southwales.

The byshop of Rome wrate to kynge John, gentilly requirynge hym to admytte Stephen Langton into the byshoprike of Cantorbury, and the monkes by hym expelled frome theyr owne abbeye, to restore theym agayne to the same: but the more hys lordes aduised hym so to do, the more was hee bente to to the contrary. So that they retourned wythout obteynynge their request.

Thomas Hauerill } Anno Reg. 6 1204
Hamond Bronde } Baylyffes.

The bishop of Rome denoũced king John with hys whole realme accursed because he woulde not admit Stephen Langton to thee bishoprike of Cantorbury: but he little regarded hys threatnynges, and would not obbey hym Englonde interdited

At this time in Suffolke a fish was takẽ like to a man, & was kept lyuynge vi. moneths vpon the lande wyth rawe A monstreus fish fleshe and fyshe: and a[illegible] when they sawe they could haue no speche thereof they cast it agayne into the sea.

1205. John Walgraue } Anno re. 7.
Richard Winchester } Bayliffes.

Kynge Philip of France subdued the countrey of Normandy, whych sens the tyme of Charles the simple (that is to say) the space of 300. yeres (was not in the possession of the kinges of France.

Normandye loste.

John Holylande Anno. re. 8
1206. Edmond fitz Gerrard Baliffs.

About this tyme the Irishemen and shortly after the Walshemen rebelled, for that he leuied on theym suche greuous taskes so that the kyng was faine to rayse a great taxe throughout Englande to wythstonde theyr force.

Wales and Ireland rebelled

He required of the white monkes sixe thousande marke: but they refused the payement of so greate a summe, so that the kyng toke great displeasure agaynst them: by reason whereof after hys return out of Ireland he exacted of them more then before he had desyred, wherby hee caused some abbottes to forsake theyr houses.

Roger Winchester Anno Reg. 9
1207. Edmond Hardell Bailiffes

King

kyng John sayled into Normandye: wher after certayn skirmisshes, he made peace wyth kynge Phylyp of Fraunce for ii. yeares.

This yere was graunted to the Citisens of London by the kynges Letters patentes, that they shoulde yearly chose to them selues, a Mayre and .ii. Shcriffes, on S. Mathewes or Mychelmas day, whose names were as foloweth

First maire of London

Anno Reg. 10

Hery fitz Alwyn	Maire	Peter duke Tho. Nele	S

1208

This yeare London bridge was begon to be buylded of stone: The originall wherof, was as foloweth. Fyrste beyng no bridge but a ferry, the Ferry man and his wife deceasynge, lefte the same to theyr daughter, a mayden named Mary Audery: who wyth the goodes left to her by her parentes, buylded an house of systers, whiche is the vppermost end of S. Mary Anderis chur che vnto the whiche house she gaue the ouersyght and profite of the same ferry but afterward the same house of sisters was conuerted vnto a colledge of priestes: who builded the bridge of tymber, and frome tyme to tyme kepte the

London bridge builded

 same

same in reparations: but consyderynge the great charges in repairyng ẏ same, in the yeare of oure Lorde. 1209. by the great ayde of the citisens of Lōdon and other, they begon to build the same of stone, and then the abouesaid college of priestes was conuerted vnto a priorie of chanons, bearynge styll the name of the mayden, whiche kept the ferry: & so called S. Mary Auderie.

Anno. 11

1209	Henry fitz Alwyne	M	Peter le Josue Williā Blonō	S

The Englishemen whiche were sente by kyng John to ayde the erle of Flanders chased the frenchemen: and in the hauen of Sluce compassed and tooke their whole nauy of ships, which was in number. 1020, sayle. Anno. 12

1210.	Henry fitz Alwyne	M	Adam Whetley Stephē le grase	S

This yere Pandolph a legat cam frō the byshop of Rome mouishing ẏ king in sharpe maner ẏ he shold restore maister Stephen Langton to hys see of Cantorbury, and the monks vnto their abbey, The king callyng to mynde the daungers he was wrapped in, bothe in his owne realme, and also in Normā-

The kinge sworn to ẏ sea of Rom

dy,

dy, made promise by othe, to be obedi=ent to the cour: of Rome,

Anno Reg.13

Hēry fitz Alwyn } M John fitz Pet John Garlonde } S 1211

STephen Langton archebyshoppe of Cantorburye wyth the other exiles landed in England: the king receyuing them ioyously, & was there assoyled of the sayd byshop: and after that, the King makyng restitution to the byshopp and other, accordyng to the thyrde article of his othe, the lande was released of the interdiction: the Kyng beyng bounden, that as well he as his heires shoulde e=uer after be feodars to the sea of Rome paying yerely tribute a thousand mar=kes, and to holde the Title of the Cro=wne by the bishop of Rome.

Anno.14.

Hēry fitz Alwyn } M { Rādolph Eilād Constātin Josue } S 1212

This yeare fell greate discention be=twene the Kyng and his lordes, partly for that he would not meynteyne the la=wes of king Edward, partli for that he would haue exiled the Erle of Chester, who oftentimes had aduised the kynge to leaue his cruelnes, and his accusto= Discentiō betwen ye kyng and hys Lords

 med

ac customed aduoutreye, whyche hee exercised with his brothers wife and others. But by meanes of the Archebyshop of Cantorbury, and other prelates, a peace was taken for a whyle.

The xi day of July, a great part of Southwarke and London was brente

Great fyre in Southwarke and London.

The kyng and his lordes mett wyth great strength on eyther partye uppon Baramdowne: where a charter or wryting was made and sealed by the kyng so that the barony was wyth it contented, and departed in peace euerye man to hys countrey

A Charter to the Barons.

Anno. 15

Roger fitz Alwyne	W	Martin fitz alis Peter Bate	S

1213.

The peace whyche in the laste yeare was agreed betwene kyng John & hys barons was thys yeare by the Kynge violated and broken. Wherfore the lordes assembled to theim great powers, and made cruell warre upon the kyng so that he was constrayned to sende intoo Normandye for ayde. Thenne camme into Englande, a Normane knight named Foukes de brente, whyche broughte wyth hym a companye of Normans, Flemmynges and Picardes. He and his cōpany were so cruell, that they destroyed as wel religious houses as other, and dyd muche harme to the lande, puttyng the lordes to the worse, the kynge made Foukes and other of his companye wardens of castels and stronge holdes in Englande. The lordes seynge the kynge, perseuer in his wronge, and that he woulde in no wyse be induced to hold his own grantes, but to do all thyngs after pleasu[re] and nothing after lawe or iustice cast in their myndes how they myght bring the realme in a better rule, and by one consent wrote to Philip kyng of Frāce that he would send som noble man into Englande, and they would yeld the land vnto hym.

This yere kynge John caused to be drawen and hanged att Warham, one Piers of Pomfrete, and his sonne, for speakyng of dyuers thynges agaynste the kyng Piers of Pomfret

Anno.reg.16. 1214

Roger fitz Alwyn } M { Salomō basing / Hugh basyng } S

Kyng John laying siege to the castell of Rochester, wanne the same, and toke therin certayn gentylmē, and sent them to dyuers prysons, placinge strangers in the same Castell. The barons held them together at London, abiding the K. John besieged ÿ castel of Rochester.

the commynge of Lewes sonne to the Frenche kyng, whiche landed in England wyth a great armye, and so came to Rochester, and wanne it with small payne: he caused all the stangers therein to be hanged: and after came to London, where certein alliances and couenants were establisshed and concluded betwene the lordes and hym, and receiued of them homage. Then he wyth the Lordes departed frome London, and gatte the castell of Rigate, of Gilforde, and of Fernham, and frome thens to Winchester, wher the Citie was yelded wyth all other holdes in those parties: and thenne hee wyth the lordes came againe to London. At whose commyng the tower of London was delyuered they slewe all straungers that hadde ben placed by the kynge in any place. The kyng beynge thus ouersett wyth his lordes sent messengers to ỹ bishop of Rome, shewyng to hym the rebellion of his lordes, and how they labored his destruction. Wherfore the bishop of Rome wyth all haste sent a Legate into

A legate frō Rome

England, called Swalo: The whyche after his commyng, commaunded Lewes to returne into Fraunce, and laboured to the vttermoste of his power: to appease the Kynge and hys baronye, but all his labour was in vayne

Anno regni.17

Williã Hardel } M { John Crauers Andrew Newlã } S 1217

This yeare Kyng John dyed of the Flixe at Newarke: hee was bowelled in the abbey of Croghton, and buried at Worcester.

He buylded the abbey of Bewley, in the new forest, in recompence of the parysh Churches, which he there ouerturned, to enlarge the forest, and an abbey of Blacke monkes in the citie of Winchester. He deceassed in the yere of our Lorde.1216. the xix. of October, when he had reigned.17.yeares.vi. moneths and 13 dayes. Bewlaye abbey builded

¶Henry the thirde

Anno Regni.i

HEnrye the sonne of John, of thee age of nyne yeares, was proclaymed Kynge of Englande, who began hys reigne the.xix. day of October, in the yeare of our 1216 oure Lorde. 1216. and deceased in the yeare. 1272. the vi. day of Nouember. So he reigned. lvi. yeres, and. xxviii. days. The noble men wyth their retinue kept sharpe warre with Lewes the frenche kynges sonne, who by the couenants made before, wyth the English men, claymed the crowne. But after certayne skirmishes and batailes, Lewys began to desyre peace, which was concluded, and Henry was crowned at Gloucester.

Crouned at Glocester.

Anno, 1

1216.

Jacob Alderman	M	Benet Couëtrie Wil, Bluntiuers	S

Swale ỹ Legat accursed Lewis ỹ frenche kings sonne. He accursed Lewlyn prince of wales, & interdicted hys lād.

At the last, Lewis toke a. M. marks (or as som authors affirm. xv. M. markes) of money, & departed this realme.

Anno. 2.

Serle mercer	M	Tho. Bokerell Rafe Holyl and	S

1217. VVhen the land was delyuered frō straungers, inquisicions were made to know what psons assisted Lewes against the kyng: of which ỹ king pardoned manye of the laye men: But the spirituall men were put to such fynes, that they were compelled to laye

al

al that they had to pledg. And also to sue to Rome to be assoyled

Raynolffe Erle of Chester, toke hys iourney to the holy land,

Anno. 3.

Serle Mercer } M { John Wayle / Joscuus Spicer } S 1218.

A parliamente was holden at London, by vertu wherof was graunted to the kyng. ii. s. of euery ploughe lande through England.

ii. s. of euery ploughe lande.

And thys yere king Henry beganne to buylde the newe worke of the church of westmynster

Westminster abbey.

Anno. 4.

Serle mercer } M { Rich. Wimbeldey / John Wayle } S 1219.

Alexander kinge of Scottes maried the lady Jane syster of kyng Henry.

This yeare was great harme doone in England by violence of whirlewindes and fiery dragons and spirits were sene flying in the ayre.

Spirites & firy dragōs

Proclamation was made that all straungers shoulde auoyde the realm excepte suche as camme wyth merchandise, and to make sale of them vnder the kynges saufe conducte, whyche was done to aduoyde Foukes de Brēt, and his complices, who kepte the ca-

Hery crouned the second tyme
The castls of Chartley Bestan, & the abbeye of Delacresse built

stell of Bedford agaynst the kyng.

This yere was kyng Henry secondly crowned at Westminster.

This yeare Rainolphe earle of Chester came out of the holy land into England, and began to buylde the castels of Chartley and of Beston, and after builde the abbey of Delacresse

Anno. 5

1220. Serle mercer } M { Richarde Renger / Josence le Josue } S

THys yeare was a counsell holden at Oxenford of the byshops of Englãd wherein one was condemned, whiche taught that he was Jesus Christ, and to confirme the same: he shewed the tokes of woundes in hys handes bodye and fete: Hee was therfore crucified on a Crosse at Alburbury, tyll he dyed

Anno. 6.

1221. Serle mercer } M { Richard Renger / Josens Josue } S

Execution

A conspiracy was made against king Henry by one Constantine, in the citie of London: for the whiche hee was drawen hanged and quartered, the morow after our Lady day assumption. Whiche conspiracie so moued the kyng, that he was in mynde to haue cast downe the walles of the citie

Anno

Anno.7.

Serle mercer } M { Richard Renger
Tho. Lambert } S 1123

This yere John kynge of Hierusalem came into Englande, and required ayde of kyng Henry to wynne againe Hierusalem, but hee returned wyth small comfort

Anno.8.

Rychard Renger } M { William Joyner
Tho. Lambert } S 1223

Thys yeare the Lordes and gentylmen of Englande fyrste graunted too kyng Henry and his heires, the warde and mariage of theyr heyres, whyche was then by learned men, called the begynnyng of euyls

The firste graunt of wardes to the king

Anno.9.

Richard Renger } M { John Trauers
Andrew Bokerel } S 1224.

Richard the brother of kyng Henry ouercame thee Frenchemen, recouered Poytiers, and kepte the Gascoynes in due obedience.

Anno.10

Rychard Runger } M { Roger duke
Martin fitz William } S 1225

This

This yeare the pleas of the crowne were pleaded in the Tower of Lōdon.

Lewis kyng of Fraunce wan certain castels in the countrey of Poytiers: & shortely after spoyled the citie of Ancowe.

Anno.11.

1226 Rycharde Renger } M { Stephen Bokerell, Henry Cobhame } S

Shiriffewike of Lōdon & Middlesex

In this yere was graunted by king Henry to the Sheriffes of the Citie of London, the Sheriffewike of London &, Midlesex for the sum of f.CCC.pound by the yeare.

Free warreyn.

It was also granted to the citie free warren, that is to saye, free libertie to hunt a certain circuite about the citie.

Toll free.

It was also granted, that the citisens of Lōdon shold passe tole free throughout all England: and also graunted by the kyng, that all weeres in ẏ Thames shoulde bee plucked vp, and destroyed for euer,

Anno.12.

1227 Roger Duke } M { Stephē Bokerell, Henry Cobham } S

The cities liberties rectified,

The liberties of the Citie were this yeare confirmed, and to eche of the sherifes was graunted to haue .ii. clerks and two officers, with oute any more.

Anno

Anno.13

Roger Duke } M { Walter Winchester / Robert fitz John } S 1228.

Kyng Henry sailed with an army in to Britayne agaynste Lewes kynge of France: where after spoyling the coütreye, a peace was concluded betwene them

Anno.14

Roger Duke } M { Richard. Fitz William / John Wodborne } S 1229

This yere was ordeined by ye Maior and rulers of the Citie of London, that no sheriffe of the citie should continue lenger in office then one yere, because they shoulde not by longe continuance of office become couetous bribers.

No sheriffe in London past one yere

Anno.15

Roger Duke } M { Michael of Sainct Cleue / Walter Suffelde } S 1230.

This yere was muche harme don in London by fyre whych began in the house of a wydowe named dame Jane Lambert

Great fire in London

Anno,16

Andrewe Bokerell } M { Henry Edmonton / Gerrarde Bate } S 1231

Variance grewe betwen kyng Hen

rye

Warre be twene the king & his lordes, ry and his lordes, because he put from hys seruice Englishemen, and trusted straungers as wel in hys counsayle as other officers nere aboute hym.

Anno.17

1232	Andrew Bocke-cel	M	Symon Fitz-marer / Roger Blunt.	S

S. Johns without Oxenford, begon

In this yere the kyng began the foundation of the hospitall of sainte John wythout the east gate of Oxenforde. In whyche yeare also fell wonderfull sore wether wyth such thunder & lightning that the lyke had not ben sene. And ther folowed an earthquake, to the gret fear of the inhabitantes of Huntingdon, and there about.

Gret tempestes,

Anno.18

1233	Andrew Bocke-cell	M	Rafe Ashewy / John Nor-man	S

This yere the kyng put from him ye strangers, and restored the English men to their officers

The Jewes dwelling in Norweche were accused for stealyng of a chylde, whom they purposed to haue crucified

Fredrike the Emperour maried Isabel sister of the kyng of England

Anno.19

Andrew

Anno.19.

Andrew Bokerel	M	Gerrard Batte / Robert Ardell	S	1234.

King Hẽry maried Elianor daughter to the Earle of Prouance.

There appeared as it were hostes of men fyghtyng in the ayre.

The statute of Merton was fyrst enacted at the parliament of Merton. The statute of Merton

Anno.20.

Andrew Bokerel	M	Henry Cobbam / Jorden Couẽtry	S	1235

Quene Elianor founded the hospital of Saint Katherins besydes the tower of London for the reliefe of poore women. S. Katherines by the Tower built.

Anno.21.

Andrew Bokerel	M	John Thesalan / Gerard cordwaner	S	1236.

Octobonea, a legat came into Englande takynge order for the churche But not all to the pleasure of the yong clergy. Wherfore as he one day passed thorow Oxeforde, the scholers sought occasion againste his seruantes, and fought with them, and slue one of the same, and put the legate in suche feare, that he for his safegard tooke the belfray of Osney, and there helde him tyll the kings officers commynge from Abingdon, deliuered hym, and conueied him to Wallingford.

Syr Symon Mountford maried the kings syster, named Elianor, countesse of Pembroke. Anno.22.

1237 Richard Kenger } W { John Welhall John Godresse } S

King Henry like to haue bene slayne. A clerk of Oxenford (or more verely a souldeor) faining himself mad: enterprised to haue slain king Henry in his chamber at Wodstocke: but he was taken and put to death at Couentry.

This yere was borne Edward the kinges sonne called Long shankes.

Anno.23.

1238 Williã Joyner } W { Reinnũd Bingley Rafe Ashewy } S

This yeare on Candelmas daye the king created syr Simõ de Mountford Erle of Leycester. Anno. 24.

1239 Gerrard Batte } W { John Gysors Michel Tony } S

The kinge subdued the Welshemen which oftentimes rebelled. An.25.

1240 Reymond Byngley. } W { Jhon Worle Tho. Duresyne } S

The fyrste aldermen in London. This yere were aldermen fyrst chosen in London, which thẽ had the rule of the wards of the citie, but were euery yere chaunged, as ẏ sheriffs are now.

Anno.26.

Rey-

Reymond Bingley } M { John Fitz John, Rafe Ashewy } S 1241

KIng Henry sayled into Normandy with a faire cōpany, purposing to recouer Poyteirs, Guian, & other contreys: but after many bickerings, somwhat to the losse of Englishmen, he treated a peace.

Anno. 27.

Rafe Ashewy } M { Hugh Blunt, Adam Basing } S 1242

THis yere the pleas of the crowne, were pleaded in the tower of Londō. And in this yere Griffeth whiche was sonne of Lewlyn, lately prince of Wales, entendyng to haue broken prison fel ouer the inner ward of the Tower of London, and brake his necke.

Griffith of wales brake his neck

Anno. 28.

Michell Tony } M { Rafe Spicer, Nicolas Batte } S 1243

THis yere Michell Tony Maior, and Nicolas Batte Shiriffe were bothe conuict of periury, by the othe of all the Aldermen. Because Nicholas Batte had bene Shirife ouer one yere, and for the same they were both deposed, and other were in their places.

Anno. 29.

1244 John Gysors } M { Robert Cornhill / Adam Beawlay } S

ROBert Grosthed bishop of Lincoln with other prelates cōplained to ŷ King, of the wast of the goods and patrimony of ŷ church, which daily was wasted by the aliant bishops, & clerks who shortly were auoided.

Anno.30.

1245 John Gysors } M { Symon fitz mary / Laurēce Frowike } S

The abbey of Hayles builded.

This yere Richarde the Kinges brother builded the abbey of Hayles.

Anno.31.

1246 Piers Alleyn } M { John Voile / Nicolas Batte } S

An earthe quake.

IN this yere was a mighty erthquake in Englande, that the lyke, was not sene many yeres before.

The kinge seised the franchises of the citie of Londō.

The kynge seised the fraunchise of the citie of London for a iudgement that was geuen by the Maior and aldermen againste a wydowe, named Margaret Viel: but shortly the Maior and sheriffes were again restored to their

Coyn chaunged.

offices: and this yere was a new coine, and the olde called in.

Anno.32.

1247 Michel Tony } M { Nicolas Joy / Geffrey winton } S

This

This yeare the wharfe of Quene-hiue in London was taken to ferme by the Communaltie of London, to paye yerely fifty pound for the same.

Anno 33.

Roger fitz Roger } M { Rafe Hardell, John Tolsan } S 1248

This yere dyed Robert Grosteed a famous clerk and byshop of Lincoln, who compiled many famous bookes, whiche remayne to this daye in the latin and the frenche tongue: the names wherof are partly declared by mayster Bale in his boke of English writers.

Anno. 34.

John Norman } M { Humfrey Basse, Williā fitz Ric. } S 1249

This yere was a great winde upon the day of Simō and Jude, whiche did muche harme in many places of Englande. A greate winde.

Anno. 35.

Adam Basyng } M { Laurēce frowike, Nicolas Batte } S 1250

The freer Augustins began to build or inhabite in wales, at Woodhous.

Kinge Henry maried his daughter Mary to Alexander king of Scots, & receiued of him homage for the realme of Scotlande.

Anno.36.

1251 John Toleson } M { Williã Durham / Tho. Wimborn } S

The maior of London sworne in therchequer.

This yere was grauted by the king, that wher before this time the citizens of London, did present theyr Maior before the kyng wheresoeuer he were, and so to be admitted, now he should come onely before the Barons of the exchequer, and they shoulde admit him, and geue him his othe.

Anno.37.

1252 Nicolas Batte } M { John Northãptõ / Richard Picard } S

Many villages drowned.

This yere in the moneth of January the sea rose in such height that it drowned many villages & houses nere vnto it in diuers places of Englande. Also the Thames sprange so highe, that it drowned many houses about the water side. And this yere was graunted of the kynge that no citizen of London should paye scauage or tolle for any beastes by them brought as they before time had vsed.

Anno.38.

1253 Ri. Hardel Dra. } M { Ro. Belington / Rafe Ashewy } S

The liberties of London seased.

The liberties of London were againe seased by the meane of Rycharde Earle

Earle of Cornwalle, because the Maior was charged, that he loked not to the bakers for their syses of bred: so that the citie was forced to please the Earle with. 600. markes or they were restored againe.

Alphonce king of Castel gaue Elinor his daughter in mariage to prince Edward the sonne of king Henry, to whō his father gaue the princedome of Wales, and gouernance of Guian and Ireland, whereof beganne that the kings of Englande ordeined their eldest sonnes princes of Wales. Anno. 39.

The kings eldest sōne prince of Wales.

Richard Hardel draper	M	Stephen Oister gate Hen. Walmode.	S	1254

The king againe seased the liberties of the citie for certain mony which the Quene claymed for her right of the citizēs, so that they gaue vnto his grace 400. marke, and then were restored to their liberties againe.

The liberties of London seased

The. 22. day of Nouēber, wer brought to Westminster. 102. Jewes from Lincolne, whiche were accused for crucifyinge of a chylde, they were sent to the tower of London: of these. 8. were hanged, and the other remayned long in prison.

Execution of the Jewes.

Anno.40.

1255 Rich. Har=dell draper } M { Mat. Bokerel John Wynor } S

This yere a peace was made betwen the citizens of London & the abbot of Waltham, who had ben long in controuersie for tol, that he demaunded of the citizens that came to Walthã faire: but at the last the citizens were set free and bound to no toll. Anno.41.

1256 Richarde Hardell Draper } M { Rich. Ewyll William Ashewy. } S

Maior Aldermen, & sherifs depriued.

Great variance was betwen ỹ king & the Londoners, in so muche ỹ the Maior & diuers aldermen & sheriffes, were depriued of their offices, and the gouernance of the citie cõmitted to certeine persons of the kings appointing.

The mad parliamẽt.

The kinge for so much as he had oftentimes promised the restitution of certayne ancient lawes, but neuer performed the same, the lords murmuryng against him, to appeace their malice, he held a parliament at Oxeforde, whiche was called the madde parliament, because many things were there enacted, which proued after to the confusion of the Realme: and death of manye noble men. In confirmation of these actes

were

wer chosen.xii.piers, who altered and changed many thinges, greatlye to the discontenting of the kinges minde.

Twelue piers.

Anno.42.

Rich. Hardell draper	M	Th. fitz Rich. / Ro. Cathelion	S

1257

This yere Hugh Bigot Justice, and Roger Turkeley, kept theyr courts in the Guildhal of London, and punished the Bakers vpon the tombrell, where in times passed they were punished on the pillorye, and they dyd manye other thinges against the lawes of the citie.

Bakers on the tumbrell.

Richarde the kings brother retourned out of Almain into England.

Anno.43.

John Gisors Pepere r	M	John Adrian / Ro. Cornhil.	S

1258

King Henry fearing some rebellion of his nobles, went into Fraunce, and there concluded a peace: After whiche peace finished, the kyng retourned.

A Jewe at Tewkesbury fell into a priuie vpon the saturday, & would not for reuerēce of his Saboth day be plucked out. Richard of Clare earle of Glocester, hearing that the Jew did so gret reuerence to his Saboth day, thought he would do as much to his holy day, which is sonday, and so kept him there

A Jewe drouned in a priuie.

tyll

tyll mondaye, at which season he was found deade.

Anno.44.

1259 Williã Fitz Richard } M { Adam brawn Ri. Couentry } S

a folk mote at Poules crosse. In this yere the king commaunded a general assembly or meting at Poules crosse, wher the king in proper person commaunded the Maior that the nexte day after he shoulde cause to be sworne before his Aldermen euery striplynge of.ij.yeres of age and upwarde, to be true unto the king & his heires kings of Englande: and that the gates of the citie shold be kept with harnissed men.

Othe to the king.

Anno.45.

1260 Wil. Fitz Richard } M { Jo. Northãptõ Rich. Pickard } S

Kyng Hēry published at Poules cros the bishops of Rome absolutiõ for him and al his, that wer sworn to maintein the articles made in the parliament at Oxforde: for whiche cause the barons of Englãd begon to utter their malice which they had long before conceiued against the kyng, and caused an insurrection that continued thre yeres. Richard erle of Glocester deceased, & Gilbart de Clare was Erle after him.

Anno

Anno.46.

Th. Fitz Thomas } M { Phi. walbroke, Rich. Tayler } S 1261

This yere was so gret a frost ye men rode on hors back ouer the thames: The barons of Englande armed them against their king, and all this yere houered about Londō & other places they robbed and spoyled aliens and certain other persons, whom they knew to be against their purpose: speciallye they slew the Jewes in all places.

A gret frost
The barōs against the king.

Anno.47.

Thomas Fitz Thomas } M { Ro. Mountpiler, Osbern Bucꝫkerell. } S 1262

500. Jewes were slain by the citizēs of Londō, because one Jew wold haue forced a christen man to haue paid more thē.ii.d. for ye vsury of.xx.s. for a weke

Jewes slaine

Hugh le Spencer with the citizēs of London, spoyled & brent the manors of Richard the kinges brother, which hitherto had ben a great stay of the warre betwen the king and his nobles.

Nere to Lewis in Sussex, king Hēry & his barons fought a cruell battel, in which the king himselfe with Richard his brother: syr Ed. his son & other noble men to the nūber of 25. wer taken: and

A battell at Lewis.

and of the commons were slaine about 20000.

Anno. 48.

1263 Tho. Fitz Thomas } M { Tho. Lamford, Edward blune } S

Debate and variance fel betwene Symon Mountford erle of Leicester, and Gilbert de clare erle of Glocester, chif capitains of ye barons: which torned to theyr great euil. For prince Ed. beyng nowe at libertie, allied hym with the erle of Glocester, & gathering to him a gret power, warred so freshly vpon Simon of Leicester, that at the end he and Hugh spencer with many others of the nobles, were slaine in the battel at Euisham in Worcestershyre.

The battel of Euishā

A Parliament at winchester

The same yere was holden a parliament at Wynchester, where all the statutes made before at Oxforde, were disanulled & abrogate. And all writinges made for the confirmation of the same, cancelled.

Lōdō like to haue ben spoyled.

The citie of London was in greate daunger to haue bene destroyed by the kyng for greate displeasure that he had conceiued againste it, because of the forenamed commotion: he gaue vnto prince Edward, the Maior of London and. iiii. of the beste Aldermen, with

with al theyr goodes & lands, and put diuers other of the moste welthy into diuers prisons.

Anno.46.

Tho. Fitz Thomas	M	Peter Armiger Greg. Rockesle	S	1264.

The kinge came to Westminster, and shortly after he gaue unto diuers of his houshold seruants, upon.60. housholdes & houses within the citie, with all such landes & tenementes, goods & catels as the sayd citizens had in any other places of Englande, and then he made one Custos or Gardein of the citie, syr Othon Constable of the tower. And after this, the kinge toke pledges of the best mens sons of the citie, that his peace should be surely kepte in the same, the whiche were put in the tower of London, and there kepte at the coste of their parentes. And shortly after, by greate laboure and suite made, all the forsayd persons whiche shoulde be in the keping of the bailife of the castel of Windsor, eyght onely excepte, and all the other londoners.31.in nūber, were deliuered and came to London. Dayly suite was made unto the kinge, to haue his grace and knowe what fine he would haue of the citye for theyr transgres-

The kinge gaue diuers citizens of London with all theyr landes and goodes to his household seruātes.

gressions, for the which the kyng asked xl. M. poundes, and stucke at. l. M. markes, but suche continuall laboure was made to ye king, that lastly it was agreed for. xx. M. marks, to be paid by the citie, for all transgressions by them done: certaine persons excepted, which the kyng had geuen his son, beynge in the tower of Windsor. Then for the leuying of this fine, were taxed as wel seruantes, couenaunte men, as householders. And many refused the liberties of the citie for to be quite of the charge.

Kenelworth castel besieged.

King Henry besieged the castell of Kenelworth, which Henry Hastinges defended against hym the space of halfe a yere. Anno. 50.

1265. Williã fitz Richard. } M { T. de la fourd / Gre. Rokesly } S

A Parliament at Northampton.

The olde franchises and liberties of London with a new graunt for the shyre of Middelsex, wer confirmed by a parliament at Northampton. Where also many noble men yt had taken part with the Barons, were disherited of their landes, and therfore fled to Ely, and strengthened it in suche wyse that they helde it long after.

Anon. 51.

Alein

Aleyn } W { John Adrian } S 1260
Fowch } { Lucas Bitecote }

About the.li.yere, was made the statutes of weightes & measure, that is to say, that.32. graynes of Whete dry and round & takē in the middes of the eare shold way a sterlig peny, &.xx.of those pens shold make an ounce, &.xii.oūces shold make a poūd troy, and. 8. pound troy shold wey a gallon of wine, and.8 gallōs of wine, shold make a bushel of London, which is the.8.part of a quarter. Also that three barley cornes drie & round, should make an inche, and. xij. ynches to a foote, and three foote to a yarde, and fyue yardes and a halfe to a perch or pole, & xl.pole in lēgth, &.iiii in bred to make an acre of lād, & thes standards of weight and mesures, wer confirmed in the.xv. yere of Edwarde the thirde. And also in the time of Hēry the sixte, and Edwarde the fourth, and lastly confirmed in the. xi. yere of Henry the seuenth. Howe be it in the tyme of king Henry the sixt, it was ordeined that the same oūnce shold be deuided into.xxx.parts called.xxx.pēce: and in kynge Edwarde the fourth hys time into.xl. partes, called xl. pence. And in kyng Henry the eight his days

The statute for weightes and measures.

Alteration of coynes.

into

into.xliiij.partes, called .iij.s. viii.d, but the weyght of the ounce troy, and the measure of the foote, was ordeined euer to be at due stint.

Anno.52.

1267. Alleyn Souch } W { Thomes Basing, Rob. Cornhyll } S

Gylbert de Clare Earle of Glocester with the exiled gentelmen and other nobles of Englande, rose againste the kyng, and held the citie of Londō, buildyng therein bulwarkes, and cast ditches and trenches in diuers places of the citie and Southwarke, and fortified it wonderously. The kyng lying at the abbey of Stratford, also assaulted the same citie, more then a moneth: but by diligent labour vpon his partie, and by the Legate and the kynge of Romains on ye other partie, Agreement was made betwene the kyng and him: In this meane time many robberies were done, wherfore foure yt bare cognisance of the Erle of Darby, were put in sackes, & cast in the Thames.

The kyng besieged London.

Foure persons cast in ye Thames

Anno.53.

1268. Aleyn Souch } W { Williā de Durhā, Walter Haruy } S

Variāce fel betwene goldesmithes & taylers

tayler of London, which caused great rufflynge in the citie, and many men to be slayne. For whyche ryot. xiii. of the chief capitains were arreigned, cast & hanged. Alein Souch was discharged of his maioraltie by the king, and Stephen Edworth made constable of thee tower, & custos of the citie.

A great ryot in London.

Execution

The disherited gentylmen were this yere reconciled to the kinges fauoure. And the fiue citesens which had remained prysoners in the towre of Wyndsor, the whych the Kynge had geuen to his sonne Edward, when they had made their end wyth great summes of money were deliuered. Anno. 54.

The maior & iiii. aldermē released out of Winsor castell.

Thomas Fitz Thomas	M	Will. Hadstock Anketill de Aluerne	S	1269

The riuer of thames was soo harde frosen from the feast of S. Andrewe to Candelmas, that men and beasts passed ouer on foote from Lambeth to Westminster. The marchandises was caried from Sandwiche, and other hauens unto London by land.

A greate frost.

The citie of Lōdon with ẏ reuenues therof was geuen to prince Edwarde.

London geuen to prince Edward

Anno. 55.

John

John Adriã vintener } W { Walter Potter John Tailour } S

1270 This yere the liberties of London were newly confirmed. And thys yeare the steple of Bowe churche in Cheape fell downe, and slue many people both men and women.

The steple of Bowe Churche blowen downe.

Anno. 56

Jo. Adrian vintener } W { Greg. Rokesle Henrye wales } S

1271. This yere deceased Richard king of Almayn and earle of Cornwal brother to the kynge and was buried at Hailes

A ryotte in Norwiche

In June began a great ryot in ẏ citie of Norwich, where through the monasterie of ẏ Trinitie, was burned. And for that fact the kyng rode downe, and made enquiry for the chiefe doers therof: whereof xxx. yonge men were condemned, drawen hanged and brent

Execution

Thys yere were diuers prodigies & strange tokens seene in diuers places of Englande. Anno. 57.

Sir walter harui } W } Richard Paris John Bedill } S

1272. In the beginning of this yere kynge Hery sickned: and he called before hym syr Gilbert Clare earle, of Glocester & caused hym to be newly sworn to kepe the peace of the lande, to thee behofe of

Edwarde

Edwarde his sonne, and then dyed the xvi day of November, in the yeare of our Lorde.1272. when he had reigned lvj.yeares and. xviij. dayes. Hee was buried at westminster upon the southe syde of saint Edwarde. Hee builded a great part of the same Churche.

Kynge Edwarde the Firste surnamed Longshanke
Anno Regni.

Edward the firste, after the conqueste, surnamed Longeshanke, began his Reigne over thes realme of Englād the xvj.day of November, in the yeare 1272. and deceased the. vii. daye of Julye, in the yeare .1307. so he reigned. xxxiiij. yeares .vii. monethes, and, xx, dayes 1273

Anno.1

Syr Walter Harvy knyght } W { John Horne Walter Potter } S 1273.

IN the ende of this yere, the kyng returned into England. There was yet busynes about chosynge of the Maior Stryfe for chosing the aior of ndon for dyuers woulde haue made suche a Maior as they had lyked. But for that tyme they were disappointed: whyche in the yeare folowynge vpon the same day toke further effecte.

Anno.2

1274	Henry Walleys	M	Nicholas Wynchester Henry Couentrie	S

The kyng of Scotts dyd homage to kyng Edwarde for the kyngdome of Scotland

The kynge ordeyned certayne newe lawes for the wealthe of the Realme, emong the which was one, that bakers making bread lackyng weighte, assigned after the price of Corne, shold firste be punished by losse of their bread, and the seconde by enprisonment: and thirdlye by the correction of the pillorye. Myllers for stealynge of corne to bee chastised by the tumberyll, and nighte walkers to be punished in the Tonne in Cornhyll. And this to be put in executiō, he gaue auctoritie to all maiors, bailiffs, & other officers through Englād, & specially to ẏ maior of Lōdon.

Anno.3.

Grego

Grego-ry Roc-kesle } M { Lucas Batecourt, Henrye Fro-wyke } S 1275

Kyng Edwarde bulded the castell of Flynte, and strengthened the castell of Rutlād, & other agaynst the welshmē. *The cast of Flyn buylded*

Anno, 4.

Gregorye Rockeslye } M { John Horne, Rafe Blunte } S 1276

The statute of Mortmayn was enacted by kyng Edward. *Aleenyng in Mortmayn.*

Michell Tony was hanged, drawe, and quarted for treason.

Anno. 5

Gregory Rockesle } M { Rob, de Bracy, Rafe Fenour } S 1277

Kynge Edwarde gaue vnto Dauyd brother to Lewlyn prince of Wales, the lordshyp of Frodesham.

Anno. 6

Gregory Rockesle } M { John Adrian, Walter Lāgley } S 1278

Michelmas terme was this yere kept at Shrewsburye. *Term kept Shrewes*

Anno. 7

Gregory Rockesle } M { Robert Basinge, Wil. Mercer } S 1279

Reformation was made for clipping of the kynges coyne: for which offence 297. Jewes were put to execution. *Execution of Jewes*

Black friers in London builte. In thys yeare began the foundation of the Church of the friers preachers or blacke Friers by Ludgate, and also Castell Baynard.

The towne of Boston was greately empaired wyth fyre.

Anno.8.

1280 Gregorye Rockesley } M } Thomas Boxe, Rafe Moore } S

Halfepens & farthings. This yeare was fyrst coyned halfepens and farthinges of syluer: where before, other coynes of other mettall ran amonge the people to theyr greate losse and noyance

Anno.9.

1281 Gregory Rockesley } M { Wil. Faringdō, Nicolas Wynchester } S

Rebellion in Wales. Dauid the brother of Lewlyn prince of Wales, vnkyndly and traiterouslye moued his brother agaynste kynge Edwarde.

Anno.10.

1282 Henry Waleys } M { Willm̄ Mazerer, Nicholas Wynchester } S

Kyng Edward sente a companye of souldiors into Wales, vnder guyding of the Earles of Northumberlande & Surry: of which company manye were

were slayn, and syr Roger Clifford taken prisoner. The Welshemen subdued certayne castelles and holdes, and of some townes threwe down the walles.

Anno.11.

Henry Waleys } M { Rafe Blunte, Haukyn Betuel } S 1283

Lewlyn prince of wales was slayn by syr Roger Mortymer: and his heade set vpon the Tower of London.

Execution

William Marton Chancellor of England about thys tyme builded Mertō colledge in ye vniuersitie of Oxenford.

Martō colledge buil

Anno.12.

Henrye Waleis } M { Jorden goodchepe, Martin Boxe } S 1284

Dauid the brother of Lewlyn prince of Wales was taken & beheaded

Prence Edward was borne in Wales, at the castell of Carnaruan, and a parliament was held at Shrewsbury

A parliament at Shrewsbury,

Laurence Ducket a citisen of London was found dead, and hanged within saint Mary Bow church of Chepe: for the whiche were condemned .vii. men, which were drawen and hanged, and one woman brent.

Laurence Ducket hanged,

This yere the greate conduite standyng againste saincte Thomas of Acres in Chepe was first begon to bee made.

Cundite in Chepe builded.

Anno

Anno.13

1285 Gregory Rockesleye } M { Stephē Cornhil Roberte Rockesley } S

Liberties London seased. This yeare the liberties of the Citie of London was agayne seysid into the kynges handes, and Stephē Sandwiche admitted for Custos, and the Maior discharged, for takynge bribes of the Bakers.

Anno.14

1286 Rafe Sādwich } M { Walter blūt John Wade } S

Parliamēt at Glocest. This yeare was enacted by ye kynge the Statutes called Additamēta Glouecestrie

Anno.15.

1287 syr John Bryton } M { Thomas Crosse Willīā Hautein } S

A hot sommer & gret cheape of corne This yere the sommer was so exceding hot, that many men died through the extrimitie thereof. And yet wheat was so plentuous, that it was solde at London for .iii.s.iiij.d.a quarter

Anno.16

1288 Rafe sandwiche } M { Williā Herford Tho. Staines } S

Greate halle fel in England, & after ensued

ensued so continual rain, that the yeare folowing, wheate was sold for .xvj. d a bushel: and so encreased yerely þ reigne of this Kyng and hys sonne, tyll it was lastly solde for xl. s. a quarter. Tempest

Anno. 17

Rafe Sandwiche } M { Williā Betain, John of Cantorbury } S 1289

Rice ap Meridoke, a welsheman, rebelling agaynst Payn Tiptoft, warden of the countreye, was by the Earle of Cornwall in the kyngs absence, taken, drawe, hanged, & quartered at Yorke. Execution

Anno. 18

Rafe Sandwiche } M { Fulke of S. Edmonde, Salomō Langford } S 1290.

This yeare kyng Edwarde returned out of Fraunce and was honorably receaued of the citisens of London.

Anno, 19.

Rafe sandwich } M { Tho. Romaine, Williā de Lyre } S 1291,

This yeare the staple of woll was ordeyned to be kept at Sandwiche. Wolstaple at sādwich

And this yeare the Jewes were banyshed the land: for the whyche cause þ cōmons gaue to the king a fyftene. Jewes baneshed.

Anno, 20

Rafe

1292 Rafe sandwiche } W { Rafe Blunt / Haimōd Boxe } S

This yere died quene Elianor ye kin-ges wife, & was buried at westminster This yere also died Elinour wyfe un-to Henry the thirde, & mother to thys Edwarde, whose hearte was buried at the graye friers in London: and her bo-dy at Ambresbury, in the house of Nun-nes

Quene Elinor deceased

Anno.21.

1293 Rafe Sādwich } W { Henry Balle / Elis Russell } S

This yere, iii men had theyr ryghte handes smitten of in the Westchep for res-cuynge a prisoner: arested by an officer of the Citie of London

Anno.22

1294 Rafe Sandwiche } W { Roberte Rockesleye / Martin Aubreye } S

The, xviii. daye of Maye fell a won-drous snow, and therwith an exceding wynde. By violence whereof greate harme was doone in sundrye places of Englande, as ouerthrowynge houses and trees. &c.

Great tempest.

Anno.23.

1295 Sir John Briton } W { Henry Boxe / Richarde Gloucester } S

Wadock

Madocke wyth the Welshemen rebelled against the kyng, wherefore he in all haste made agaynst them, and ouer came them:

Thys yeare the frenchemen arriued at douer, and spoyled the towne, and brente a parte of it, in which skirmishe was slayne one Thomas of Douer.

Douer spoyled by frenchemen.

Anno. 24.

Syr John Bryton	M	John Dunstable Adam Harlyngbury	S	1296

John Baylel was by kyng Edward admitted to be kynge of Scotts, & hee for the same dyd his homage, & sware vnto hym fealtie.

Thys yeare was taken Madocke of Meredoke capitayne of the rebelles in Wales: hee was drawen and hanged at London.

Rebellion in Wales.

Anno. 25

Sir John Bryton	M	Thomas Suffk Adã de Fullam	S	1297.

John Baylell kyng of Scots cõtrary to his allegiance, by the settinges on of the Frenchmẽ, rebelled agayn kyng Edward, Wherfore kyng Edward hasted him thither. He wan from him the castels of Barwicke and Dunbarre,

Barwike wonne.

Hee

The slewe of the Scottes. xxv. M, and toke prisoner syr William Douglas & other noble men. Hee conquered also Edenbrough, where he found the regal ensignes of Scotlande: that is to witt, the Crowne, the Scepter and clothe of estate. Anno. 26

1298. Syr John Britton } M { John de Stortforde William de Stortforde } S

Certain persons brake vp ye Tonne in Cornehyl, and toke oute prisoners, that thither were cōmitted by syr John Britton: for the whyche .ix. of theym were greuously punyshed by longe imprisonemente, and great fines. The tunne aboue named is nowe the cundit in Cornhell

Liberties of London graunted.

The kyng cōmyng agayn into England, and so to Winchester: the citizens of London made suche labour that they obteyned their liberties that had in som part be kept from theim by the terme of xii. yeares or more Anno 27

1299 Henrye Walleis } M { Richard Resham Thomas Sely } S

Thys yere the kyng made cruel war vpon the Scots, & had of them a greate victorie, and then yelded theym selues agayne to his grace and mercy.

Thys

This yere also the king called in certayn coynes of money called pollardes Crocardes and rosaries:

Anno.28

Elis Russell } M { John Armencer / Hery Fringrith } S 1300

Kinge Edwarde hearinge of the untruth and rebelliō of the Scotts, made his third voyage agaynst them, wherin he subdued a greate part of the land, and toke the castell of Estrivelyn wyth other, and made the lords sweare to him fealtie and homage

Anno.29

Elis Russell } M { Luke Haverynge / Rich. Champnes } S 1301

This yeare the kyng gave unto Edward his son, the princedom of Wales and ioyned thereunto the dukedome of Cornwall, and the erledome of Chester.

Anno.30

John Blunt } M { Roberte Caller / Peter Bosham } S 1302.

This yeare the kynge helde a greate parliament at Cantorburye. Parliamēt at Cātorb.

Anno 31

John Blunte } M } Huge Pourte / Symon Parys } S 1303

Thys yeare kyng Edward made greate warres in Scotland, where hee had many ny greate victories,

Anno.32

1304 John Blunt } M { William Combmartein John.de Burforde } S

This yere the kyng caused greate inquirie to be made of ẏ behauior of his Justices throughout his realme, which was called Troyly Baston.

Anno.33

1305. John Blunt } M { Roger Paris John Lincolne } S

William Wales which had done so many displeasures to kynge Edwarde in Scotland, was taken, drawen, hanged and quartred at London on Sainct Bartholomewes eue, and his head sette on London bridge:

Execution at London.

And the nobles of Scotland in a parliamente at Westmynster voluntarilie swore to be true to the kyng of Englād and kepe the land of Scotlande to hys vse agaynst all persons.

Anno.34.

1306 John Blunt } M { Raynold Doderel William Causon } S

Roberte le bruse contrarye to his oth assembled ẏ lords of Scotlande & caused hym selfe to be crowned. When kynge Edward hearde of this treason, he went into Scotlande, where he chased syr Roberte le Bruse, and al the power of Scotlande, and toke manye of the noble men prisoners.

Anno. 35

John Blunt	M	Symon Belet Godfrey de la conduite	S 1307

The warres contenuinge in Scotlande, the noble kyng Edwarde ended his lyfe, the seuenth day of July, in the yeare. 1307. when hee had reigned. 34. yeres. 7 monethes, and 21. dayes. Hee lyeth buried at westminster in the chapell of saynct Edwarde vpon the south syde in a playne tombe of marble at the head of his father. Kyng Edwarde deceased

King Edward the secōd

Anno Regni. i

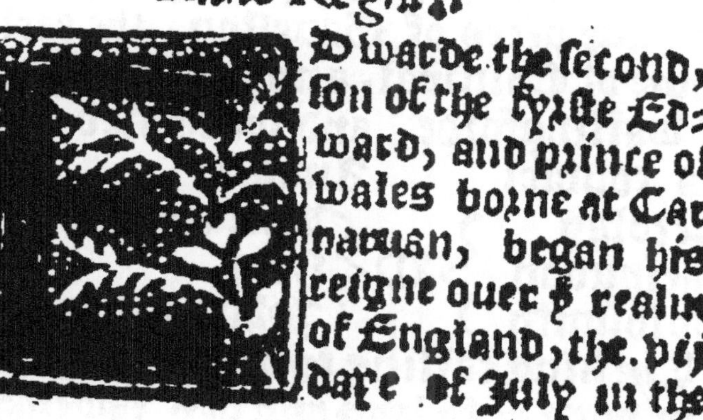

Dwarde the second, son of the fyrste Edward, and prince of wales borne at Carnaruan, began his reigne ouer ye realm of England, the. vij daye of July in the yere 1307

yere of our lord.1307. who was depo=
sed the.25. day of Januarye: and in the
yere.1326. so that he reigned,.9. yeres
He was fayre of bodye, but unstedfast
of maners, and disposed to lyghtnes: he
refused the company of his lordes, and
men of honour: haunting ye company of
vile persõs. He gaue hi self to ouermuch
drinkinge, and lyghtly would disclose
thinges of great councell: Piers of Ga
ueston, Hugh Spencer, and others,
whose wanton counsel he folowynge
gaue hym selfe whollye to the appetite
and pleasure of the body, not regarding
to gouerne his common weale, by sad=
nes discretion, and iustice.

Anno.1

1307. Syr John Blunt } M { Nicolas Pigot / Michell drury } S

Kyng Edwarde toke to wyfe Isabel the daughter of Phillip king of France he gaue piers of Gaueston, the earle=dome of Cornwal, and the lordeshypp of wallingforde, and was ruled al by his counsel

Anno.2.

Nicolas Faringdon
3081. Goldsmith } M { William Basyng / John Butler } S

The king calling to mynd the disple sure done unto hym and hys familiar,

Piers

Piers Gauestō, by ỷ bishop of Chester commanded him to the tower of London, where he was straytlye kepte many dayes after. But the lordes perceauing the king geuen all to wantonnesse, and that he was much prouoked therunto by ỷ meanes of Piers Gaueston, caused the kyng to banish hem the realme, into Ireland, where the kynge notwithstandynge comforted him wyth many riche giftes and made him chiefe ruler of that countrey.

Anno.3.

Thomas Romayn } M { James of S. Ed. Roger Palmer } S 1309

The kinge and his lordes were at great strife for the banishmēt of Piers of Gaueston, in so much that the kinge woulde not be pleased untill he were again restored.

This yere was the Isle of Rhodes recouered from the Turke, by the knightes of the order of saint John Baptist. the Rhods wonne

This yere the crouched friers came first into England. Crouched friers.

Anno. 4.

Ry. Reffā Wint. } M { Simō Croppe Pet. Blackney } S 1310

Piers of Gaueston more and more encreased: in so much that he had the custody of all the kynges iewels and tre=sure of the which he tooke a table and a payre of tressels of golde, and conueig=hed them with other iewels out of the lād. He also brought the kyng to many folde vices: as adultery & suche other. Wherefore the lordes againe banished him out of Englande into Flaunders, to the kinges great displeasure.

Anno.21.

1311 John Gysours Peperer } M { Symon Mer=wood, Rich. Welforde } S

Piers of Gaueston, was againe by the king called out of Flanders, wherfore the lordes being confederate, besie=ged him in the castel of Scarborough, where they toke him, and brought him to Gauersyde besyde Warwicke, and smote of his heade. This yeare the kynges fyrst sonne, named Edwarde, was borne at Windsore.

Execution in Gauer=syde.

Anno. 6.

1312 John Gysours Grocer } M { John Lam=byn, Adam Lucekyn } S

This yere was manye good lawes made in the parliamente at London, wherunto the kyng and his lordes were sworne. Anno.7.

Nicolas

Nicolas Faringdon goldsmith } M { Adam Burden Hugh Bayton } S 1313

The Englishe men encountered with Robert le Bruse and his Scottes, at Estriualen, where was foughte a strong battel. In the ende wherof, the Englishmen were discomfited and so egerly pursued by the Scottes, that many of the noble men were slayne: as Gilbert de Clare Earle of Glocester, syr Robert Clyforde, syr Edmonde of Maule, with other lordes and barons, to the nūber of .xlij. knightes, & .lxviij. barons, besyde .xxij. men of name, whiche were taken prisoners, and .x. M. common souldiours slayne. After this tyme Robert le Bruse reigned as Kyng of Scotland.

The battel at Estriualen.

Anno. 8.

John Gysors Grocer } M { Stephen of Abingdon Hamōd Chikwel } S 1314

A villayn called John Poydras, a tanners son of Excester, in diuers places of England, named himselfe the son of Edward the first, & said that by a false nourse he was stolne out of his cradel, & Edward that was now king put in his place, which was but a carters son

A barkers son made clayme to the croune.

but shortly after, he was conuict of his vntrueth, and confessed, that he dyd it by the motiō of a familiar sprit, which he had in his house in likenes of a cat, whom he had serued.iii. yere, & he for his seruice was drawen and hanged at Northampton. Anno.9.

1315 Stephē abingdō } W { Hamōdgoodchep Wil. Reading } S

The castel of Barwike was yelded vp to the Scottes by the treason of Peter Spaldyng.

Two cardinalles beyng sente from Rome to conclude a peace betwene the king of England & the Scots: as they went through Yorkshiere, were robbed by two knightes called Gilbert Midleton, & Walter Selby, with.600.men, which had don many robberies in those partes, or they were taken, the two knightes were drawen & hanged at Londō. And the kinge recompensed the Cardinalles double so muche as they lost.

Notable theues in Friers apparell.

Shortly after syr Gosslen Deinuile and his brother Robert, with two hundred in habite of Friers, goynge about as outlawes, did many notable roberies, they robbed and spoyled the byshop of Durhams palaces, leauyng no

thing

thing in them but bare, walles, & such Execution
lyke robberies, for the which they were after hanged at Yorke.

Anno. 10.

John Wengraue	M	Wil. Caston Rafe Palmer	S	1316

The Scottes entred the borders of Northūberland and most cruelly robbed and spoyled the countrey, sparynge neither man, woman nor child.

To this mischief was ioyned so exceding dearth and scarsitie that wheate was sold for. iiii. mark the quarter: the cōmō people did eat hors flesh, & other vile beastes, & many died for hunger. Great famine.

Anno. 11.

John Wengraue	M	Jon Prior Wil. Furner	S	1317

Kinge Edward layde siege to Barwike. But in the meane time the scots by an other wey inuaded the borders of England, & wasted the countrey euen to Yorke, & slew a great nūber, specially of religious people: Wherfore it was called the white battel. King Edward was constrained to break vp his siege, & returne againe into England. The white battell.

Syr Hugh the Spencers, the father and the sonne were, of great power in Englād, and by the fauour of the king

 practi-

practised suche crueltie, and bare them selfe hautie, that no lorde in this lande durst contrary them in any thynge that they thought good: whereby they were greatly hated of the nobles.

Anno.12.

1318 John Wegraue } M { John Poutney, John Dalling } S

The Lords and nobles of England, detestynge the outragious pryde of the Spencers, in suche wyse conspired against them, that they caused the kinge halfe against his mind, to banish them the Realme.

Anno.13.

1319 Hamond Chikwel peperer } M { Symon Abingnon, John Preston } S

This yere King Edward contrary to the mind of his lords reuoked the Spencers from banishment, and set them in like authoritie as they before had bene, to the greate disturbance of the realme. and not long after pursued the barons and chased them frō place to place: as fyrst at Ledes castell in Kent: after in the marches of Wales, where he tooke the Mortimers, and sent them to the Tower of London.

Anno.14.

Nichos

Nicholas Faringdon goldsmithe } M { Reynolde at cundit Wil. Prodham } S 1320

This yere kyng Edwarde ouercam the barons in many battels and tooke many of them, whome he put to death in diuers partes of this realme, to the numbre of two and twentye noble mē. Maister John Baldocke, a man of euil fame was made Chancelor of Englād, who extremely pilled the commons of this realme: for the which he was wel rewarded after.

Great execution.

Anno.15.

Hamond Chikwel Grocer } M { Richard Constantine Rich. Hakeney } S 1321

This yere the sonne appeared to mens sight as red as bloud, and so continued the space of vi. houres. The Irishemen by the ayde they had out of Englande, droue the Scottes out of theyr lande. At whiche time many noble men of Scotlande were slayne. Among whiche was Edwarde le Bruze the kinges brother.

The sunne appeared as bloud

Anno.16.

Hamond Chikwel Grocer } M { John Grantham Rich. of Ely } S 1322

King Edward with a great army entred Scotland: but with sicknes and other misfortunes that chanced amonge the soldiors, he within short space was forced to returne: wherof syr James Douglas, & the Scots hauing knowledge, pursued him in such wise, that they slew many englissh men, and had welnere taken the kyng at an abey called Beighland, frō the whiche he was forced to flee, and leaue his treasure behinde him.

Anno reg. 17.

1323 Nicolas Faringdon Goldsmith } M { Adam Salisbury, Jo. of Oxford } S

Charles of France warred vpon the lands of king Edward in Gascoyne to Guien, and tooke there many townes and castels. Wherfore king Edwarde sent his wyfe Isabell to entreate wyth her brother Charles for peace, or (as Froissard saith) the Quene her selfe fleyng the tyranny & mischief of the Spencers, fled with her yong son Edwarde into France, and was gently receiued of her brother, which made greate promise to ayde her againste the tyranny & iniury of the Spencers.

Anno. 18.

Hamond Chikwel Grocer } M { Benet of Fulham John Canston } S 1324

Quene Isabel by the ayde and helpe of syr John of Haynold with a smal company of Henoways returned into England: to whome the nobles and the commons gatheringe in great number pursued the kinge, the Spencers, and other enemies so egerly, that shortlye after they toke them, and kept the king in prison at Kenilworthe. King Edward taken prisoner.

And after at Barkley, they toke maister Robert Baldock, the Chancellor both ye Spencers, the father, and the sonne, the earle of Arundel, with diuers other, & brought them to the town of Hereford. Robert baldocke, the spencers taken prisoners.

Anno. 19.

Richard Betain Goldsmith } M { Gilbert Mordon John Cotton } S 1325

The morow after Simon and Jude, syr Hugh Spencer ye father was put to death at Bristowe, & on saint Hughes day folowing was syr Hugh his sonne drawen hanged & quartered at Hereford, & his head sent to London, & sette emong other vpon the bridge. After Robert Baldock the Chancellor was sent to London to Newgate, where he dies Great execution.

misera-

miserably. The earle of Arundell was put to deth at Hereford: and kinge Edward was by perliament deposed frō his kingdom, when he had reigned. xix yeres, syxe monthes & .xviij. da's, and not longe after was marthered by syr Roger Mortimer, and was buried at Glocester.

King Edward deposed.

Edwarde the third.

Anno Regni. i.

1329

Edwarde the thirde after the deposing of his father was crowned king of England, he began his reigne ouer this realm the .xxv. day of January: in the yere of our lord. 1326. and deceased the. 21 day of June in the yere. 1377. so he reigned. 50. yere, and. 5. monethes lacking 3. daies. In feates of armes he was very expert, as the noble enterprises by him atchieued, du well declare. Of his liberalitie & clemencie, he shewed many greet examples. Briefly, in al prince ly vertues he was so excellēt, that few noble men before his tyme were to be compared to him. At the beginninge of his reigne he was chiefly ordred by syr Roger Mortimer and his mother Isabell.

In this fyrst yere of his reigne he cōfirmed the liberties of the citie of London, and ordeined, that the maior of the city of London should syt in all places of iudgemēt within the liberties of the same for chiefe Iustice, the kinges person only excepted, and that euery alderman that had ben maior shold be iustice of peace of al London and Middlesex: and euery Alderman that had not bene maior should be iustice of peace within his owne warde. Diuers other priuileges be graunted to their citie.

The liberties of London cōfirmed.

The king went towarde Scotland hauing understandinge that the scottes were entred into England, as farre as Stanhop parke. He beset them rounde about, hopynge to haue broughte them under his subiection. But when he thought to be most sure of them by treason of some of his host, the scottes escaped cleane, & returned back into scotland. About the .xxj. day of September Edward ỹ second was murdered in the castell

Edward ỹ secōd murdered.

castell of Barkley by syr Roger Mortimer, and was buried at Glocester.

Anno. 1.

1326	Richard Britayn Goldsmith	M	Ric. Roting Roger Chāscellor	S

The King maried the lady Philip the earles doughter of Henaude in the citie of Yorke.

A Parliament at Northampton.

The kinge helde his parliament at Northampton, wher through the counsaile of syr Roger Mortimer, & the old Quene his mother, he made with the scots an unprofitable and dishonorable peace: For why he restored to them all theyr writings, charters, and patentes wherby the kynges of Scotlande had bounde them selues to be tributarye to the crowne of Englande, with other like unprofitable conditions.

Anno. 2.

1327	Hamonde Chikwell Grocer	M	Henry Darcy John Hawden.	S

Dauid the yong prince of Scotland maried Jane, the syster of Kynge Edwarde, whome the scottes in dirision called Jane make peace. The scottes made many rymes againste thenglishmen, for the fond disguised apparell by

them

them at that tyme worne, amongest the which this was one.

Long beardes hartlesse,
Paynted hoodes witlesse,
Gay Cotes gracelesse,
Makes England thriftlesse.

Scottishe tauntes

Anno.3.

John Grantham Grocer	W	Simō Frācēs, Henry Combmarten.	S		1328

Edward erle of Kent, vncle to king Edward of England, beynge falselye accused of treason, was by syr Roger Mortimer put to death at Winchester.

Execution

Prince Edward was borne at Wodstock. The .xvii. of October, syr Roger Mortemer was taken in Notingham castell, and sent to the Tower of London.

Anno.4.

Symonde Swalond	W	Richard Lazar, Henry Gysors	S		1329

Syr Roger Mortimer was accused, for diuers points of treason, as y^t he murdered king Edward the second, & that through him the Scots escaped at Stanhope parke, for receiuynge summes of money of the Scottes: for which accusations he was shortly after drawen and hanged at London.

Execution

Edward Baylel, the sonne of John

Baylel

Bayliol late kinge of scottes by lycense purchased of King Edward, entred into Scotland, clayming the crowne by the right of his father, where he vanquished the Scottes, and was crouned at Stone. Anno.5.

John Pountney Draper. } M { Robert Ely, Thomas whorwod. } S

1330

The king with a great army wente into Scotland, and at Halidō hil gaue the Scottes battaile, wherin he obteined a triumphant victory, and slew of them. viii. erles 900. knightes & of barons, and esquires. 400. & .33000. cōmon souldiors: he wan Edenborowe, Barwike, and many other castels, and gaue the gouernance of Scotlande to Edward Bayliel. Anno.6.

Barwike wonne.

John Pountney Draper } M { Jon Mocking, Andrw Aubery } S

1331

The king of France sent .x. shyps toward Scotland, which wer so wether driuen into Fleunders, that they were little worth after that time.

Anno. 7.

John Preston Draper } M { Nicolas Pike, John Husbande. } S

1332

Kyng

Kyng Edwarde wente agayne into Scotlande, and layd siege to the castel of Kylbridge: he wan it by strength, set the countrey in quietnes, and came back to the castell of Tyne where shortly after Edward Baylel kyng of Scottes, came and dydde hym homage, and sware vnto hym fealtie.

Anno. 8.

John Pountney draper	M	John Hamond William Hansarde.	S	1333

Embassodors wer sent from Philip de Valoys king of Fraunce, for to conclude vpon certein articles of variãce betwene their lord and the kyng of England, but it toke none effecte.

Anno. 9.

Reignold at Cõduit vintner.	M	John Hyngston Walter Turke	S	1334

This yere kyng Edward sent ambassadors into Fraunce, to cõclude a peace which likewise toke none effect.

Anno. 10.

John Pountney draper	M	Walter mordon Richard Uptõ	S	1335

This yere kyng Edward made claime to the

to the crowne of France, and therfore proclaimed open warre betwene England and France.

Anno.11.

1336 John Pou̅tney draper } M { William Brickelsworth John Northhal } S

This yere the kyng consideryng the charge he had with warres in Scotlād and also that he intēded to haue against the Frenchmen, gathered togither treasure by diuers and sundry ways, wherof the maner is not expressed: but suche greate plentie came to his handes, that money was very scant throughout the whole Realme: by reason of whiche scarsnes, vitaile and other merchandise were exceding good cheape: for at London a quarter of wheate was solde for.ij.s. A fat oxe for.vj.s.viij.d. A fatte shepe for vj.d.and.viij.d.six pigeons for one peny, a fat goose for ij.d.a pyg for a peny: and so all other victuals after the rate.

Cheape of vitailes.

This yere appered a blasing sterre.

Anno.12.

1337 Henry Darcy } M { Walter Neale Nicolas Crane } S

King Edward sent Embassadors beyond

yond the sea, to allie with hym the earle of Heynault, and other lordes, whiche obeye not the french kynge: of whō by the meanes of Jaques Dartuel he had great comfort bothe of the Flemmings & diuers lords & princes of those parts This yeare the kyng granted, that the officers of the Maior and Sheriffs of London should beare maces of syluer.

Anno.13.

Henry Darcy } M { Williā of Pomfret, Huge Marbre } S 1338

Kyng Edwarde for establishement of amitie betwene hym and the Hollanders, Selanders, and Brabanders, sayled to Andwarpe where he concluded the matter with his aliances, & by the consent of ÿ emperor Lewys was proclaimed vicar generall of the empire.

Southhāpton robbed

In this mean time certain frenchmē had entred the hauē of Southhamton and robbed the towne, & brent a greate part therof, and vpon the sea they toke ii great ships, called the Edward, and the christopher. Anno.14.

Andrew Aubery grocer } M { William Thorney, Roger Frosham } S 1339

Great subsidye.

The Kynge helde a perliamente at Westminster: he demaunded thee fythe

part of euery mans goods. The custo=
mes of the wolles to be paid .ii. yeares
before hand: and the nynthe sheafe of e=
uery mans corne. Which was granted
hym. But before it were all payde, the
loue of the people dyd turne into hatred
and their prayer into cursing. &c.

Coyn changed

The kyng changed his coyn, & made
the noble, and half noble. The noble at
vi.s. viii.d.

Armes of Englande and Fraunce entermedled.

Kyng Edward entred the borders of
Fraunce, and made clayme to the whole
realme of Fraunce, as his rightefull in=
heritance: and for more auctoritie na=
med hym selfe kynge of Fraunce, and en
termedled the armes of Fraunce, as it
remayneth to this day.

Anno. 15.

1340 Andrew Aubery grocer } M { Adam Lucas, Bartholomew marys } S

John of Gaunt.

The quene of England wife to kyng
Edward beinge at Gaunt, was deliue=
red of a sonne, which afterwarde was
called John of Gaunt, which was first
earle of Richemounte, and after Duke
of Lancaster

Battayl on the sea

Kyng Edward saylyng into Flaun
ders nye to the towne of Sluce mett
wyth the Frenche kyngs nauye, wher

was

was foughten a cruell battaill, Wherof the kyng of England had the victorye, and the Frenche flete that was in number. 400. sayle was welnere destroyed and the souldiors taken slayne & drouned, so that of. 33000 four escaped aliue

After this victory kyng Edward besieged Turney, and the towne of saint Omers. At the ende of xi. wekes after the siege, a peace was concluded for xii monethes and the kyng returned.

Anno. 16

John Oxenford vintener } M { Rich. barkinge John Rockesley } S 1342

This yeare came into Englande. ii. cardinals to treat a peace betwene the kynges of Englande and of Fraunce, who concluded it for iii. yeares, but it lasted not so longe.

This yere the quene was deliuered of a man child at Langley, who was named Edmund of Langley

Anno. 17.

Symond Francys mercer } M { John Lukyn Rich. Rysingbury } S 1343

Thys yere died John duke of britayn be reason of w hose deathe war & strife grewe, and parts takyng by ye French kyng and kyng Edwarde.

Anno.18

1343. John Hamond } M { John Sewarde / John Aysesham } S

This yere ye king made a coin of fine gold, and named it the Florentine, yt is to say, the peny of ye valu of.vi.s.viii.d ye halfpeny of the valu of.iii s.iiii.d. & the farthing of the valu of.xx.d. which coyn was ordeined for hys warres in France, for the gold therof was not so fyne as was the noble before named

A newe coyne.

Anno.19

1344 John Hamōd } M { Geff. Wichingham / Thomas Legget } S

Thys yere ye king held a solemn feast at his castel of Windsor: where he deuised the Order of the garter, and stablished it as it is at this day. And then hee sayled into Sluce, & so into little Britain with a strōg army. He sent ye earle of Derby with a strōg army into Guyā for to ayde the earle of Northamton.

The order of knights of the garter.

Anno.20,

1345 Richard Lacer Mercer } M { Edmonde Heuenall / John Gloucester } S

king Edward made a greate preparation for the warres of Fraunce: and Philipp de Waloys kynge of Fraunce made as great preparatiō to defend hys land agaynst him

Anno.21

Geffrey Wichinghā	M	John Croydon / Wil. Clopton	S 1346.

Kynge Edward sailed into Normādy with.1100. sayle. wyth his son Prince Edwarde, they ouer rode spoiled & destroyed ŷ coūtrey before them unto Paris: & gathered wōderful riches of plat which he sēt into Englād. Shortly after, he encoūtred ŷ French kyng nye the forest of Cresse, when he had not in his hoste the eight man in comparison of ŷ Frenche army, and obteyned of theym a triumphant victorie. Wher was slain the kynge of Boheme wyth tenne other great princes.80.baners.1200.knightes, and .3000.common souldiors After this victory kyng Edwarde wente toward Caleys, and beseeged it. In the meane whyle Dauid of Scotlād made warre upon the borders of Englande: but the bishop of Yorke with other lordes gathered a great companye aswell spirituall as temporal, and nere unto Durham did byd the kyng of Scottes battaile, where was fought a cruel and fierce battaile. But in the end the victorye fell unto the quenes syde, & there was taken thee kyng of Scottes, wyth many of his greatest lordes, and there was slayne one an other aboue, 15000. souldiours.

K. of scots taken.

Anno, 22

1347	Thomas Legget skinner	M	Adam Bramsō Richa. Basing stoke,	S

Caleys yelded.

This, yere after kyng Edward had lien afore Calais a yere & more, it was yelded up to hym, as yee maye reade in John Frosarde.

Anno, 23

1348	John Lufkyn fishmōger	M	Henrye Pycarde Symō Dolell	S

Gret plage

In the ende of this yeare about August the pestilēce begon in dyuers places of England, and specially at London, and so continued tyll that tyme twelue moneth

Anno. 24

1349	Walter Turke fyshmonger	M	Adame Bury Rafe Lynne	S

Alteration of coyne

The king caused to be be coyned grotes and halfe grotes, the whych lacked of the weyght of his former coyn. ii. & vi. di. of. pound troy, And about ȳ end

of

of August ceased the death in London, whych was so vehemēt and sharp, that ouer thee bodyes buryed in churches and churchyardes: monasteries, and other accustomed buryng places, was buried in the Charter house yarde of London. l, M. persons. Great pestilence

Anno. 25

Richarde Kyllyng bury:	M	John Notte Wylliam Wocestre	S	1350

This yeare kyng Edwarde hadde goodly victory vppon the sea agaynste the Constable of France, where he toke xxii. of their ships. Anno 26

Andrew Aubery grocer	M	John wroth Gibbon Staindrope.	S	1351.

This yere the castel of Guynes was yelden vnto ẏ englyshmen, dwellinge in Calice, by treason of a French man,

Also the englishmen beinge in Britayn had a goodly victory ouer ẏ Frēch men wher they toke manye noble men prisoners. Anno. 27

Adam Francis mercer	M	John Peache John Stodeney	S	1352

This sommer was so long dry, that it was called after, the dry sommer: for from

Dry Sommer — from March till the latter end of July fell litle rain or none: by which reason corne that yere folowyng was scant,

Anno.28

1353	Adam Francis mercer	maior	John Welde John Lytle	S

The duke of Brunswike made an appeale agaynst Henry duke of Lancaster: for whiche was waged battaile in the frenche kynges courte, and beynge bothe ready with in the lystes to fyght, the french king staied the matter, and toke the quarell into his hands, so that either of them departed the field without any stroke striken. Anno.29

1354	Thomas Legget Skinner	M	William Totingham Richar. Smelt	S

Woll staples at Westmin. Chichester Lincolne, Bristow & Cãtorbury — For so much as the townes in Flãders brake their promyse before tyme made by Jaques Dartuel, and now fauored the French partie, kyng Edward remoued the market and staple of wol out of Flanders into Englande: as to westminster, chichester, Lincolne, Bristow & Cantorbury.

Fryer Augustines — Also this yeare was the house of the Friers Augustins in London finished which was reedified by syr Humfreye Bo-

Bohune Erle of Herforde and Esser, whose bodye lieth buried in the quier of the said hous before the high aulter. — *churche in London builded*

Anno.30

Simond Francis Mercer	M	Tho. Forster / Thomas Bran=don	S	1355

Edwarde prince of Wales, nie to the city of poitiers ioined battel with king John of Frãce: of whõ ẏ prince by hys marcial policy wan a noble victory not with stãding ẏ he had in his army but 800. souldiors: & on the frẽchpart were 6000. fightig mẽ. In this cõflict king John was takẽ with his yong son Phi=lip, and many of his nobles, & brought into England.

Anno .31

Henry Picard vintener	M	Rich. Noting=ham / Thoma Dosell	S	1356

Great and royal iustes were holdẽ in smithfield before the king of Englande the Frẽch king being prisoner the king of Scotts, and diuers other nobles. — *Justes in smithfield*

Anno 32

John Stody vintener	M	Stephẽ Cãdish / Barthol. Frost lyng	S	1257

This yere Dauid le Bruze kinge of Scots was set at libertie, when he had put

Nj

put kynge Edwarde suretie of. 10000. marke for his ransome.

Anno.33

1358	John Lukyn fyshmonger	M	Joh. Barnes John Burys	S

The Englishemen in Britain toke the towne of Ancore, and diuers other, and put them to great raunsome

Anno.34

1359	Symon Dolel grocer	M	Simon Bedington John Chichester	S

A fynall peace was concluded betwene the kynges of Englande and of Fraunce, on this condition, that kynge Edward should haue to his possession, the countreis of Gascoyn and Guyen, Poetiers, Lymosyn, Baleuile, Xantes Calice, Guines, and diuers other lordshyps, castels, townes, and al the landes to them belonging, without knowledge of any soueraigntie or subiection for the same: and the kyng of Fraunce should pay for his raunsome. 30000. crownes: and so kyng John returned into France.

Anno.35

1360	John Wrothe fishmonger	M	John Denis Walter Burney	S

Kinge

Kyng Edward returned frō Caleys into England, and broughte wyth hym many noble mē of Frāce for hostages. Thys yeare men and beastes perished in Englande in diuers places, wyth thunder and lightenynges: and fiendes wer sene in mans likenes & spake vnto men as they trauailed by ẏ way Anno 36

John Pech fishmonger } M { Williā Holbeche James Tame } S 1361

Thys yeare was great death and pestilence in Englād, whiche was called the seconde mortalitie: in whyche dyed Henry duke of Lancaster: & then was John of Gaunt the kyngs sonne which had maried the dukes daughter, made duke of Lancaster The secōd pestilence.

Also there were sene this yeare in the ayre Castelles, and hoostes of menne fyghtynge,

Anno 37.

Stephen Candishe } M { Jo. of S, Albons James Andrewes } S

This yeare was a greate wind in England, wher with manye steples & towres were ouerthrowen. 1362 Great wynde.

Kynge John of Fraunce came into England, & shortly after died at ẏ Sauoy in London. Also this yere was a greate froste Great frost

frost in England, whiche lasted frome the myddest of September, to the moneth of Aprill

Anno.38

John Notte peperer — W — Rychard Croydon / John Hiltofte — S

63 Prince Edward sayled into Burdeaux, & receiued the possession of Guyen that kyng Edwarde, had newly gyuen vnto hym

Anno 39

Adam Burye Skinner — W — Symon Mordant / Jo. of Motford — S

1364.

S. stephẽs chapell. This yere the kyng began the foundation of sainct Stephens Chapell at Westmynster, which was fynished by Richarde the second, & sonne of prince Edward

Anno.40

Adam of Burye Skinner — W — John Bukillsworthe / John Irelande — S

1365

Adam of Bury was maior one par's of the yere, & John Lukayn ye residue.

This yeare the kyng commanded that Peter pence should no more be gathered nor payd to Rome

Anno

Anno.41.

John Louekyn fishmõger } M { John warde, William Dikman } S 1366

This yere was borne the second son of prince Edward, named Richarde.

Anno 42

James Andrewe Drape. } M { Rich. Torgold, William Dickman } S 1367

This yere appered a blasing starre. And the Earles of Armenak, of Brett, and of Perygort, with other nobles of the Duchye, of Guyan, appealed the Prince of Wales in the Frenche kings courte, that he had broken the peace, & wronged them, as in exacting of theym ouer great summes of money. &c But the French kyng deferred it for certayn causes

Blasynge sterre.

Anno, 43

Symon Mordon fishmõger } M { Adã Wimbingham, Rob, Girdler } S 1368

This yeare the Frenche kynge proceded in iudgemente vpon the appellation before made by the earle of Armenak, the lord of Brett, and earle of Perygort agaynst prince Edward. Wherupon, discorde and variance began to

take

take place betwene the two kynges: & those lordes whiche before was sworne to kyng Edward, dyd nowe yelde dyuers townes of the countrey of Poytiers vnto the Frenche kynge.

Anno 44

1369 John Chichester goldsmyth } M { John Pyell, Hughe Holbitch } S

Quenes colledge in Oxeforde

This yeare dyed Quene Phelyppe wyfe to Edward the thirde, she builded the colledge in Oxeforde, called quenes colledge.

In this yere was the third mortality or pestilence, wherof died much people

Anno. 45.

1379 John Bernes mercer } M { William Walworth, Roberte Gayton } S

John Barnes maior of London, gaue a cheste with three lockes, and a .1000 markes, to be lent to yonge men vppon sufficient gage, so that it passed not one 100. markes: and for the occupying therof, if he were lerned, to say Deprofundis for the soule of John Barnes: if he were not lerned, to saye Pater noster. But how soeuer the money was lent, at this day the chest standeth in the chamber of Londō, with out eyther money or ple-

ges

ges for the same. Anno.46.

John Barnes mercer } M { Robert Hatfielde, Adam Staple } S 1372

The erle of Pembroke, as he passed the sea to reskue the castell of Rochell, was encoūtred with a flete of Spaniardes, which kynge Henry of Castell had sent to ayde the Frenche kynge. Of these Spanyardes after cruel fight, the Erle was taken, and syr Guystarde de Angle, and other, to the number of .160. persons, and the more parte of his men slayne and drowned.

Anno.47.

John Pyel marchant } M { John Philpot, Nicolas Brember } S 1372

John Duke of Lancaster, entred by Calays into Fraunce, & passed throughe out the realme, by Vermendoys and Chāpayn, nigh to Burdeaux in Aquitayne without battaile.

Anno. 48.

Adam of Burye Skenner } M { John Aubery, John Fyshed } S 1373

Dyuers entreaties of peace were made betwene the kyng of England, & Fraunce, by meane of the byshoppe of

Rome

Rome, but none was concluded.

Anno. 49

1374 William Walworth Fishmonger } W { Richard Lions William Wodhouse } S

The entreatie of peace cōtinued, but not concluded but for foure monethes at the moste: in which time of entreatie the Frenche Kyng wan many holdes, & townes of the Englishmen, as wel in Guyen as in Britayn, and in other places:

Anno. 50.

1375 John Warde grocer } W { John Hadleye William Newe-port } S

Many wonderfull sycknesses fell among the people, aswel in Italy as in England, whereof there died an exceadyng great number.

Anno. 51.

1376 Adam Staple Mercer } W { John Northampton Roberte Launde } S

Prince Edward departed out of this life, who was in his time the flower of chiualrie. Hee was buried at Cantorbury, and then kyng Edwarde created Richard son of prince Edwarde prince of Wales: and because the kyng waxed feble and sicklye, he betoke the rule of the land to syr John of Gaunt duke of Lancaster, who so continued durynge his fathers lyfe, who deceased at Richemond, the. xxi. day of June, in the yeare of our Lord 1377. When he had reigned. 50. yeres fyue monethes lackyng foure dayes, and was buried at Westminster. He buylded a house for studients in Cambridge called ẏ kings halle, the abbey of our lady by ẏ tower of London, the house of fryers at Lāgley, and the nunnery of Dertforde. He lefte behynde hym foure sonnes: Lionel duke of Clarēce, John of Gaūt, duke of Lancaster, Edmonde of Langley, duke of Yorke, and Thomas of Wodstocke, Earle of Cambridge.

The kings haull in Cambridge new abbey by ẏ tower of London buylded.

Richarde the seconde

Anno regni. 1.

Ichard the second, son of Prince Edward of Wales, was ordeyned kyng of England, beynge as yet but eleuen yeares of age. He began his reigne the. xxi. 1377.

O.j. day

day of June, in the yeare of our Lorde 1377. and left the same the. xxix. daye of September. in the. yeare. 1399. so he reigned. xxii. yeres. iij. monethes and eight dayes. In bountie and liberalitie he farre passed all his progenitoures: but he was ouermuche geuen to rest & quietnes, and loued litle dedes of armes, & marciall prowesse, and for that he was yonge, he was moste ruled by yong counsayle, and regarded nothing the aduertisementes of the sage & wise men of his Realme: for the chiefe about hym were of no wisedome nor estimation. Whiche thing tourned thys lande to great trouble, and himselfe in fine to extreme miserie. Of hym John Gower writeth these verses folowing.

Vox clamantis.

When this king first began to reigne,
 the lawes neglected were:
Wherfore good fortune him forsoke
 and thearth dyd quake for feare.
The people also whom he poulde,
 against him did rebell,
The tyme doth yet bewayle the woes,
 That Chronicles do of tell:
The foolishe c[illegible]uncell of the lewde
 and yong, [illegible] dyd receyue:
And graue aduice of aged heds:

he did

he dyd reiect and leaue.
And then for gredy thirst of coyne,
some subiectes he accusde:
To gayne their goodes into his hande
thus he the Realme abusde.

Anno regni. 1.

Nicolas Brember grocer	M	Andrewe pickmã, Nicolas Twyforde	S	1377

By the enticement of the Frenchmẽ, the Scots began to rebel, and a squire of theyrs, called Alexander Ramsey, with. xl. persons, in a nyght toke the castell of Barwike, whiche was rescued and recouered by therle of Northumberladde.

Barwyke taken.

Anno. 2.

John Philpot grocer	M	John Boseham, Thomas Cornewalis.	S	1368

This John Philpot gaue to the citie of London certain tenementes, for the whiche the Chamberlayne of Londõ, payeth yerely for euer, to. xiij. poore people of the same citie, euery of thẽ iij pence the weke, which is payd to them at the. iiij. quarter feastes, of the yere.

Charitable dedes of John Philpot.

Anno. 3.

1379 John Hadley grocer } M { John Heylisdom, Wyllyam Barret } S

The Frenche men entred into the Thames and burnt diuers townes, & at the last came to Grauesende, where they spoyled the towne, and set it on fyre, and returned into Fraunce wyth muche riches. This yere was suche a pestilence in Englande that most people dyed. Also a parliament at Westminster, where was graunted, that all men and women, beynge of the age of xiiij. yeares or vpwarde, should pay to the King. iiij. d. by reason wherof great grudge and murmure grew among the commons: and this was graunted towardes the warres in Fraunce.

Newe colledges in Oxforde, & Winchester

About this time Willyam Wicham bishop of Winchester buylded the new colledge in Oxeford, and the new colledge in Winchester.

Anno. 4.

1380 Willyam Walworth Fishmōger } M { Walter ducket, Will. Knightshode } S

Tis yeare the makynge of gunnes was fyrst found in Almayne

Gunnes inuented.

By the meane of the parlimēt aboue named, this yere ẏ cōmons of this lande, specially

specially of Kent & Essex, sodeinly rebelled & assembled together vpõ black Heath, to the number of. 60000. and aboue, whiche had to their captaines, Watte Tyler, Jacke Strawe, Jacke Shepard, Tom Myller, Hobbe Carter, and suche other: whiche were animated to this rebellion, by one John Wall or bal, a seditious precher. They caused muche trouble and busynes in the realme: and chiefly about the citie of London, where they practised muche villany, and destroying many goodly places of the nobles, as the Sauoye, Saint Johns in Smithfield, & other. They let foorth al prisoners, and sette them at libertie: they spoyled all the bookes of lawe in the Innes of court, the Recordes of the Counters, and other prisons. They fet the king forth of the tower of London, cõpelling him to graunt al bondmen fredome, & that he shold neuer demande tribute or taxe of his commons: and also required Jacke Straw, & Wat Tyler to be made dukes of Essex, and Kent, and gouernours of the kynges person from thens foorth, both in peace & warre: which thinges he granted, for he durst in no point deny thẽ. But William Walworth fishe-

The Sauoy burnte and Saint Johns spoyled.

monger Maior of London beynge in Smithfielde, nere vnto the kinges person, seynge him stande hoodlesse afore Jack straw, rebuked the said Straw of his great leudenes, and with a dagger slew him, & brought the kyng into the citie: Wherupō the rude company was dispersed, & fled as shepe, som one way and some an other. In memory of this dede, the city geueth the dagger in their shield of armes.

Jack straw slayne.

Why ỹ city of London geueth the Dagger.

Anno. 5.

1381 John Northāpton Draper } M { John Rote, John Hynde } S

This yere was a terrible earthquake throughout all England, which threw downe many castels, steples, houses, and trees.

An earthquake.

Anno. 6.

1382 John Northāpton Draper } M { Adā Baume, John Selye. } S

A combat

This yeare was a combat foughten at Westminster, betwene one Garton appellant, and syr John Ansley knight defendant, the knight was Victor and Garton was from that place drawen to Tyborn, and there hanged for his false accusation.

Anno. 7.

Nicolos

Nicolas Brember grocer	M	Simon Winchcombe John Moore	S	1383 Execution at S. Albons

This yere was one Wall, or Ball taken at Couentre, by Robert Treuilian, and hanged at saint Albons, for that he was the animator of the rebels spoken of in the fourth yere of this kyngs reigne. Anno. 8

Nicolas Brembre grocer	M	Nicholas Exton John Frenche	S	1384

The kyng went toward Scotland with a great army, but when he drewe nere the borders, suche means was sought that a peace was concluded.

Anno. 9.

Nicolas Brembre grocer	M	John Organ John Churcheman	S	1385

Kyng Richard maried the daughter of Winceslaus, emperour of Almayn.

Anno. 10.

Nicolas Exton fishmõger.	M	William Stonden Williã More	S	1386.

The Erle of Arundel went into the Duchy of Guyan, for to strengthen suche souldiors as the: kyng at that tyms had in those parties, or to scoure the sea of Rouers. The erle keping his course encountred with a mighty flete of Flemynges laden with Rochell wyne, and tooke them, & brought theim to dyuers portes of England: wherby wyne was sold for.xiij.s.iiij.d.and xx.s.a tonne, of the very choyse.

Anno. xi.

1387	Nicolas Exton fishmonger	M	Wylliam Venour Hugh Fostalfe	S

Thomas of Wodstocke duke of Glocester, the erles of Arundel, Warwike, Darby, and Notingham, consyderinge how this lande was misgouerned, by a few persons about the kinge entendyng reformatiō of the same, assembled at Radecocke bridge, where they toke their counsell, and raising a strong power, cam to London, where they caused the kyng to cal a parliament wherof hearyng Alexander Neuyll, archbyshop of Yorke, syr Lionel Vere, marques of Deuelen, & syr Michael de la Poole, Chācellor & Erle of Suffolke fearing punishment, fled the lande and died in strange countreis. The kynge by consaile of the aboue named lordes during the parliament, caused to be taken sir Robert Tresilian, chief Justice of En-of Englande, sir Nicholas Brembire, late Maior of Lōdon, sir John Salisbury knight of houshold, sir John Beauchampe steward of the kings house, sir Symon Burley, sir James Barnes and syr Roberte Belknappe knightes and a sergeant of armes, named John Wske, the whiche by authoritie of the sayd parliament, were conuict of treason, and put to death at the tower hil, & at Tyborn. And John Holt, John Locton, Richard Graye, Willīā Burgth, and Robert Fulthorpe iustice, with the other foresayd lordes, which before had voided the lande, were exiled for euer. Anno. 12. Execution

Sir Nico. Twyforde goldsmith	M	Tho. Austen Adam Catshyll	S	1388

This yere the kyng kept a great iustes in Smithsfeld, whiche continued xxiiij. days. This yere on ye fifth day of August, was the battayle of Ottirborn where syr Henry Percy slewe the erle Douglas of Scotlande, and after was taken prisoner. Anno. 13. Iustes in smithfielde Battaile at Ottirborn.

William Venour grocer	M	John Walcot John Loueney	S	1389

An esquire of Nauarre accused an en- A combat.

englishe esquiere called John Welsh of treason: for the triall wherof, a daye of fyght was taken, to be in the Kinges palais at Westminster: where John Welshe was victor, and cõstrained the
Execution the other to yelde. He was despoyled of his armour, and drawen to Tyborne, and hanged.

Anno. 14.

1390	Adam Banlome goldsmith	M	John Francis Thomas Vicent	S

The duke of Lãcaster uncle to king Richard sailed with a company of souldiors into Spayn, to claim the realme of Castile: for so much as he had taken to wife the eldest daughter of kyng Peter, that was expelled his kingdom by Henry his bastard brother: he conquered the countrey of Galice, and made league with the king of Portugal: but by great mortalitie, which fell among his people: he was fayn to desmisse his army and shortly after loste all that euer he had wonne. Anno. 15.

1391	John Hynde Draper	M	John Chadworth Henry Vamer	S

A fraye in Fletestrete — A bakers man bearynge a basket of horsebread in Fletestreet, one of the bishop

bishop of Salisburies men toke out a lofe, ye baker requiring his lofe, ye byshops man brake ye bakers head: wherupõ folowed such partles taking, yt the Maior and sheriffes and all the quiete people of the citie coulde not order the unrulynes of the multitude, but yt they wold haue him deliuered to them, who brake the bakers head, or els to breake open the gates of the saide bishops palace, who was the kings highe treasorer: for the which the kyng seased the libertie of the citie, and discharged the Maior and Sheriffes of the rule of the Citie, and committed the gouernement therof to a knyght of the courte called syr Edward Dalingrige.

Anno.16.

William Stonden Grocer } M { Gilb. Mãsfield, Thomas Newenton } S 1392

This yere by the great sute & labour of doctor Grauesend then bishop of Lõdon, the liberties were shortly restored to the citizens of London. The liberties of Lõdõ restored

Anno.17.

John Hadley grocer } M { Drew Barentin, Richarde Whitington } S 1393

A truce prolonged betwene Fraunce and

and Englande for thre yeares.

This yeare died Quene Anne, wyfe to kyng Richarde.

Anno.18.

1394 Jonh Frenche Mercer } W { William Bramton, Tho. Knolles } S

John Wikliffe. Aboute this tyme was Wikliffe famous in England.

Kyng Richarde made a voyage into Ireland, whiche was more chargeable thē honorable. And this yere was great tempest of wynd in England.

Anno. 19.

1395 William More vintener } W { Roger Elys, William Sheringham } S

A truce for .xxx. yeres was made betwene England and Fraunce: and kyng Richard toke to wife Isabel the daughter of Charles the Frenche kyng.

Anno.20.

1396 Adam Bame goldsmith } W { Thomas Wilforde, Will. Parker } S

The duke of Glocester kyng Richardes uncle with the erle of Arundel and

Execution other was put to cruell death: for so muche as they rebuked the kyng in certain matters ouer liberally.

Anno.

Anno.21.

Richard Whittingtō Mercer } M { Wil. Askham John Wood-cocke } S 1397.

This yeare deceased John of Gaūt duke of Lancaster: He was buried in Poules Churche, on the north syde of the quier.

The Duke of Hereford and also the Duke of Norffolke were bothe banyshed the lande. the duke o Herefords banished.

Anno.22.

Drewe Barentine goldsmith } M { John Wade John Warner } S 1398

Kinge Richarde lette the realme of Englande to Ferme, to syr Willyam Scrope Erle of Wyltshyre, and to.iij. knyghtes, Bushye, Bagot and Grene. Englande let to ferme. And then in Aprill he wente with an army into Irelande, leauynge for hys Lieuetenaunt in Englande, syr Edmund of Langley his uncle, Duke of Yorke.

Kynge Richard beynge occupied in Irelande, Henry Bolyngbroke, Duke of Herefords, and of Lancaster: whiche was banyshed into France, beynge sente for of the Londoners, came into Englande with a small power, and

landed

landed in Holdernesse in Yorkeshire, to whome the Commons gathered in greate number: whereof Kynge Rycharde hearyng, about September hee returned and landynge at Wylforde hauen, he went to the castell of Flynte in Wales, where he rested hym entendynge to gather more strengthe: In the whych tyme, Henry Duke of Lancaster came vnto Bristowe, where he tooke syr William Scrope, Erle of Wylteshire, and Treasourer of Englande, syr John Bushy, and syr Henrey Grene Syr John Bagot was there taken but he escaped and fledde the other thre were put to Execution. king Richard beyng in the castell of Flynte was taken: and by Henrye Duke of Lancaster, sente to the Tower of London: where shortly after hee yelded vp and resygned to the sayde Henrye, all hys power and Kyngely tytle to the Crowne of Englande and Fraunce, knowledgynge, that he worthily was deposed for his demerites and misgouernyng of the common weale.

Kyng Rycharde takē prisoner.

Kyng

¶ Kynge Henry the fourth.

Anno regni. 1.

Henry the fourth was ordeined kinge of Englande more by force, then by lawful succession or election: which thinge tourned him to much unquietnesse, & caused often rebellion in this realme, He began his reigne ouer this realme, the. xxix. of Septēber, in the yere of our Lord. 1399. and lefte the same the. xx. daye of Marche, in the yeare. 1412. So he reigned thirtene yeres. vi. monethes, lackyng. ix. dayes. 1399

Henry the sonne of kynge Henry was chosen prince of Wales, and duke of Cornewall, Earle of Chester, and heire apparant to the Crowne: he deposed three Dukes, that is to saye, of Albumarle, Excester, and Surrey, and the marques of Dorset.

Anno. 1.

Thomas Knolles Grocer } M { William Walderne / William Hyde } S 1399.

Syr

A conspiracie against King Henrye.

Syr John Hollande duke of Excester brother to Kinge Richarde, the duke of Albumarle, ỹ duke of Surrey with the Erles of Salisbury & Gloucester, and other that fauored Richard of Burdeux, conspired against Kynge Henry, and appointed priuely to murder him at a feaste, whiche shoulde be holden at Windsore: but theyr treason was disclosed, and they al put to death with as many knightes & esquires as were of that aliance and confederacie.

Execution

King Rychard murdered

Kyng Richard was put to death in Pomfret castel, by a knight called syr Piers of Erton, and after brought to the tower of London, & so through the citie to Poules barefaced, & ther stode iij. dayes for all beholders: and from thence to Lãgley, and ther buried in a house of Friers: but he was since remoued by Henry the. v. and lieth at Westminster. Vpon the deathe of this King Richard, John Gower doth write as foloweth.

Vox clamantis.

O myrroure for the worlde mete,
Which shouldest in gold be bette,
By whiche all wise men, by forsight,
Theyr prudent wittes may whette:
Lo God doth hate suche rulers as

hem

Were viciously do lyue
And none ought rule, that by theyr life
Doo yll example gyue.
As this King Richard witnesseth wel
His ende this playne doeth showe,
For God allotted hym such ende
and sente hym so greate woo,
As suche a lyfe deserude as by
The chronicles thou mayst knowe,

Anno 2.

John Fraunceis Goldsmith } M { John Wakel, William Ebot } S 1400

Whyle the kyng was yet in Wales, certayne persons enuying that he had so shortelye obtayned and possessed the Realme, blased a broade amongeste the vulgare people, that kynge Richarde was yet liuing, and desyred ayde of the common people to reposesse his royal dignitie. And to þ furtherance of their inuention, they sette vpon the poastes, and caste about the stretes raylyng rimes agaynst Kyng Henry. He beynge netled with those vncurteous prickes searched out the auctors and amongest other were found culpable, syr Roger Claryngdon knyght wyth two of his seruauntes, the Priour of Launde, and eyghte Freyers Mynours, or graye

Freers who were drawen, hanged an quartered at Tyborne

Execution

Owen Glendour of Wales rebelled and kyng Henry went thither with a strong armye, but they fledde to theyr mountaynes.

Rebellion in Wales

This yeare was greate scarsitie of wheate and other graine, so that wheat was sold at Lōdō, for, xvi.s, a quarter

Dearthe of corne

Anno.3.

1401	John Chadworth Mercer	M	Wil. Wenour John Fre=mingham	Ve= n	

This yere the condite standyng pon Cornehill in London was bego to be made (wher as before tyme it was a pryson for preestes called the Tonne in Cornehill.

Condite in Cornhill builded

A great battaile at Shrewsbury, began by sir Thomas Percy, erle of worcester, and other agaynste the kynge, where syr Thomas Percie was taken and beheaded, and syr Henry Percye slayn, wyth many other noble men.

Batayle at Shrewsburye

Execution

Anno.4

1402	John Walcot Draper	M	Richarde Mar=lowe Robert Chicheley	S

The Lorde of Castell in Britayne

landed

landed within a mile of Plymmouthe, with a greate company, hee lodged all nyght in Plimmouthe, and on the morow robbed and spoyled the town, and returned agayne to their shyps. Plimmout spoyled

Anno. 5.

William Askham. fishmonger } M { Thomas Fauconer Tho. Poole } S 1403

The Britaynes and Frenchemen, which the yere before had spoyled and robbed the town of Plimmouth, were discomfited and slayne by the englishe men, in a battayle on the sea nere thee towne of Dartmouth.

This yere one William Serle was taken in the marches of Scotland, and brought to London and there hanged drawen and quartered for murdrynge the duke of Gloucester at Calice. Executio

Anno. 6

John Wood Draper } M { Wil Lowsche Ste. Spelmā } S 1404

Syr Rychard Scrope then archbyshop of York, and the Lord Mowbray then marshall of England with other, gathered greate strengthe to haue put down the Kyng, but they wer taken at York, where they were bothe beheaded Executio

Anno. 7.

1405 Jo. wodcock Mercer } M { Hēry Bartō Wil. Cromer } S

Rochester bridg builded. This yere was the bridge and Chapel of Rochester finished by sir Robert Knols, who also new reedified the body of ye church of white friers standing in Fletestrete, and there was buried: That Church was first founded by the auncestores of the Lord Gray Cotner.

Anno. 8

1406 Richard Whittingtō Mercer } M { Nicolas Wotton Geff. Broke } S

Thys Richarde Whittington aboue named, builded in London Whittingtons colledge, A great parte of the hospitall of sainte Bartholomewes in weste Smithfielde: the librarye at the gray friers and a great part of the east end of the guyld hall.

Whittington college

This yere syr Henry Erle of Northumberland, and the lord of Bardolfe commyng out of Scotland: with a strōg company, were met & foughten with, and discomfited, and theyr heades were stryken of, and sent to London.

Execution

Anno,

Anno.9.

William Stonden Grober	M	Henry Pomfret / Henry Halton	S	1407.

This yere was a great frost which began in December, and lasted fyftene wekes. Gret frost

Edmond Hollande Erle of Kent and admirall of the sea, scouring the sea landed in Britayn, and besieged the Castell of Briake and wan it: but he was ther wounded with an arrow, wherof he dyed.

Anno.10

Drewe Barentine Goldsmith	M	Thomas duke / William Norton	S	1408.

This yere in Smithfielde was held a great Justes betwene the Henowayes and Englishemen, in the whiche were many feats of armes done. Gret iustes in Smith field

Anno.11.

Richarde Marlowe Ironmonger	M	John Lawe / William Chichley	S	1409

John Badley Taylour was brent in Smithfield for the Sacramente of the Aulter. Execution in Smithfield

This yere the market house called the

[Th]e stocks [b]uilded — the Stockes in London was begon to be builded.

Anno. 12

Tho. knolles Grocer.	M	Jo. Penne Tho. Pike	S

1410 This yere a squire of Wales named Rice ap Dee, which had long tyme rebelled agaynst the kyng, was broughte to London, and there drawen, hanged and quartered.

[E]xecution

[G]uild hal [i]n London [n]ew builded.

This yere was the Guilde Hall of London begon to be new built: and of an olde and lyttell cotage, made into a fayre & goodly house as it now apereth.

Anno. 13

1411	Robert Chicheley Grocer	M	John Rainwel William Cotton	S

This yeare the xii. day of October, the Thames flowed thrise in one day.

And this yere the kyng caused a new coyn of nobles to be made which were of lesse valu e then the olde by. iiii. d in a noble.

Anno. 14

1412	William Waldren Mercer	M	Rafe Leuehind William Seuenoke	S

This yere after the great and fortunate chaunces happened to kinge Henry, being deliuered of al ciuile diuisio[n] and discentiō, he minded to make a vo-age agaynst the infidels, and especially for the recouery of Jerusalem: and for that cause prepared a great army, and gathered muche treasure, entendyng to set forward in the same spryng. When he had thus prepared al thinges necessary for his voyage: he was taken with an Apoplexie, of the whiche he languished till his appoynted hower, and departed, in a chamber of the Abbotts of Westminster, called Jerusalem, the xx. day of Marche, in the yere of oure lorde. 1412. When he had reigned .13. yeres, syxe monethes and nyne dayes, he was buried at Cantorbury

Kyng Henry the fyfth

Anno Regni. 1

Enry the fyfth began his reign ẏ xx. day of March in the yeare of our lorde, 1412. and deceased ẏ last day of August in the yere 1422 so he reigned. ix. yeres, fyue monethes and ten dayes. He was a prince of great noblenes & prowes, of stature and personage tall and sclender, of nature gentle and liberal, 1412

in

in dedes armes experte and cunnynge, whereby he cōquered manfully his enemies, and brought Fraunce to his subiection: before the death of his father he applied and gaue him self to al vice and insolencie of life, and drewe vnto him riotous and wildly disposed persons: but when he was admitted to the rule of the laude sodaynly he became a newe man, and turned all the rage of wildnes into sober and wise behauior, and vice into vertue: and that he might not be agayne corrupted, he charged al his olde companions, that vpon payne of their liues none of them shold come within ten myles of the place that he was lodged in.

Oldcastel. Thys yere about haruest tyme, was syr John Oldecastle knight appeached for an heretike and committed to prison, but he brake out of the tower, and wente to wales, where hee lyued .iiii. yeres after

Anno.1

1413 Wil. Crowmer Draper } M { John Sutton, John Mycol } S

Certayne adherentes of the forenamed syr John Oldecastell, assembled them in Thickets fielde, nere vnto S. Giles in greate number, wereof the

kynge

kynge being informed, toke the felde
afore them, and toke of them so many,
that all the prisons in and about Lon
don, were filled. The chief of thē whiche were xxix. wer condempned by the
Clergie of heresie, and attaynted of
high treason, as mouers of war against
theyr kyng, by the temporal law in the
Guild hall, and adiudged for treason,
to be drawen and hanged, and for here
sye to bee consumed with fyre, whiche
was executed accordyngly in January
folowyng. The chiefe wherof was syr
Roger Acton knyghte, John Browne
Esquier, and John Beuerley priest.

Anno.2.

Thomas Fauconer Mercer } M { John Michell, Thomas Alleín } S 1414

This yere the king made great prouision to sayle into France with an ar
my, & while he was shipping of his pe
ple, syr Richard erle of Cambridg, syr
Richard Scrope treasorer of England
and syr Thomas Graye knight, were
arrested for treason, and so straightlye Execution
examined, that it was cōfessed that they
were purposed to haue slayn the king,
by the corrupting of the Frenche men:
wherfore they were all three adiudged

to dye, and were headed at Hampton.

The kyng toke shipping wyth a greet power, and sayled into Normandye and toke the town of Harflew, where he was compassed about wyth a great host of frenchmē, to ye nūber of .40000 he hauinge but 13000. footemen, and 2000 speares. He slew of his enemies 10000 and toke prisoners nie as many This was called ye battel of Agincourt

Battell of Agincourt

Anno. 3.

1415 Nicholas Wotton Draper } M { William Cambridge. Allein Euerard } S

This yere the Emperour Sigismond came into England: to entreat a peace betwene the kynges of Englande and France: but all was in vaine, for in the ende no peace could be concluded, and kyng Henry went agayne into France

Anno. 4.

1416 Henry Barton Skinner } M { Robert Wodington John Couentre } S

This yere in Fraunce kyng Henry obteyned many victories, and gotte al the townes and holdes in Normandy sauing Rohan, whyche he strongly besieged.

On Ester daye was a great fraye in saynct Dunstons Church in the Easte parte of London: the beginners thereof was the Lorde Strange, and syr John Trussel knight through the quarell of theyr owne wiues: through the whych fraye many people were sore wounded and hurte, and one Thomas Pet warden Fishmonger, slaine oute of hande, wherfore both the fraiers wer brought to the counter in the Pultrie, and the lord Strange for beginning the sayde fray, was yͤ next sōday accursed at Paules crosse.

A fraye in saint Dunstons Church

Anno. 5

Richard Marlow Iremonger	M	Henry Reade, John Gedney	S	1417.

This yere syr John Oldcastel was sent vnto London by the Lord Powes out of Wales, the whyche syr John for heresie and treason was conuicte, and for the same was drawē to saint Giles fielde: where he was hanged and consumed wyth fyre.

Execution

About this tyme the person of Wrotham in Norfolke, whiche had haunted newe Market heath, and there robbed & spoyled many of the kinges subiects was with his concubine brought vp to

The persō of Wroth

New

Newgate where he lastly died,

Anno 6.

Wil. Seue- } M { Rafe Barton } S
noke grocer } { Jo. Parnesse }

1418 Kynge Henry conquered Roan, subdued all Normandy, and was proclaimed Regente of Fraunce for terme of the lyfe of Charles beyng then kynge. And after his decease ỹ croun of Frãce wyth all rightes belonging to ỹ same to hym and his heyres. For confirmacion wherof, he toke to wife Catherin the daughter of Charles.

Anno. 7

Richarde } { R. Whitting- }
1419 Whittingtõ } M { ham } S
Mercer } { John Butler }

This yere king Henry returned into England & so to London, and at Westminster Katherin his wife was crowned the xxiiii. day of February.

Anno. 8.

1420 Wil Cam- } M { John Butler } S
bridge gro } { John Welles }

The duke of Clarence king Henries brother was ouerset by the Dolphin of France, and slayn, to the kinges greate displeasure.

Kyng Henry went againe into France and made warre vpon the Dolphin.

Anno

Robert Chichely Grocer } M { Richard Gosselyn / Wil. Weston } S 1421

This yeare. Quene Catherin was deliuered at Windsor of a yong prince whose name was Henry, and the tenth daye of Auguste was the newe wether cocke set on Paules steple.

This yeare the Quene returned into Fraunce to Kynge Henrye, where was a ioyfull meting, but after folowed sorow: for the king beyng at Bois in Vincente, waxed sicke and deed, the last day of August, in the yeare of oure lorde. 1422. when he had reigned nine yeares fyue monethes & ten dayes, hee builded the Shene and Sion, and lyeth buried at Westminster.

Shene & Sion builded.

Kyng Henry the sixt

Annno. Regni. 1.

Enry the syxte beeing but viii. monethes of age, began hys reigne ouer this Realme of Englande the last day of August in the yeare of our Lorde 1422 1422

lord 1422. hee was deposed the fourthe day of Marche in the yere 1460. So he reigned .xxxviii. yeres, syxe monethes & foure days, continuing the time of his youth, he was committed to the gouernaunce of Duke Humfraye of Glocester hys uncle: when he came to mans state he was of wit, and nature, symple, gentle, and meke, & loued better peace then war, quietnesse of mynd then busines of the world al trouble, vexation, unquietnes, and iniuries, that euer happened to hym, (whiche were many and great) hee suffred soo paciently that he reputed theym to bee worthely sente of God for his offences Hee fauored good letter, excellentlye well: in token whereof he erected two famous Colledges, the one att Cambridge, called the kynges colledge, the other at Etō: by meanes wherof good learnyng greatly encreased.

Kings colledge at Cambridg and the colledg at Etō builded

In the beginning of his reigne died kyng Charles of France, by reason wherof, the kingdome of Fraunce should come unto kyng Henry, and ẏ nobles of Fraunce (except a fewe that helde with the Dolphin) deliuered the possessiō therof unto the Duke of Bedforde

Lord Regent of Fraunce, to the vse of kyng Henry.

Anno. 1

William Waldern e Mercer } M { William Estfield R. Tatter sale } S 1422

A subsedie was graunted for three yeres, fiue nobles of euery sack of wol that should passe out of the lande.

A priest was burned for heresie, called William Tayler. Execution

The weste gate of London, nowe called newegate, was newlye buylded by the executors of Richarde Whittington late Maior of London, Newgate builded

Anno. 2

William Crowmer Draper } M { Nic. James Tho. Wadforde } S 1423

This yere the duke of Bedford wan from the Dolphin of Fraunce, manye strong holdes and townes, and nere to a towne, called Vernel, he discomfited the Dolphins whole power, for in that fighte were slayne .iii. erles and many other noble men, and 5000: common souldiours.

This yere James kyng of Scottes was

was deliuered who had remayned prisoner in England. xviii. yeres, and hee maried the ladye Jane daughter to the erle of Somerset, cosyn to kyng Hery.

Anno. 3

1424 John Michel Fishmonger } M { Symon Seman Jo. Bywater } S

This yere the Kinge of Portingale came into England, and was honorably receaued.

The fyrst custome.

This yere by the parliament holden at Westminster, was graunted to the kyng for three yeres to help him in hys warres a subsedy of. xii. d. in the pond of all marchandizes brought in, or caried out of this realm, and. iii. s. of euery tonne of wine, the which was then called tonnage and poundage, but since it hath bene renewed at sundry parliamentes, and nowe is called custome. Furthermore, it was enacted that all marchant strangers shoulde be lodged within an english host, within. xv. dais of their comeng to their port sale, & to make no sale of any marchādise or they were so lodged: & then within. lx. days folowyng, to make sale of all that they brought, and if any remayned vnsolde at the sayd. lx. dayes ende, that then ale

such

such marchandise so vnsold, to be for=
feyte to the king.

Anno. 4.

Jo. Couen=tre Mercer } M { Wil. Milrede, John Brokel } S 1425

Great grudge & variance was betwen the duke of Gloucester protector of England and his halfe brother the byshop of Winchester, which was appeased by the regent of Fraunce, and debated by a parliament at Leicester. Parliamēt at Leicester

Anno. 5.

John Raynewell Fishmonger } M { Jo. Arnold, Jo. Heigh=ham } S 1426

This John Raynewel before named, gaue certain landes or tenementes to the citie of London, for the whiche the same citie is bound to pay for euer, all suche fyftenes as shall be graunted to the Kyng (so that it passe not three fyf=tenes in one yere) for three wardes of the same, that is to say, Dowgate, Bel=linsgate, and Algate warde. Fiftenes discharged.

Anno. 6.

John Sidney Draper } M { Henry Fro=wicke, Rob. Otley } S 1427

This yere a woman dwelling in whit Chappell parishe withoute Algate of

London, was in the night murdred by a Brytayne or Frenchman, whom she had cherisshed and brought vp of almes Who conueying such iewels and stuffe as he might cary, was taken in Esser, and brought vp to London: but as sone as he came in the parishe where he had committed the murder, the wiues caste vpon him so muche fylthe and ordure of the strete, that notwithstandinge the resistaunce made by the Constables, they slew him out of hande.

Murder quite with murder.

Anno. 7.

1428 Henry Barton skinner } M } T. Dufhoue John Abbot } S

This yere duke of Norfolk, was like to haue byne drowned, passing through London bridge, his barge beyng set vpon the piles whelmed ouer, so that he and very few escaped, beyng drawē vp with ropes, the rest were all drowned.

Anno. 8.

1429 William Eskeld Mercer } M { William Russe Rafe Holslande } S

This yere was kinge Henry crowned at Westminster.

Anno. 9.

1430 Nicholas Wotton Draper } M { Walter Chertsey Robert Large } S

This

This yere at Abington, began an insurrection of certain lighte persons, that entended to haue wrought muche mischiefe, but they were quieted by the lorde protector, and the chiefe authour beyng bayly of the towne, named William Maundeuil, a weauer, otherwise naminge himselfe Jack sharpe of Wigmores Land in Wales, with other were put to death. Commotiō at abingtō.

This yere was one Richard Russel a woolman, drawen, hanged, and quartered at Tiborne for treason. Execution at Tiborn.

Anno. 10.

Joh. Welles grocer } M { John Adelee, Step. Browne. } S 1431

This John Wels of his goods caused the condite named the Standard in chepe, to be builded in Anno. 1442. This yere king Henry was crowned at Paris, The standard in cheape.

Anno. 11.

Jo. Paruels Fishmonger } M { John Olney, Jo. Paddesley } S 1432

This yere was sene in the southwest, a sterre called a Comete or blasing sterr. A comete.

Anno. 12.

John Brokley Draper } M { Thomas Chalton, John Kyng } S 1433

The erle of Huntington, was sente with a companye of souldiours into Fraunce, where he atchiued many great feates of armes.

Anno. 13.

1434 Roger Otsley Grocer } M { Th. Barnwell, Simond Eyre } S

A gret frost. This yere was a gret frost, that such marchandise as came to the Thames mouth, was caried to London by land. This frost endured from the .xxv. daye of Nouember vnto the .x. day of February, which was .x. wekes.

Anno. 14.

1435 Hen. Frowike mercer } M { Th. Catworth, Ro. Clopton } S

Charles of Fraunce recouered the citie of Paris, and wanne by force the town of Harflew, and of saint Denis expelling and murdring the Englishemen in great number.

Anno. 15.

1436 John Michell Fishmonger } M { Th. Worsted, William Gregorie } S

This yere on the third day of January, dyed Quene Catherine mother to King Henry the syxt, and wife to Henry the fyfth, and lyeth at Westminster vnburied.

This

This yere on the fourtene day of January the gate of London brydge with the tower upon it next to Southwark fell downe, and ii. of the furdest arches of the said bridge: but as god would no man ther with perished.

A parte of London bridge fell downe.

This yere all the lyons in the tower of London dyed, which had bene there a long tyme.

Anno. 16.

William Eastfield Mercer } M { William Chapman / Williā Halles } S 1437

The King caused a great obite to be kept in Pouls church, for Sigismund the Emperour, who was knight of the Garter.

Anno. 17.

Stephen Browne Grocer } M { Hugh Dyker / Nicholas Yoo } S 1438

This yere on new yeres day, a stacke of wodde fel downe at Baynardes castel, and slew three men, and hurt many other.

Three men slayne.

Ther was so great a dearth in Englande, that the poore people made them bread of fetches, peason, & fern rootes.

Greate dearth.

This yere by the fall of a stayre at Bedford. xviii. persons wer slayne.

People slaine.

In this yeare the Cundite in Flete-

The cōdit in fletestret — strete was begon by syr William Eastfield late Maior of London, & finished of his owne cost, without any one penny charge to the citie.

Robert Chicheley. — This yeare dyed Robert Chicheley grocer, & twise maior of London, who willed in his testament, that vpon his mind day, a good competēt diner shold be ordeined for.2400.poore men, housholders of the Citie, if they mighte be found.and.xx.li. in money distributed amongest them, whiche was to euery man.ii.d.

Anno.18.

1439	Robert Large Mercer	M	Robert Marshall	Philip Malpas	S

Erectiion at Tower hill. — A prieste was burned at the Tower hyl on the.xvii.day of June, whiche of the cōmō people was counted an holy man, for ye he sayd, the postern shold sinke, and such like things: they made theyr prayer to him, and reysed a great heape of stones, and pight ther a Crosse by nyght, vntyl a cōmaundement was geuen by the king to the contrary.

The postern sanke — The posterne of East Smithfielde against the tower of London sanke by night.vii.foote into the earth, the.xviii. of July.

Anno

Anno. 19.

John Paddisley goldsmithe } M { John Sutton, William Wetinghale } S 1440

Elienor Cobham wife to Humfrey duke of Glocester, Roger Bolinbroke a conning negromancer, and Margery Jourdemain cōmonly called the witch of Eie were accused, that by sorcery & enchantmentes, they practised the kinges death, as by an image of waxe, whiche through their deuilish incantations should little & litle wast and consume, and so likewise the king to weare out of his life. Wherfore being examined & conuict, Elianor Cobham was iudged to do penaunce, as to beare a taper .iii. days, through the chiefest stretes of the Citie of London, and so to be exiled to the Ile of Man, Roger Bolinbroke was drawen hanged and quartered at Tiborn, and Margery Jourdemain the witch was burnt in Smithfield.

Sorcery.

Execution

Anno. 20.

Ro. Clopton Draper } M { Wil. Combis, Rich. Riche } S 1441

This yere was a fray in Fletestrete betwene the Innes of Courte, and the inhabitantes of the same strete: which fray began in the night, and continued

A gret fray in Fletstret

tyll the next day wher were many men slayne and hurt on both parties.

Anno. 21.

1442 John Thirley Jronmonger } M { Tho. Bew-mount Ri. Nordon } S

Paules steple a fyre.

The steple of Poules church in London was set on fyre wyth lightning, & lastly quenched by greate deligence of many men: but chiefly through the labour of a priest of Bowe in cheape.

Anno. 22.

1443 Thomas Catworth Grocer } M { Nicolas Welford John Norman } S

An acte was made by the Common counsell of London, that vpon the sonday should no maner of thinge within the franchises of the Citie be boughte or solde.

Anno. 23.

1444 Henry Frowicke Mercer } M { Stephen Foster Hugh Wyche } S

King Henry toke to wife Margaret, the Kinges doughter of Sicile.

Alsoules college and Barnarde colledge builded.

Henry Chicheley byshop of Cantorbury died, who in his life time builded two houses for students in the vniuersitie of Oxeforde, called Alsoules colledge, and Bernard colledge.

Symon

Anno.24.

Symond Eyre dra. } M { John Derby / Godf. Feldinge } S 1445

This Simond Eyre builded the Leaden hal in Londō, and also a beautifull chapell in the east end of the same.

Leadin hal builded.

Anno.25.

John Onely mercer } M { Robert Horne / Godf. Boloine } S 1446

Humfrey duke of Gloucester, and protectour of England was at the parliament of Bury, arrested, and. vi. days after he was found dead in hys bed. He was buried at saint albones.

Duke of gloucester arested.

William Wamflete byshop of Winchester and Chancelour of England erected the famous college of Mary Magdalen in Oxeford.

Magdalen colledge builded.

Anno.26.

John Gidney draper } M } Wil. Abraham / Tho. Scotte } S 1447

This yere was taken the towne of Fogers from the Englishmen, whiche was the cause that Normādy was lost afterwarde.

Anno.27.

Stephen Browngro } M { Wil. Catlow / Wi. Marlow } S 1448

This yere Roan was yelded to the Frenche king.

Roan yelded.

Anno.28.

Tho. Chalton mercer } M { Wil. Hulyn / Th. Caninges } S 1449

The

The Marques of Suffolke was banished the land for. v. yeres who saylyng towarde France, was met on the sea by a ship of warre, and there presently beheaded, by the capitayn called Nicholas of the tower, & the dead corps cast vp at Douer vpon the sande.

A murder

The commons of Kent in great number assembled on black Heath, hauing to their capitaine Jacke Cade, Against whom the king sent a great army, but by the sayd rebelles they were discomfited, and syr Humfrey Stafford and William his brother with many other slayne: After this victory the capitayne and rebelles came to London, and entred the citie, and stroke his sworde on London stone, saing: Nowe is Mortimer lorde of this citie. Vpon the third day of July, he caused the Lorde Say to be brought to the stādard in cheape & smote of his head. He also beheaded sir James Cromer at the myles end: And pitching these two heades on two polles entred the Citie: and in despite caused them (beynge borne before hym in euery strete to kysse together. After this murder, succeded open robberie within the citie: But the Maior and other sage Magestrates, perceauinge them

A cōmotiō in Kent.

them selues; nother to be sure of goods nor life, determined to repulse this vngracious company, & sente to the Lord Scales, keper of the tower, who promysed his ayde, with shoting of ordenaunce: and Mathew Gough was appointed to assist the Maior: so the capitaines of the Citie tooke vpon them in the nighte to kepe the bridge, prohibyting the Kentishmen to passe. The rebelles hearing the bridge to be kept, came with great force to open that passage: where betwene both partes was a fierce encounter. The rebelles draue the Citezens from the stoulpes at the Bridge foote, to the drawe bridge, and set fyre on diuers houses: In conclusion, the rebels gat the drawe bridge, and drowned and slewe many. This conflict endured tyll .ix. of the clock in the mornyng, in doubtfull chaunce: so that both partes agreed to desiste from fyght tyll the next day, vpon condition that neyther Londoners shoulde passe into Southwarke, nor the Kentishmen into London. Then the archebishop of Cantorburye beynge Chauncelor with the bishop of Winchester, passed into Southwarke, wher they shewed a generall pardon for all offenders, vnder the kinges greate seale, whiche they caused to be proclaymed, whereupon the whole multitude retyred home: but through a proclamation beyng made, that who so coulde apprehend the saide Jacke Cade, should haue a thousand markes, one Alexander Iden founde him in a gardeyn, who in his defence slew the sayd Jacke Cade and brought his body to London, where his heade was set on London bridge.

Bishop of Salisbury murdred. About that time, The Byshop of Salisbury was murdred by the commons of the west countrey.

Anno.29.

1450 Nicolas Wilford Grocer } M { John. Middleton. William Dere. } S

The whole duchie of Normandye was yelded to the frenche kynge by meanes of the Quene, and the duke of Somerset: whiche caused so muche trouble in England, that mortall war ensued.

Anno.30.

1451 William Gregory Skinner } M { Mathew Philip Christopher warton } S

The duke of Yorke began a commotion. A commotion began this yere by the duke of Yorke, and other noble men, which was appeased for a time, and the malice

malice dissembled. mocion.

Anno.31.

Godfrey Feldyng Mercer	M	Richard Lee Richarde Al=ly	S	1452

This yeare the Quene was delyuered of a Prince, who was called Edward.

Anno.32.

John Norman Draper.	M	John Wal=derne Thomas Coke	S	1453

Before this Maiors yere, the maior sheriffes, and commons were wont to ryde to westminster, when the Maior should take his charge: but this maior was rowed thither by water.

The maior of London first rowed to westminster.

The fire of enuye that a good space had couertly smouldered betwene the Duke of Yorke, and the duke of Somerset, with other of the quenes counsayle, at this tyme brake oute, in hot & fierce flames of warres. In so muche that betwene the Kyng, who defended these persons, and the Duke of Yorke, with his alies, at saint Albons a cruell battaile was foughte: In the ende whereof, the victory fell to the duke of Yorke. And on the kynges partie was slayne the Duke of Somerset, the erle of Northumberland, the Lorde Clyfford.

Battails at S. Albons

ford.

ford, with many other honorable men, knightes and Squyers. After which time, the Duke with greate reuerence brought the Kynge from Saincte Albons to London. Where by a Parliament, he was made protector of the realme; the Erle of Salisbury Chauncellor, and the erle of Warwike Capitayne of Calice.

Anno.33.

1454 Stephen Foster Fishemonger } M { John Field, Williā Taylor } S

Fraye in London.

This yeare in London was a greate fray at saint Martins le grād, by saintuary men, who issued forth and hurte diuers citisens: but it was appeased by the Maior and other. There was suche greuous complaintes made thereof to the kyng by the Deane of Saint Martens, that the liberties of the citie were in peril to be seised.

Anno.34.

1455 William Marrow Grocer } M { John Yong, Thomas Oulgraue } S

By meanes of the Quene and other lordes, the duke of Yorke was discharged of his protectorship: whiche thinge was cause of newe grudge and malice.

A great

A great riot cōmitted in London against the Lombardes and Italians, because a mercers seruant was caste in prison for strikyng an Italyan — A ryote in London.

Anno. 35.

Thomas Canyngs Grocer	M	John Steward / Rafe Verney	S

1456

At Erith within. xii. myles of London were taken. iiii. wonderful fishes: whereof one was called Mors Marina, the seconde a swordfishe, the other two were whales. — Great fyshes taken.

A Fleete of Frenchemen landed at Sandwich, & spoyled the towne with great crueltie. — Sandwiche spoyled.

Anno. 36.

Godfrey Boleyne Mercer	M	William Edwarde / Tho. Rayner	S

1547

A fained agremēt was made betwene the Kyng, the Quene, and the Duke of Yorke with his retinue: for ioy whereof a generall procession was celebrate in saint Poules at London. At which solemne feast, the kyng in habite royall, and his diademe on his head, kept his state in procession: before whom went hand in hand, the Duke of Somerset, the Erle of Salisbury, the duke of Exeter — A generall

cester, and the erle of Warwike, and so one of the one faction, an other of the other sect. And behind the King, the duke of Yorke ledde the Quene, with great familiaritie to all mens syghtes. But wo worth dissimulation: for theyr bodies were ioyned by hande in hande, whose heartes were farre in sunder, as appered shortly after.

Anno. 37.

1458 Thomas Scotte Draper } M { Rafe Josselin Richarde Wedtham } S

Printinge first inuented.

The noble Science of printynge was founde in Germany at Magunce by one John Cuthenbergus, a knyght: he found moreouer the Inke by his deuice, that printers vsed. xvi. yeare after printing was foūd, which was the yere of our Lorde. 1458. one Conradus an Almain brought it into Rome: & Nicolas Johnson a Frenche man did greatly polishe and garnishe it. And now it is dispersed thorough the whole worlde. William Caxton mercer of Lōdon firste brought it into England: about the yere of our Lord. 1471. And first practised the same in the abbeye of saynt Peter at Westminster.

The duke of Yorke, the Erles of Salesbury,

lisburye and Warwike, wyth a greate host met the kynge and other lordes of England vpon Blore heath nere to Lōdon: wher because Andrew Trollop a captain of Calice, the night before the battaile should haue ben, fledde with a company of the beste souldiours to the Kynges parte. The duke of Yorke, the Earles of March, Salisbury, and Warwike, mystrustyng them selues to bee to weake, departed wyth a priuye company, and fledde: The Duke into Ireland, the .iii. erles into Gerneseye, & after into Calayes without any notable battaile — Blorehethe field

Anno 38

William Hulyn fishemonger	M	John Plummer Jo. Stocker	S	1459

The .iii. erles cōming frō Calice with a puissant army, the .ic. day of July met kyng Henry at Northampton, & gaue hym strong battayle, In the end where of, the victorie fell to the Earles, and the kynges host was dispersed, chased, and many slayne: amonge whiche was the Duke of Buckingham, the Erle of Shrewesbury, the lord Egremounte, wyth other, and the kyng taken in the fielde. — Bataile at Northāpton

The Duke of Yorke made claim to ye crown — The duke of Yorke returnyng into Englande, made suche clayme to the crown, that by consent of a parliamēt he was proclamed heyre apparant, and all his progenie after hym.

Battaile at wakefield. — The quene in this meane tyme, had gathered a company of Northern men: & nere to Wakefielde, slew ye duke of Yorke, wyth hys sonne the earle of Rutland the erle of Salisbury. was taken prisoner wyth dyuers other noble mē.

Anno. 39

1480 — Rich. Lee Grocer } M { Rich. Flemyng John Lamberd } S

Second battayle at S. Albons. — The Quene with her retinue neare sayncte Albons, discomfited the erle of Warwike and the duke of Norfolk, & delyuered kyng Henry her husbande.

Edwarde, Earle of Marche, and eldeste sonne to thee Duke of Yorke: came vp to London wyth a myghtye, power accompanied wyth the Earle of Warwike, and by agrement of a councell was proclaymed kynge of Englande: and called Edwarde the fourth

Battaile at Sherborne — shortely after, he pursued kyng Henry to warde Yorke, where hee gaue a sore battayle to the kynge and his company. This fyghte was soo cruell and

fierc

fierce, that in the fyght and chase were slayne. xxx. thousande of the commons besyde menne of name: the whych wer the Earles of Northumberlande, and westmerlande, the lorde Clyfford, Andrew Trollep, and other, to the num of eleuen and kynge Henrye loste all, and was fayne to flee the lande, when he had reigned eighte and thyrty yeres vi. monethes and foure dayes. And Quene Margeret wyth þ yong prince fled to her father, the duke of Angeow.

Kyng Henry fayne to flie the lād

Kyng Edwarde the fourth

Anno Regni. i

Edward the fourth, began hys domenion ouer thys Realme of Englande, the fourthe day of Marche, in the yere of our lord. 1460 and lefte the same the ix. day of Aprile, in the yere. 1483. soo he reigned xxii. yeres, one moneth and fiue daies. He was a man of noble cou- 1460

cage & great wyt: but in this time was muche trouble and vnquietnesse in the Realme. Anno.1.

Hugh Wich grocer } M { John Looke George Ireland } S

1461 This yere the Staplers of Calcis demaunded of kyng Edward .xviii. thousand poundes, which they had lent him to mainteyne his warres agaynst king Henry: but their sute was smally regarded, and lastly denied.

Anno.2

1462 Thomas Cooke Draper } M { Williā Hampton Barth James } S

Margarete the Quene, and wife to Henry the sixt, lāded in England, but hauyng smal succour and euil fortune was fayn to take the seas again, and by tempeste of weather, was dryuen into Scotland. Anno.3.

1463 Mathewe Philippe goldsmyth } M { Robert Basset Thomas Muschampe } S

Batayl at Exam. The lorde Mountague hauing the rule of the North, discōfited king Hēry, commyng out of Scotland with a great power, to recouer ẏ crown: this is called ẏ battaile of Exham, in whi

the

the were taken the Duke of Somerset the lorde Hungerford, the lord Roas, whiche were after put to deathe with many other.

Kynge Edwarde was secretly maried to Elisabeth Grai, late wife of sir John Gray. For whych maryage rose greate variance betwen the king and the erle of warwicke, his chiefe frende and mainteyner.

This yere was kinge Henry taken in a wodde in the north countrey, by one named Cantlowe, and arested by the erle of Warwike, and presented to thee kyng Edward, and sente to the tower, where hee remayned longe after in the Dungeon. King Henry take prisoner

Anno. 4.

Rafe Josselyn draper } M { John Tate John Stone } S 1464

This yere the king ordeyned a newe coyne, as the ryall, the angell, the halfe aungell, and the farthing : ryals were x.s. y angel. vi.s. viii, d. And the grotes were made of lesse value then they were by viii. d. in an ounce, The sylver that before was at ii s. viii. d. the ou͂ce was now inhanced to iii, s. iiii. d the ounce, and fyne golde that before was xxx. s. the ounce was now inhaunced to xl. s. the ounce. New coyn

And this yere was quene Elizabeth crowned at Westminster on whitsonday, or the xxvi. day of May.

Anno.5

1465 Rafe Verney Mercer } M } Sir. Hen. weuer, William Constantine } S

This yeare the xi. day of Februarye, the quene was deliuered of a daughter who was named Elizabeth.

Anno.6

1466 S. Jo Yōg Grocer } M { John Browne, Henry Bryce } S

John Darby Alderman, for that hee refused to pay for the cariage awaye of a dead dogge lying at his gate, and for vnmete language, which he gaue vnto the Maior, was by a courte of Aldermen assessed wyth the fyne of l. pound whiche he payde euery peny.

Anno 7

1467 Thomas Owlegraue Skynner } M { Humf. Heyforde, T. Stalbrok } S

Syr Thomas Cooke alderman of London, was accused of treason, and arraigned of the same, and founde not gyltie: but yet by reason of the Lorde Treasorer, who was not his frend, he was deteyned in prison, and could not be be delyuered ,untyll he had fined with the kynge for, 8000 poundes, which he payde.

A great Justes was in Smythfielde betwene the lorde Scales, and the bastarde of Burgoyn.

Anno.8.

William Tayler Grocer	M	Symond Smith William Hariot	S	1468

This William Tayler afore named, gaue to the Citie of London certayne tenementes, for the whiche the citie is bounde to pay for euery fyftene to bee graunted to the kyng, for al such peop.e as shall dwell in Cordwainer strete ward, that shalbe sessed at xii.d. the pece, or under Whiche charitable worke ought not to be forgotten. Charitable dedes of William Tayler

The earle of Warwike adioyned him wyth the duke of Clarence the kynges brother, and by their meanes stirred so the Northern men, that they diuers tymes rebelled and turned the kynge & ye realm to much trouble. But shorty ye kyng demeaned hymselfe, y^t ye rebels were suppressed & ye erle of warwik Battaile at Badbery

with

wyth the duke of Clarence, and other fled into Fraunce.

Anno. 9.

1469 Richarde Lee grocer } W { Rich. gardiner / Robert Drope } S

The Duke of Clarence, the Erles of Warwike Pembroke, and Oxforde, landed at Darthmouthe, to whome by meanes of proclamations, that wer publyshed in the name of kynge Henry, the commons gathered in so great companies, that Edward fearing his part fled into Flanders to the duke of Burgoyn. Then was Henry the sixt set at libertie, and agayn proclaymed kynge by meanes of the erle of Warwike and other, & Edwarde proclaimed usurper of the Crowne: but that continued not longe, the Earle of worcester was beheaded at the tower hyll.

K. Ed. fled into Flanders

Execution

Anno. 10.

1470 Jo. Stokton mercer } W { John Crosby / John warde } S

Quene Elisabeth wife to Edwarde the fourth beynge in the sanctuarye of Westminster, was deleuered of a prince who afterward was Edward ye fifthe. King Edward being returned out of Flaunders arriued in the north parts of of England, wyth a very smal company of souldiors: but by meanes that he vsed and through his brother the duke of Clarence, who turned nowe to hys part, he came to London entred the citie, and toke kynge Henrye in the byshops palace, and then went agaynste the earle of Warwike, whom hee vanquished and slewe wyth hys brother Marques Mountague, on Gladmore heath nere Barnet, ten miles frō London. Shortly after, at Teukesbury, he ouerthrew Quene Margaret, the wife of Henry. In which battaile was takē the sayd Margaret, with Edward the Prince her sonne the duke of Somerset, and diuers other. King Edward agayne receiued his royaltie, & was taken for kyng, and vncurtouslye slewe prince Edward sonne of Henry þ. vi. after he had taken hym prisoner.

Barnette, field on Ester day.

Battaile at Teuksbury

The bastarde Fawcombridge, and the commons of Kent and Esser, robbed and spoyled the suburbes of the citie of London and fyred Bishops gate and Algate.

The suburbes burnt,

Henry the sixt was murdered in the tower of London, and buried at Chertsey, and after remoued to wyndsor.

Murder

Anno, 11.

william

1471 Willia Ed } ward gro. } W { John Alleyn } { John Chelly } S

The erle of Oxeforde was sent prisoner to Guynes, where he remayned
prisoner so long as Edward the fourth
reigned, which tyme the lady his wife
myght neuer come to hym nor hadd a-
ny thyng to lyue vpon, but what people of theyr charities would geue her,
or what she got by her nedle.

Anno.12

1472 William Hampton fyshmonger } W { John Brown, Tho. Bledlowe } S

This Maior was a good iusticer, he
punished baudes and strompettes, &
caused theym to ryde with raye hoodes
and made a payre of stockes to bee set
in euery ward of the citie.

Anno.13

1473 John Tate mercer } W { William Stocker, Rob. Bellisoon } S

In this yere the erle of Excester was
founde dead in the sea, betwene Douer
and Calays.

One John Gose, was burned at the
Execution tower hyll for heresy.

Anno.14.

Ro. Drope draper } M { Edmōd Shaw / Thomas hyll } S 1474

Thys Robert Drope maior of London, buylded the east ende of the Cundyte in Cornhyll. The cōdite in Cornhil

Kyng Edward required of his subiectes a beneuolence, and soo hee sayled into France with a great army, to ayde the Duke of Burgoyn: but by sute of the Frenche kyng, a peace was concluded for vii. yeres.

Anno. 15.

Robert Basset Salter } M { Hugh Prince / Ro. Colwich } S 1475

This maior dyd sharp correccion vpō Bakers, for makyng of lyght bread, in so muche that he set dyuers of them on the pillory, And a woman named Agnes Deintie was also ther punished for sellyng of false mynged butter. Agnes deintie,

Anno. 16

Rafe Josselyn Draper } M { Richard Rauson / William Horne } S 1476

By the diligence of thys Maior, the new wall of London, from Creplegate to byshopps gate, was made, the Maior wyth hys companye of thee Drapers, made all that parte betwixte All hallowes Churche in thee same wall London walle wall and byshops gate of their owne proper costes: and the other companies made the other dele, which was a gret work to be don in one yere, cōsidering the purueyance of the stuffe.

Anno.17.

1477 Humfrey Heyforde Goldsmith } M { Henry Colet John Stocker } S

This yere the duke of Clarence second brother to the kyng beyng prysoner in the tower was secretely drowned in a barell of maluesye, wythin the sayd tower.

Anno.18.

1478 Richarde gardiner Mercer } M { Roberte Herdynge, Robert Byfelde } S

Great pestilence. This yeare was a greate dearth, and also a great death at London, and in diuers other partes of this realme.

Anno.19.

1479 Bartholo. James Draper } M { Tomas Ilam John Warde } S

Execution This yeare at Tower hyll wer foure felons hanged and burned for robbing of a churche.

Anno.20

John

John Browne Mercer } M { William Daniell, william Bacon } S 1480

The kyng required great sommes of money to be lent hym of the citisens of London, who after diuers assemblies graunted to lende hym .5000. marke, whych was repayde agayne in the next yere folowyng.

Anno.21

William Hareet Draper } M { Robert Tate, wil. wikyng, Rich Chawry } S 1481

This yeare the Scots began to stirre, agaynst whom kyng Edwarde sent the Duke of Gloucester, and diuers other which returned agayne wythout any notable battayle.

Anno.22.

Edmonde Shawe goldsmith } M { wil, white, John Mathew } S 1482

Kyng Edward makynge great prouision for warre into France, ended his life the ix. of Aprill, in the yere of oure lord.1483, when he had reigned xxii. yeres, i. moneth, and v dayes. He was buried at wyndsor, leauynge after hym two sonnes, Edward the prince, & Richard Duke of Yorke, wyth v, daughters, as Elizabeth y^t after was quene, Cicelie, Anne, Katherin, & Bridget

King Edward the fifth

Anno. Regni. i

1483 Edward the fyfth, of the age of eleuen yeres began his reign ouer this Realm of England the ninth of April, in the yere of our Lord .1483. & was murdered by Rycharde Duke of Glocester, the same yere the xxii. day of June, so he reigned ii. monethes and xi. dayes

Richarde duke of Glocester named

King Richard the third

Anno. Regni. i

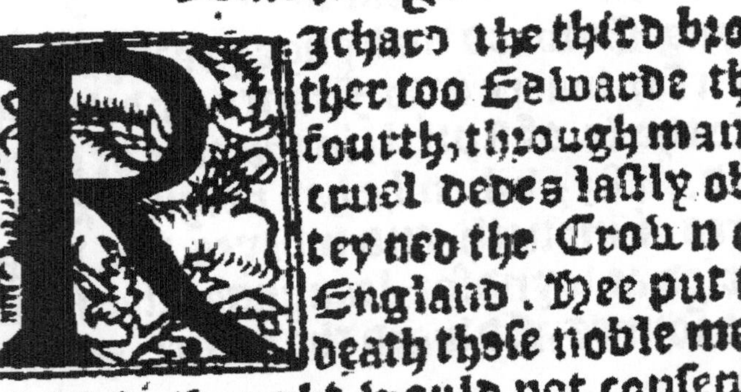

1483 Richard the third brother too Edwarde the fourth, through many cruel dedes lastly obteyned the Crown of England. Hee put to death those noble men which he thought would not consente to

to his mynde: the other hee corrupted wyth riche gyftes: then he wrested frõ the quene Elizabeth (beynge then in saintuarie) Richard her yonger sonne and brother to the Prince: Thirdly he caused to bee publishede att Paules Crosse, by one doctour Shaw that Edward the fourth, his elder brother was not rightly begoten of his mother, but by aduoutrie: and therfore that neither he, nor hys chyldren hadde ryghte to ŷ crowne: or as some write, he caused to bee publisshed, that the prynce and his brother were not rightefully begotten of Quene Elizabeth: and therefore the ryght of the crowne to be his, whiche he toke vpon hym, and shortly murdered ŷ two yong chyldren in ŷ tower of London, and vsurped the crowne two yeres and two monethes,

Quene toke saintuarye.

Murder

Anno Regni. 1

Robert Bilisdõ haberdasher	W	Tho. Norlãd Williã Martyn	S	1483

Grudge began betwen king Richarde & the duke of Buckingham: in so much that for displeasure therof, the Duke cõspired with diuers other noble men agaynst hym, and intended to bring into the lande Henry erle of Richmond, as rightfull heyre to the crown: This Hery had fled into Britayne, fearynge the crueltie of Edward the fourth: for whiche conspiracie, the said duke of Buckingham with diuers other, was shortly after taken and put to death

Anno. 2

1484 Thomas Hyll Grocer	M	Rich. Chester Tho. Britayn Rafe Astrie	S

Henry erle of Richmount, wyth a small company of frenchemen, landed at Mylford hauē, nygh Pembroke, whose commynge when it was hearde of in wales, dyuers noble men wyth theyr retinue, forsakyng Richarde, gathered to hym in great number: so that his strength in short space greatly increased. At Bosworthe, he mette wyth his enemies: where betwene them was foughten a sharp battaile In conclusion, Kyng Richard wyth diuers other, was slayn, and Henry obteyned a noble victorie: he was immediatly crowned in the fielde: and the dead corps of kynge Rycharde was broughte to Leicester, and there buryed at the Graye Friers

K. Richard slayn

King

Henry the seuenthe began his reigne ouer this Realme of Englād the xxii. day of August, in the yere of our Lorde. 1485. and deceased in the yere 1509 the xxii. day of Aprill: So he reigned xxiij. yeres, & viii. monethes: hee was a prince of meruailous wisedome and policie, and of greet iustice, temperāce and grauitie. He so behaued him in the tyme of his reigne, that notwithstandyng many & greate occasions of trouble vnquietnesse and warre, hee kepte his realme in right good rule & order. Wherfore hee was greatly estemed and reuerenced of foreyne princes. 1485

This yeare maister Thomas Ilam Alderman of London, and marchaunte of the Staple, newe made the greate Cunduite in Cheape of hys owne goodes.

This yere was the sweating syckenes of the whiche a wonderfull multitude dyed: And in London besydes other, there dyed Thomas Hyll Maior,, on the. xxvii. daye of September in whose place was chosen syr Wylliam Stocker Draper, who receyued his othe at the vtter gate of the tower of London: but hee lykewyse deceased about seuen dayes after, in the whyche seuen dayes, departed other foure Aldermenne as Thomas Ilam, Rycharde Rawson, Thomas Morlande, and John Stocker, brother too Syr Wylliyam Stocker, And thenne was chosen for Maior, John Warde Grocer, who continued that office the full of Thomas Hylles yeare, that is to saye, tylle thee feaste of Symon and Jude.

Anno. i.

1485 Hugh Brice goldsmith } M { John Tate John Swan } S

The xxx. daye of October, the kynge was solempnely crowned at westminster, hee ordeyned a number of chosen Archers, and other stronge and hardye persones, to geue dayely attendaunce on his person, whome he named Yeomen of his garde.

Yeomen of the garde.

The kyng sent the Lorde Treasourer and other, vnto the Lord Maior of London, requiryng hym and hys Citisens of a prest of vi. M. marke: wherefore the Maior wyth his brethern and cōmon counsel of the Citie, assembled theym selues and by theyr auctoritie,

granted

graunted a prest of .MM, poundes, the whych was leuied of the fellowshyps, and not of the wardes: for more ease of the poore people.

Thys yere the beautifull Crosse in Cheape was newe buylded and made. Towarde the buildyng wherof, Thomas Fysher mercer, gaue vi. C. marks

The crosse in Cheape builded

Thys yeare wheate was at iii. s. the bushell. bay salte at. ii. s. viii. d. and iii. s. the bushell

Anno. 2.

Syr Henry Colet Mercer	M	John Perciual, Hughe Clopton	S	1486

This yere ỹ king maried Elisabeth eldest daughter of Edward the fourth: by which meanes the two families of Yorke and Lancaster, the whiche had longe caused deuysion, was knyte together in one.

K. Henrye maried.

About this tyme Francis Louel, & Humfreye Staffords rebelled in thee north: with them was Martin Swart which cõmotion was quieted by ỹ policy of the Duke of Bedforde, but there was slayn ỹ Earle of Lyncolne, ỹ lorde Louell, Martyn Swart, and other,

Battaile at Stoke

boue iiii.thousand

Thys yere was borne Prynce Arthur, in the moneth of September.

Anno.3

1487	William Horn Salter	M	John Fynkell Willia Remington	S

This yere was Quen Elisabeth crowned at westminster vpon S. Katherins day. In July was an other prest for the king made in ẏ city of London of .iiii. thousand pouds which was sessed on ẏ craftes or felowships: shortly after was the thirde prest of .ii. M li. whiche was lewied as the other, whiche were bothe repayed agayne the next yere folowing These summes of moneye with many mo, whiche he borowed of hys lordes, and other, was to ayde the archduke of Burgoyn, agaynst the duke of Britayne. In the ende of this Maiors yere

Execution was John Ashlieye, the sonne of syr John Ashley knight with .ii. other drawen frome westminster, to the tower hyll, and there beheaded.

Anno.4

1488	Roberte Tate Mercer	M	Wyllyam Isake Rafe Tinley	S

This yeare was a taxe of the ten peny

peny of all mens goodes and landes: through whiche the cōmōs of the north slew the Earle of Northumberlande, wherfore John Chamber their captain with other was hanged at Yorke.

Anno. 5.

William Whyte Draper } M { Wyllliam Capell, John Brooke } S 1489

This yere one Roger Shauclocke a taylor dwellynge wythin Ludgate, slewe hymselfe: For whose goodes was muche busynes betwene the kynges amner and the sheriffe. *Desperation*

Anno. 6.

John Mathewe mercer } M { Henry Coote, Ro. Reuell, Hugh Pēbertō } S 1490

Syr Roberte Chamberlayn beheaded *Execution*

Thys yere the kynge required a beneuolence, whyche was to hym graunted toward his iourney into Fraunce.

This yeare Creplegate of London was new buylded at the costes & charges of syr Edmund Shaw goldsmyth late maior of thee same citie. *Creplegate buylded*

In July was Henry the kynges seconde sonne borne at Grenewiche.

This yere the beautiful cundite in Gracious stret was begō to be builded *Cundite in Gracious stret.*

of

of the goods & by he executoures of sir Thomas Hil grocer: as it doth appere by certayn verses written on the same

Thomas Hyll knight, late Maior of this Citie,
Wyth his wife Dame Elisabeth, of their charitie,
For the loue of God, & werle of the commonaltie
Of theyr costes only, this thing did edifye,
Out of the grounde, with all thynges necessarye.

In this Maiors tyme wheate was at xx.d & xxii.d. þ bushel which was then accompted deare Anno.7

1491 Hugh Clopton mercer } M { Tho. Wood / Wil. Brown } S

This yere kinge Henry toke his voyage into Fraunce with a great army to aide þ Britōs agaynst the french kyng Anno.8

1492 Wil. Martin skinner } M { Wil. Purchas / Wil. welbecke } S

This yeare was a peace concluded betwene the kinges of Englande and Fraunce, and king Henry returned agayne into England.

In the moneth of January, two pardoners wer set on the pillorye.iii market dayes, for forgynge of a false pardonne wher with they had deceaued meny people, and for that one of them had fayned hym hymselfe to be a priest, hee was sente to Newegate, where hee dyed, and the other was driuen out of the citie wyth shame ynough. And this yeare was a fraye made vpon the Easterlinges or Stilliard men, by Mercers seruants & other: For the whyche diuers of the wer sore punished, & the chiefe aucthors wer kept long in prison. Anno. 9.

A fraye agaynste the Stillarde men

Rafe Astry fishmonger	M	Rob. Fabian John Winger	S	1493

This yere wheat was solde for. vi. d the bushell, and bay salt at iii. d. ob the bushell: white hearing at ix. s ye barel red herring at. iii. s. the cade of ye beste, red sprots at vi. d a cade and gascoyn wyne at vi li ye tonne. Anno. 10

Cheape of wheat & salt.

Ric. Chawry Salter	M	Nico. Alwin John Warner	S	1494

This yeare white herring was solde at. xl. d a barell beyng good

Perkyn Warbecke whyche by thee counsayle of Margerete of Burgoyne namyng hym selef Rychard of Yorke: Kyng Edwardes seconde sonne, arriued in kente: where hee was dryuen backe by thee uplandishemen, and other of the inhabitauntes of thee countreye, wyth the losse of diuers of hys men: and shortly after were hanged an hundred

Perkyn Warbecke

Great execution

hundred and threscore persones of the fore named rebels, in dyuers and sundry costes of England. The. v. capitaines were Mountford, Corbet, Whitbelt, Quintin, and Genyne.

Anno. 11

1495 Sir Hery Colet mercer } M { Thomas Kneisworthe Henry Somer } S

The Scots brake into ꝧ north partes of Englād by ꝧ setting on of Perkin Werbeck, & dyd much harme to ꝧ borderers.

Anno. 12.

1496 John Tate mercer } M { John Shawe Rich. Haddon } S

Blacke heath field

By meanes of a payment that was graunted to the kyng by acte of parliament) a newe cōmotion was made by the cōmons of Cornwall: which vnder the leadyng of the lorde Audeleye, with Mighell Joseph ꝧ blacke smith, and diuers other came to Black heath where the king met with them, & discomfited the rebels, and toke their captaines, which wer shortly after, drawē hanged, and quartered: The lorde Audeley was beheaded at the tower hyll, the xxviii day of June.

Kyng Hēry sent an army into Scotland vnder the guiding of the Earle of

Sur-

Surrey and the Lorde Neuell, which made sharpe war vpon the Scots.

A mariage concluded betwene prince Arthur, and lady Katherine the kings daughter of Spayne.

Perkin Werbeck lāded again in Cornwal, & assaulted the town of Excetour & other places: but finally he toke the saintuary of Beaudley, and was after pardoned his life. Excetour besiged

Anno. 13

William purchase mercer	M	Bartho. Rede Thomas wind-ought	S

1497

Perkyn Warbecke, endeuoured to steale away secretly out of the lād: but he was takē agayn by his kepers, and by the kynges commandement cast in the Tower of London: where after he was shewed at Westminster, and in Chepe on scaffolds, and stocked, to the great wonderment of many people

This yeare the Englishe marchants (beyng long absente out of Flaunders comming into Flaunders with marchādise, were receiued into Andwarp with generall procession: so glad was the towne of their returnynge, whiche was by theyr absence sore hindred & impouerished. Englishe marchants receyned wyth procession.

Anno. 14.

Sir

1498 Sir John Perciuall mar. tailer } M } Th. bradbury Stephen Jenyne } S

At saynct Thomas Watring a stryplyng was put to execution, which called hymselfe Edwarde Earle of Warwyke, and sonne of George Duke of Clarence: which George sence the beginning of kyng Henries reigne was kepte secretly in the tower of London

Execution

This yere master John Tate alderman of London began to edify S. Anthonis church in London with a notable free schole to the same adioynynge, and also one almes house for poore people.

S. Anthonies

The xvi. daye of July, beynge sondaye, and the nexte sonday folowynge xii. persones bare fagottes at Paules crosse.

Thys yeare good Gascoyne wyne was solde for xl s the Tonne: wheate for iiii. shyllynges the quarter, and baye salte for iiii. d. a bushell, and better cheape.

Anno 15

1499 Nicholas Alwyn mercer } M { James Wylforde Rich. Bronde } S

This yeare the xvi. day of Nouember was arraigned at Westmynster,

Par-

Parkyn Warbeek, & iii. other, whyche Perkyn, and one John a Water, were executed at Tyborne, the xxiii. daye of the same monethe of Nouember. And soone after, on the. xxviii. daye of Nouember was the erle of Warwike put to deathe at the Tower hylle, and one Blewet and Atwood at Tyborne.

Execution

Thys yeare was a greate deathe in London: wherof (after Fabyan) dyed xx. thousande, but after Hall his chronicle. xxx thousand.

Greate pestilence.

In May the king and Quene sailed to Calaice: and at saincte Peters they met with the duke of Burgoin.

Anno. 16

William Kenington fishmonger	M	John Hawes Wil. Stede	S	1500

This yere the kyng builded new his manour at Shene, & changed the name therof, and named it Richmont: & he buylded new his place called Baenardes castell in Lõdon, and repaired his place at Grenewich, with much other buildinge.

Richmond Baenardes castell and Grene wiche buylte

King Henry trouthplighted his daughter Margaret to James the kyng of Scots: and the 4. day of October landed at Plimmouth, Katherin daughter

Anno.17

1501 Sir John Shawe goldsmith } M { Syr Laurence Aismer, Henrye Hede } S

This syr John Shawe caused the kitchens and other houses of office to be buylded at the Guilde hall of London, and sens that tyme the Maiors feastes hath bene there kept: where as before that tyme they were kepte eyther at the Grocers, or the marchant Taylers hal

Prince Arthur maried.

Prince Arthur beyng but .xv. yeres old, was maried vnto Katherin: daughter to Ferdinando king of Spayn, the xiiii. of Nouēber, which Arthur shortlye after departed thys mortall life at Ludlow and was buried at Worcester

The diche of London from Themes to Holborne bridge was new caste: so that boates wyth victuals fuelle, and other stuffe were broughte vpp to Holborne bridge.

Anno.18

1502 Bartholo. Rede Goldsmith } M { Hēry Keble, Nicholas Nines } S

In thys yere began the newe worke of the kinges chapell at Westminster, and Elizabeth Quene of England died at the Tower of London in childebed, and was buried at westminster, Shortly after was dame Margeret the kynges daughter, maried to thee kynge of Scottes.

The deathe of Quene Elizabethe

The kinge of Scottes maried.

This yere the felowship of Taylers in London purchased of the king to be called Marchantes Taylours.

Anno 19.

syr Wil. Capell Draper	M	Christo. Hawes Robert Wattes Tho. Granger	S.

1503

This xxi. day of Nouember, was a dreadfull fyre vpon the northe ende of London bridge. And vpon the vii. day of January were certayne houses consumed with fyre against S. Botulpes church in Thames strete, & the xxviii. day of March was an house burned against saint Martins le grand, and the same day was hurt don wyth fyre in ye parish of saint Peter the poore.

Fyre on London bridge.

This yere was holden a parliament wher was ordeyned a new coyn of silver: as groates, halfe groates, and shillings with halfe faces: and in the same parliament was graunted to the kyng the loane of .36000.li.

A newe coyne.

Anno.20

John

1504	John Winger Grocer.	W	Rogger Achil- ley Wil. Browne	S

Thys yeare the liberties of the Citie of London were agayn confirmed.

Anno.21

1505	Thomas Kneisworthe fishmonger	W	Richard Shore Rog. Groue	S

The condit at Bishops gate buil- ded.

This Thomas Kneisworthe of his owne goodes, builded the Condite at Byshoppes gate. Moreouer, hee gaue to the companye of the Fishmongers, certayn tenementes, for the which they bee bounde to fynde iiii. scholars. that study art, two to be at Oxeford, the o- ther: ii. at Cambridge euery of them to haue iiii. li. the yeare for theyr exhibiti on, They be bound also to geue to xiii aged poore people of theyr companye euery of them euery weke viii. d. and to euery of theym at Bartylmeutide a winter garment of friese, or suche like for euer. And also to geue to the priso ners of Newgate and Ludgate, euerye yeare xl.s. whose notable workes by hym don, are well worthye of remem- brance, and to be folowed of others

The kinge of Castile

This yere Philip king of Castil and his wife, were wether driuen into En

glande

gland, as they were passyng towarde Spayne who wer honorably receiued by the Erle of Arundell at the kynges apoyntment with.iii.C.horses all by torchelight

Anno.22.

Syr Ric. Hadden mercer	W	Wil. Copinger Tho. Johnson Wil. fitz Wil,	S	1506.

This yere the king of hys goodnesse deliuered out all prisoners in London which lay for xl s and vnder. Prisoners deliuered

Anno.23

William Browne mercer	W	William Butler John Rykebe	S	1507

In the ende of Aprill dyed William Browne maior, and for him was chosen Laurence Ailemer draper, who serued out that yere.

Anno 24,

Stephen Genings W.tayler	W	Thoma, Exmeu Richard Smith	S	1508

This yere was finished the goodlye hospitall of the Sauoy, nere vnto Chating Sauoy buylded ring crosse, which was a notable foundation for the poore don by king Henry the seuenth.

The newe chapell at Westminster builded.

This yere died this most noble and famous prince king Henry the seuenth whiche was in the yere.1509.the.xxij day of Aprill, when he had reigned.23. yeres and viij.monethes, and was buried at Westminster in the new chapel, which he had caused to be builded: and left behind him Henry prince of Wales, whiche after him succeded, ladye Margaret quene of Scottes, and lady Mary promised to Charles kynge of Castile.

Kyng Henry the eyght.

Anno regni.1.

1509

Enry the eyghte, beynge.xviii. yeres of age, succeded his father in the gouernaunce of this realme, and began his reigne the.xxij.day of Aprill, in the yere of our Lord.1509.and deceased in the yere.1546.the.xxviii.

day of January: so he reigned. 37. yeres ix. monethes and. vi. dayes.

Margaret mother to Henry the. vii. builded. ii. colledges in Cābridg, the one called S. Johns colledge, and the other Christes colledge: and William byshop of Lincolne builded Brasenos in Oxford. S. Johns colledge & Christes colledge builded.

King Henry maried the Lady Katherin late wife to prince Arthur. Kyng Henry maryed

Richard bishop of Winchester builded Corpus Christi Colledge, & William Smith byshop of Lyncolne builded brasenos colledge in Oxforde. Corpꝰ christi colledge & brasenos builded.

Anno. i.

Thomas Bradbury Mercer	M	George Monoxe John Doltet	S	1509

This yere syr Richarde Empson knight, and Edmond Dudley Esquier who had bene great counselours to the late King Henry the seuenth, were beheaded at the tower hyll the. xvii. daye of August.

This yere maister doctor Colet dean of Poules erected a free schole in Paules church yarde in London, and committed the ouersighte therof to the maisters and wardeins of the company of Mercers, because himselfe was borne Paules schole builded.

T.j. in

in London, and sonne of Henry Colet, who was a Mercer and Maior of London.

Anno. 2.

1510 Henry Kebel mercer } M { Jo. Milborn, John Reste } S

Henry, the first son of kinge Henry was borne on new yeres daye: for ioy wherof, a greate iustes was kepte at Westminster: and on saint Mathewes day folowing the child died.

Anno. 3.

1511 Roger Achley Draper } M { Ni. Shelton, Th. Merfin } S

Syr Edmond Haward and the lord Thomas Haward toke Andrew Barton, and. 150. Scottes, with two great shyppes.

The xv. day of January was holden a parliament, in the which two fiftens and ii. tenthes of the clergy were graunted to ayde the king in his warres, that he entended against the French king.

Anno. 4.

1512 William Copinger fishmonger } M { Robert Holdernes. Rob. Fenrother } S

William Copinger deceased, and for hym Richard Haddon serued the rest of that yere.

This

This yere was finished the beautifull steple with the lanterne at Bowe churche in Chepe.

The nauies of England and France metyng at Britayne Baye, fought a cruel battell, in the whiche the regent of England and a Caricke of Fraunce beyng crappled together, were burned and theyr captaines with their men all drowned, the english capitayn was syr Thomas Kneuet, who had with him 700. men, in the frenche carricke was syr Piers Morgan with. 900. men. Battel on the sea.

Anno. 5.

William Browne mercer	M	Johns Dawes John Bridzes Reg. Basforde	S	1513

This William Brown deceased, for whome was chosen to serue as Maior the rest of that yere. John Tat mercer.

Kyng Henry being confederate with the Emperour and the kyng of Spain, passed with a gaeat power into France where hauing in wages vnder his banner the Emperor Maximilion, & al the nobilitie of Brabant, Flanders & Holland: he discōfited the whole power of France, & conquered Turwin and the great citie of Turney. In this tyme the king of Scots, notwithstandinge that Turney Turwin he was sworne to kepe peace, inuaded this lande with a mighty army, but by the good diligence of the Quene, and the policie and manhod of the Erle of Surrey the kynges lieuetenaunt, he was him selfe slayne with. xi. of his erles, and the Scottes discomfited, but not without great losse of Englishmē.

The townes about London, as Islington, Horden, and suche other had so enclosed the common fields wyth hedges and diches, that neyther yonge men of the citie mighte shoote, nor ancient persons walke for their pleasure, except either theyr bowes and arrowes were broken or taken away, or the substantial persons arested or endited, saying: That no Londoner should go out of the citie, but in the high wayes. This saying so greued the Londoners, that suddenly a great number of the citie, assembled in a mornyng, & a Turner in a fooles cote came cryinge through the Citie: shouels and spades: & so many people folowed, that it was wonder, and within a short space all the hedges about the townes were cast downe, the dyches filled, and euery thing made plaine. When the kynges counsell hard therof, they commanded

the

the Maior to see that no other thynge were attempted, and to call home the citizens, whiche when they had done theyr entrerprise came home without any more harme doynge: and so after the fieldes were neuer hedged.

Anno. 6.

George Monox Draper } M { James Yarforde, John Mundye. } S 1514

A peace concluded betwene Englãd and France, & Lewes the frenche king coupled in mariage with lady Mary ye kinges sister: on new yeres day folowing he ended his life, wherfore king Henry sent againe for his syster by the duke of Suffolke and other.

This yere Richarde Hunne a marchant taylour of London was founde hanged in Lollers tower.

Anno. 7.

syr Wil. Butler grocer } M { Henry Worley, Richard Gray, William Bayly } S 1515

Lady Mary king Henries daughter was borne at Grenewich in February. Lady Mary borne.

Lady Mary the kinges sister before maried to the Frenche kinge, returned into England, and shortely after was maried to the duke of Suffolke.

Margaret the Quene of Scots, kinge Henries eldest syster, fled into Englād and laye at Harbottel, where she was deliuered of a child, called Margeret. In maye she came to London, where she taried a whole yere before she departed into Scotland.

Anno.8.

1516 John Rest Grocer } M { Tho. Seimer Rich. Thurstō } S

Great frost This yere was such a froste, that all men with cartes might passe betwene Westminster and Lambeth

Euil maye day. On May euen, the beginning of the ix. yere of Kinge Henry was an insurrection in Londons of yonge persons, An.reg.9 againste aliens: of the whiche diuers were put to execution, with their capitaine John Lincolne, a broker, and the residue came to Westminster with halters about their necks and were pardoned. This was called euil May day

Anno.9.

1517 syr Thomas Exmew Golsmith } M { Th. Baldrie Richard Symon } S

The sweating sicknes. Many died in England of the swettynge sicknes, and in especially aboute London: wherfore the terme was one day kepte at Oxforde, and adiourned again to Westminster.

The admirall of Fraunce came into England as embassadour with a great company of gentilmen and the Citie of Turney was delivered againe unto the Frenche kinges hand, for the which he should pay. vi. C. thousende crownes: and for the castell that the kynge buylded. xxii. C. thousand and 23000. poundes turnoys, and a peace was cōcluded betwene the kynges of Englande, Fraunce, and Castile for terme of their lives.

Turney yelded french.

Anno. 10.

Thomas Wyzkin Skynner	M	John Alleyn James Spencer.	S	1518

This yere the Erle of Surrey was sent into Ireland as deputie, and the Erle of Kyldare was of his office discharged.

Anno. 11.

syr James Yarforde Mercer	M	John Wilkenson Nico. Partrige	S	1519

As kyng Henry was at Cantorburye with the Quene, in a redinesse to haue passed the sea, he heard of the Emperours cōming, with whome the met at Dover, and accompanied hym to

Can-

Cantorbury: where after the Emperor had saluted the quene his aunt: he toke shipping into Flanders: the last day of Maye king Henry passed ouer to Calais, and met with Francis the French king at the campe betwene Arde and Guisnes. Immediately after he met with the Emperoure, with whom he went to Grauelyn, and the Emperour returned with him vnto Calais, wher he had great cheare: after whiche tyme they departed, and king Henry returned into this Realme.

Anno.12.

1520 syr John Bruge Draper } S } John Skeuington John Kemble } S

An.reg.13. In this Maiors yere the.xvii.day of May, which was in the.13. yere of the kinge, was the duke of Buckingham beheaded at London.

Duke of buckingham.

King Henry wrate a boke against Luther, and therfore the byshop of Rome named him defender of the faith. To whiche booke Luther aunswered very sharply, nothing sparyng the auctoritie or maiestie of the king.

King named defender of the fayth.

All frenchemen were attached in the citie of London, and cast in prison.

The.v.day of July the cardinal Wol-

ses

tees rode through London to Douer to mete with the Emperour, being accompanied with. ii. Erles. xxxvi. knightes an. C. gentilmenne. viii. bishoppes. x. abbots. xxx. chaplaynes all in veluet and saten. and. 700. yeomen.

This yere was a great pestilence & death in London, and other places.

Anno. 13.

syr John Wilborne Draper	M	John Britayn Thomas Pargeter	S	1521

This syr John Wylborne buylded certain almose houses, nere to ÿ crouchyd friars in London, wherin be placed. xiii. aged poore people, who haue theyr dwellings rent free, and also. vi. s. vi. d. the piece payd to them the fyrst day of euery moneth for euer. Almes houses builde

An. reg. 14

Charles the fifte Emperor of Rome came into England, and was honorably receiued into London, by the maior the Aldermen, and Commons of the Citie, the syxt of June, the kynge him selfe accompanyinge him: from thence he went to Windsor, and sate in the stal of the garter. After great feastes, iustes and honourable enterteynemente, he departed to Hampton, and sayled from thence into Spaine. Duryng this tyme the The Emperours comming to london.

the Earle of Surrey Lorde Admirall brent Morles in Britain, and then returned into the Realm. Not long after he passed ouer to Calaice, and entred Picardy, and brent diuers tounes and castels. He besieged Hesding, but because winter drewe nere, he returned home. Anno.14.

1522 Syr John Mondye goldsmith } M { John Rudston, John Champneis } S

The Lord Rosse and lord Dacres of the North, burned the towne of Kelsey in scotland, with foure score Villages and also ouerthrewe eyghtene towers of Stone, with al their bulwarkes.

The Emperor Charles king Henry of England, Ferdinando duke of Austrige, the bishop of Rome, the citie of Venice, and diuers other in Italy wer confederate against the french men.

Rhodes taken. The Turkes besieged the Rhodes, and on Christmas daye tooke it, to the greate shame and rebuke of Christen men.

An.reg.15.

Kinge of Denmarke came into England. The.xv. daye of June the Kynge of Denmarke, and his Quene arriued at Douer, and the.xxii. day of June, they came to London, and lay at the bishop of Bathes place.

The

The Earle of Surrey burned. 37. villages in Scotlande, and despoyled the countrey from the Easte marches to the Weste, and ouerthrewe diuers holdes and castels.

Anno. 15.

1523

Syr Tho. Baldrie Mercer	W	Wic. English Michol. Jenninges	S

In December at the citie of Couentry one Philip, Scholemaster to the kynges hanchmen Christopher Pikering clarke of the Larder, and Anthony Maynuile gentleman, entended to haue taken the kinges treasure of his subsedye, as the Collectors of the same came toward London, and therwith to haue araysed men and taken the Castel of Kilingworth, and thē to haue made battell against the kyng, for the whiche they wer drawen, hanged aud quartered at Tyborne, the reste that were taken were executed at Couentrie. Executio

The souldiours of Guines tooke a great bootie at a fayre in the towne in Morguison, and syr Robert Jerningham and certaine dimilaunces of Calays toke diuers Frenche prisoners. An. reg. 1

Anno. 16.

1524 Syr Wil Baylie Draper } W { Raufe Dodmer Wil. Roche } S

The golden rose.

Clement bishop of Rome, sent vnto king Henry in token of great loue, the golden rose.

Great triumphe in Englande for the takynge of the Frenche Kynge by the Emperor.

Religions houses supressed.

The Cardinall obteined licence of the bishop of Rome, to suppresse certain small houses of religion, to the intent to erect two colledges, one at Oxeforde, an other at Ipswich, and to indue them with landes: whiche colledges he began so sumptuously, that it was not like they would come to good ende.

Kyng in iopardy.

King Henry was like to haue bene drowned by leaping ouer a diche in folowing his hauke.

This yeare was the castell or tower, set vp at Grenewiche.

Coyne enhaunced.

This yere the coyne was enhansed in England.

A murmuring was in all partes of the realme for payment of money, and in Suffolke. 4000. men rose against the Duke and other commissioners, which were appeased by the duke of Norfolk

and

and other.

A truce betwene England and Fraunce

Anno. 17.

Syr John Allen mer	M	John Calton Christ. Askew	S	1525

The. xi. of Febuary, fyue men of the Stiliarde, did penaunce at Paules And an Austen fryer, called Doctor Barnes bare a fagot at Paules, ye same daye, the byshop of Rochester made the sermon againste Martin Luther & his doctrine.

The syxt day of September, was a proclamation for golde, the Frenche crowne was valued at iiij.s.vi.d. the Angel at.vii.s.vi.d. the Ryall. at xi.s. iii.d and so euery piece after that value — An.reg.15 Gould enhaunced

Anno. 18.

syr Th. Seymer Mercer	M	Ste. Pecock Nic. Lābert	S	1526

The thirde day of July, the Lorde Cardinall of Englande rode towarde Fraunce, where he concluded a league betwene kinge Henry and the Frenche kinge, whiche both sente their defiance to the Emperour, and a strong armye into Italy, to deliuer the byshop, and driue the Emperors power out of that countrey. — Anno.19.

The. xv. day of July, was one Hatman — Executed

man drawen and hanged, for coynynge false golde.

Scarsiti of bread. This yeare was suche scarsitie of bread at London and al England, that many people dyed for default thereof. And the bread cartes that came from Stratford to London, were met by the way at Miles end by the cytizens, that the lord Maior and Sheriffes of London, were fayne to go and rescue the sayd cartes, and se them brought to the markets appointed for the same.

Anno. 19.

1527	Syr James Spencer Vintener	M	John Hardy William Hollis	S

Peace proclaymed. The fyrst day of November, the lord Cardinall with the Ambassadours of France, were at Paules, and ther was proclaymed a general peace betwene kyng Henry of England and Frances the frenche king, durying their lyues, & twelue monethes and a day after.

The eyght daye of December, three scholers of Cambridge and one Forster a gentilman of the court, bare fagots at Paules.

Generall procession. The syxth of Januarye, the Cardinall with many bishops, abottes, an priors, went a procession at Paules,

sa

sang Te deum, for the escaping of the Pope from the Emperor.

This yere a French Crayer of. xxx. tonne, beynge manned with. xxxviii. frenchmen, & a flemish crayer of. xxviii tonne, and xxiiii. fleminges, meting at Margate, the one chased the other alōg the riuer of Thames to ye tower wharf of London: wher the lieuetenaunt stayed them, and toke both the captaynes and their men.

A ship chased to the tower. wharfe

The. xvii. day of June, the terme was adiourned to Michelmas after, because of the sweting sicknes that then reigned in Londō, and other places of this Realme: and also there was no suche watch in London at Midsomer, as before time had bene acustomed.

An. reg. 20

A sweting. sicknes.

The vii. day of October, came to Londō a legate frō Rome, called Cardinal Campegius, who afterward with Cardinall Wolsey, sate at the Black friers in London, where before them was brought in question the Kings mariage with Quene Katherine, as to be vnlawfull, but they long time protracted the conclusion of the matter, which delaye king Henry tooke very displeasauntly: in so much that shortly after, the Cardinall Wolsey was deposed frō the

A legate frō. Rome.

the Chauncelorship of England

Anno.20.

S.John Rud-stone Draper	W	Ra.warre / Joh Long	S

1528

The xxix, day of November the parysh, priest of Hony lane, and the usher of saynct Anthonies schole, bare fagottes at Paules, and two other bare tapers of waxe, The 8, day of may a pouchmaker bare a fagot at Paules.

An.reg.22

A peace was agreed betwen kyng Henrye of Englande, the Emperour, the French kynge, the kynge of Boheme, and Hungary. The third day of October, the kyng came to his place of Bridewell, and there he and his nobles put on theyr robes of parliament, and so came to the blacke Friers, and there sate in theyr robes, and began the parliament.

A parliament at the Blacke friers.

The.xviii.day of October, was the Cardinal discharged of his Chauncelorship & ye kyng seased all his goods and his palais at Westminster, called Yorke place into his handes.

Cardinall discharged

The xxvi.daye of October, was syr Thomas More made Chauncelour of England

S. Thomas more chancelor.

William Tyndale translated the

new

new testament into Englishe, and printed the same beyond the seas, New testamente in englishe

Anno.21

Syr Rauke Dodmer Mercer	M	Nic. Dormer. Walter Champion,	S	1529

Commaundement was geuen by kyng Henry to the Bishops, that Tyndales translation of newe testament shoul be be called in, and that they should se an other set forth to the profit of ẏ people.

Execution

The xxiiii. of January wer.iii.men drawen from newgate to the tower hil and there hanged and quartered, for counterfeyting the kinges coyne.

Anno.22

The xvi.daye of Maye was a gybet set vp in Finsbury field, & a man hanged in chaynes for murderinge doctor Miles Vicar of saint Budes, and the .v day of July, was one hauged in chaynes in Finsbury field, for murderynge mistres Kneuets mayde at sainte Antolins.

Execution

Execution

Kynge Henry, vpon occasion of delay that the bishoppe of Rome made in his controuersie of deuorcemēt, caused proclamation to be made in Septēber forbiddinge all his subiectes to purchase any thing from the court of Rome.

Sute to Rome forbydden

Anno.22.

1530 xxi To. Pargitour salter } M { Wil, Dauncie J. Chopinge } S

The cardinall beynge before caste and conuict in a premunire in Nouember was arrested by the earle of Northumberlande at Cawood and dyed at the abbey of Leicester, the 28. daye of Nouember and was ther buryed

The cardinal deceased

The vi. day of April, was a cooke named Richarde Rose, boyled in smithfielde, for poysonyng the byshop of Rochesters seruantes and other,

One boyld in Smithfield

The whole clergie of England, being iudged by the kings lerned councel to be in the premunire, for mainteyninge the power legatiue of the Cardinall, were called by proces into the kinges benche to answere: wherfore in theyr conuocation, they concluded a submission, wherein they called ẏ kyng suprem head of the church of England, & were contented to gyue the kyng, 10000. li. to pardō them their offences, touching the premunire by act of parliameent

Anno, 23 Clergie in premunire.

The kyng named supreme hedd

The kings palaice builded at saint James, whyche before was a house of systers

The xix day of August a batcheler of law called Thomas Bylney was burned

burned,

The xxii. day of October, one Pat mer a marchant and a glasier, bare fagottes at Paules crosse.

Anno. 23.

s. Mich. Lambert Grocer	M	Ri. Gresham Edw. Alton	S	1531

The xxvii day of Nouember, was a monke of Bury bur..ed in Smithfield Execution

The iiii day of December, was one Ryce Grifyn of Wales, beheaded at ÿ tower hil: and his man hanged, drawen and quartered at Tyborne for treason. Execution

An. reg. 24 Execution

The xxvii. day of January a Duche man bare a fagot at Paules crosse, and the last of April: was one Baynam burned in Smithfield.

The xxv day of May, was taken betwene London and Grenewiche, two great fishes called Herlpoles, both a male and a female. Gretfishes taken

This yere, the othe that the clergie, was wonte to make to the byshoppe of Rome, was made voide by statute and a newe othe confirmed, wherin they cōfessed the king to be supreme head. Clergie swozne

s. Thomas More

Syr Thomas More after sute made was discharged of the Chauncelorship the xvi. day of May. And the fourth of

June, the kynge dubbed Thomas Audeley knighte, and made him keper of
the great seale. And not long after, lord
Chauncelor of England.

Execution

The xv daye of June, were fiue men
drawen frō Newgate to the tower hil
and ther hanged and quartered for coy-
ning of syluer, and clipping of golde.

Execution

The fyfth day of July, was a priest
drawen hanged, and quartered for clipping of gold.

Crichurch put downe

Also in July, the kyng put downe the
priory of Christchurch in Londo.

Tower of London repayred

In August and Septemer, the kynge
repayred the tower of London.

The fyrste of September, was lady
Anne Bulleyne, made Marques of
Pembroke at Windsor.

The vii, day of October the Kyng
went to Caleys and to Bulleigne, and
came ouer agayne the xiii, daye of Nouember.

Anno. 24

1532 syr Stephē Pecocke Haberda. } M { Ric. Reinold, John Martin, Nic. Pinchō } S

The xv daye of December, was a
great fyre at the byshop of Lyncolnes
place in holborne.

The lady Anne Bulloyn, on the xii day of Aprill beynge Easter eue, was proclaymed Quene of England. Henry maried 2

The twelfth day of Maye, one Pauier beinge the towne clerke of London hong him selfe Anno. 25 Desperate

On Whitsonday beyng the last day of May, was the lady Anne Bulleine solemnely and honorably crowned at Westminster. Quene Crowned.

The xvii daye of July, were two Marchauntes slayne on thee water of Thames towarde Westminster, by one Wolfe and his wife. A murder

The 7 of September, was the lady Elizabeth daughter to Kynge Henrye borne at Grenwich, and ther christned at the friers church, the x day of September. The v. day of October, was a great fyre at Baynardes castell Lady Eliza bethe borne

The 24 of October, beinge sundaye a scaffold beyng set vp at Paules crosse there stode a nonne, named Anne Barton of Courtopstrete besyde Cantorbu torbury, two Monkes of Cantorbury two obseruaunte friers, the person of Aldermary in London, an other priest and two laye men : there preached at that tyme thee byshoppe of Bangor, Fyre at bay nardes castell Anne bart shewed theyr offences, and from thence they wer sente to the tower of london.

Anno. 25

syr Christopher Askew Draper	M	William Forman Tho. Retson	S

1533 This yere Pope Clement cursed king Henry and the realme of England the curse beyng hanged on a church dore at Dunkirke in Flaunders, was taken down by one William Locke, a Mercer of London

A gret fish taken — The xxviii. day of Januarye, was a great fysh taken at Blackewall, called a whale, whych was brought to Westminster for the king to se, & so brought down to broken wharfe, and cut out to be sold

An othe to the kyng — Commissioners were sente all ouer England, to take the othe of al persons to the acte of succession, for the refusall of whiche acte, doctour Fysher byshop of Rochester, and syr Thomas Moore late lord Chancer of Englande were sente to the tower of London.

Wolfe and his wife hanged. — The fyrst day of April Wolfe and his wife wer hanged on two gybets: at the turninge tree in Lambith marshe, for murmardringe of the two marchant stran=gers afore named

The xx day of Apriel two monkes two friers, the person of Aldermary the ho=ly Mayde of Courtopstrete in Kente: all these were drawen from the tower of London unto tyborne, and there han=ged and beheaded, theyr heades sette on London bridge, and other gates of the Citie, the same day all the craftes and companies in London were sworne to the kynge to Quene Anne, and theyr heyres. Execution

Othe to the kyng

The xv day of May was a gret fyre at Salters hall in Breadstret. An. reg. 16

Tha v day of June were all seruants and prentises of the age of 20 yeres, or aboue sworne to the king and Quene Anne his wefe and to their issue.

The ix day of July was ye lord Da=cres of the north arrained at Westmin=ster of high treason, where he so witti=lye and directlye confuted his accu=sers that hee was founde by hys peres not giltye. Lorde Da=cres

The xxii. day of Julye, was John Frith, burned in Smithfield for hys o=pinions, and with him on yong mācal Frith brent led Andrew Hewet a taylors seruante

Frier houses suppressed

The xi. day of August was all the places of the obseruant Friers put down, and Austen Friers set in theyr places, and the same obseruantes were put in places of gray friers &c.

Fyre at tempel barre

The thyrtenth day of August was a great fyre at Temple barre, and muche hurte done, and certaine personnes burned

The kings stable brent

The xvi daye of August was burned the kings stable at Charing crosse called the mewes, wherein was burned many great horses, & gret store of haye.

Thomas Cromwel was appointed maister of the Rolles the ix, daye of October

Anno. 26

1434 Syr John Champneis Skinner } M { Nic. Lewson William Denham } S

Bishop of Romes autoritie abrogated

In Nouember by a parleamente the byshop of Rome with al his authoritie was cleane banished this realme, and commaundement geuen, that he should no more be called Pope but bishop of Rome, and ye king should be reputed as supreme head of ye church of Englãd

Also

First frutes geuē to the king.

Also the firste fruites and tenthes of al spirituall dignities were graunted to the kynge.

An. reg. 27

The xxix daye of April the prior of the Charter house of London, the prior of Beual, the prior of Exam, and a brother of the same called master Reignoldes, and a prieste calle master John Haile, vicar of thistilworth wer al cōdemned of treason, who wer executed the fourth daye of Maye, theyr heades and quarters set on the gates of the citie of London, and at the Charter house of London, was set one quarter

Execution

Polled heads

The eight day of Maye the kynge commaunded all aboute his courte to poll theyr heades and to geue them ensample, he caused his owne heade to be polled likewise.

Examination of Hollanders

The xxv day of May was a gret examination of heretikes, born in Hollād to the number of xix. men, & xvi womē.

Execution

The iiii day of June a man and his wife borne in holland wer burned in Smithfield for the arrians heresie:

Execution

The 18 daye of June were iii monkes of the Charter house named Exmewe, Midlemore, and Nudigate drawen too Tyborne and there hanged and quartered

The

Bishope of Rochester beheaded

borne and there hanged and quartered

The xxii. daye of June was doctor Fysher byshopp of Rochester beheaded at tower hill.

Syr Thomas More beheaded

Thee vi. daye of Julye syr Thomas More was beheaded at the tower hill for deniall of the kings supremacie.

Visitation of abbeis

In October the king sent doctor Lee to visite the abbeis, priories and nonneries in England, & to put out al religious persons that would go, and al that wer under the age of xxiiii yeres

Anno.27

1535 syr John Aileyn mercer } M { Hūfrey Monmothe, John Cotes } S

A generall procession

The xi. day of Nouember was a great generall procession at London by the kings cōmandemēt, for the recouering of thee Frenche kinge to his health. The number of copes that wer worne in thys Procession, was seuen hundred and fourtene.

Chantries

The laste daye of December, the Lord Maior of London gaue commaundement to all parishes in the same, to bring in before him the names of al the Chauntries in their parishes, and who had the gift of the same.

The viii day of Januarye died lady

Kath

Katherin dowager at Kimbalton, and was buried at Peter borowe.

Ladye Katherine deceased

The .4 daye of February wer geuen to the kinge by a parliamente with the consente of the abbottes all religious houses that were of .300. marke, and vnder.

Smal houses of religion geuen to ye kynge An reg. 28.

On May day king Henry being at a Iustes at Grenewich, sodenly departed to Westminster, hauing only with him 6. persons. The next day An Bulleine Quene was had to the tower: and ther for things layd to her charge, beheaded the xix day of May.

The same time were apprehended the Lord Rochefords brother to the sayd Quene, Henry Noris, Mark Smertō William Brierton, & Francis weston all of the kings priuie chamber, which also about matters touching the quene were put to death the xvii day of May

Execution

Execution

The xx day of Maye, the kynge maried Ladye Jane daughter to syr John Seymor knyght, whiche at Whitsontide was openly shewed as Quene.

The viii day of June the kyng helde his court of parliament, & the bishops and clergie of this realme held a conuocation at Paules church in Lōdon: where

K. Henrye maried. 3.

where after muche debatynge of many matters, they publyshed a booke of religion, entitled, Articles deuised by the kynges highnes. In this boke is specially mentioned but iii. sacramentes, with the whiche the Lincolnshire men were offended, and fearing the vtter subuersion of theyr olde religion, raised a great commotion, against whi the kynge dyd sende a stronge power, wherof when the rebels hadde knowledge, they desyred pardon, brake vp theyr armie, and departed home: but their capitaines wer apprehended and executed.

Cōmotion in Lincoln shire.

The men of Lincolnshire beinge pacified, within sixe dayes after, began a newe insurrection in Yorkeshire, for the same causes: for they were persuaded, that all theyr syluer chalices, crosses, iewels, and other ornamēts shold be taken out of theyr churches. These people were gathered togyther, to the number of forty thousand.

Anno. 28

1536 Sir Rafe Warren Mercer } M { Rich. Paget William Bowyer. } S

The xii day of Nouember, sir Thomas Newman bare a faggot at Pouls les Crosse for that he song Masse with good ale

The xiii day of Nouember, one mayster Robert Pagyngton: a Mercer of London, was slayne with a gonne as he was goyng to Masse at saynct Thomas of Akers.

Mayster Pagynton slayn

Agaynst the rebelles of Yorkshyre, the kynge sente the Duke of Norfolke the Duke of Suffolke, the Marques of Excester, and other with a great army, by whom after the daye and place was appointed to fyghte, the Capitaynes of bothe parties had communication of peace: and promyse was made to the rebelles, that suche thynges as they wer greued wyth, shold be redressed by the kyngs auctoritie, wher with they beyng cōtented, departed without bloudshedynge. Aske, that was chiefe of this rebellion, in December came to London, and was not onely pardoned, but also receiued and rewarded wyth other gyftes of the kynge, but hee dydde not longe enioye his prosperitie

Execution

Aboute the same tyme a priest and a boucher were hanged at Wyndsor, for speakyng in the behalfe of the Yorkeshyre men.

Great frost

This yeare in December the Thames at London was all ouer frosen

Execution

The thirde daye of Februarye was Thomas Fitzgarret late Earle of Kildare, & fiue of his vncles, drawen hanged, & quartered at tyborne, for treas[on]

A new commotion in Yorkshire.

In this moneth of Februarye, Nicolas Musgraue Thomas Gilbye, & other, stered a newe rebellion, & besieged the Citye of Carlile, from whense they were driuen, and many of them taken, and put to death. Sir Francis Bigot, sir Robert Constable, and other, began an other conspiracie, and for the same were attainted and executed in the moneth of June folowyng.

Execution

The xxix daye of Marche beyng Maundy thursdaye, were xii. men of Lincolne, drawen from Newgate to tyborne: and there hanged and quartered Fiue were priestes, and vii. were laye men

Anno reg, 29

Execution

In June the Lord Darcye, the lorde Hussy, sir Robert Constable sir Thomas Percy, sir Fraunces Bigot, syr Stephen Hamelton, sir John Bulmer and his wife Wylliam Lomley, Nicolas tempest the abbots of Jerney and Ryuers, and Roberte Aske were all put to deathe: sir Roberte Co-

stal

stable was hanged atte hull ouer ye gate commenlye called Beuerley gate Aske was hanged in chaynes on a tower at Yorke: Syr John Bulmers wefe burned in Smithfield, the lord Darcy be beheaded at tower hyl, the lord Hussey at Lincolne, and the other suffred at tyborne.

In October on saynt Edwards eue was borne at Hampton court, Prince Edward & shortly after, Quene Jane left her lyfe, the. 14 daye of October, Birthe of prince Edward.

Anno. 29

Sir Rich. Gresham Mercer	M.	John Greshã Thomas Lewen	S.	1537

The viii. day of Nouẽber the corps of the Quene was caried to Windsor, and buried with great solemnitie.

The xviii daye of January a salter of London was set on the pillory for sellyng rotten hearyng and vsyng of fals weightes Execution

The xviii. day of February a seruant of my ladye Margetors was drawen, hanged and quartered for cleppynge of gold Execution

The xxv day of February sir Allein

Epriesste and a gentylman were drawen to Tyborn, and ther hanged and quartered for treason

Execution

The xxi. day of March Henry Hadsam customer of Plimmouth was drawen from newegate to Tyborne, and there hanged and quartered for treason, And one Thomas Ewel likewise was hanged and quartered

An. re. 30
Execution

The xxii. day of May frier Forest was hanged and brent in Smithfield for denyinge the kynges supremacie, wyth hym was brent ÿ Image of Deuell Gatherne of Wales

Fyre in London

The .xxvii day of May was a great fyr at sainte Margarete Pattens, called Roode lane, where were many houses burned and ix persons

Execution

In July was Edmonde Conyngsbe attainted of treason, for counterfeating of the kinges signe manuel. And in August was Edwarde Clyfford for the same cause attaynted, and bothe put to execution at Tyborne

The fyrst day of September beyng the sonday after Bartilme w faire was one Cratwell hangman of London, & two persons more hanged at the wrestlyng place beside London for robbing of a bouthe in Bartylmew faire

The hangman hāged

In September by the speciall motiō of the lord Cromwel, al ÿ notable images, unto whiche were made any speciall pylgremages and offeryngs wer utterly taken away, as the images of Walsyngham, Ipswich, Worcester, the Lady of Wilsedon, with many other, and lykewise all shrines. &c. Images taken down.

In October and Nouember the abbeys wer suppresed, & al friers, monkes, chanons, nonnes, and suche lyke were desplaced. Abbeys suppressed

Anno. 30.

Sir wil. Forman Haberd.	M	Wil. Wilkinson Nic. Gybson.	M	1538

This Nicolas Gibson sheriffe and Grocer of London afore named, buylded a free schole at Ratcliffe, nere unto London, appointynge to the same schole for ÿ instruction of. lx. pore mēs children in lernyng and vertuous educatiō, a scholemaister & an usher, with a stipend of ten pound by the yere to ÿ maister: and. vi. poūd. xiii. s. iiii. d. to ÿ Usher. He also builded certain almesse houses, adioynyng to the said schole, for xiiii. poore and aged persons, suche as through impotencie and age are not able to susteyne the trauell and toyle of the worlde: who quarterly do receiue vi.s.viii.d.a pece for euer.

The friers in London suppressed.

The.xvi. daye of Nouember, was the Black friers in Lōdon suppressed, and the next day the white fryers, the next day the Gray friers, and the monkes of the Charterhouse, and so all the other immediatly after.

Lamberte burnt.

The.xxii.day of Nouember, was one John Nicolson, otherwise Lambert a priest, burnt in Smythfield.

Also in Nouember, wer Henry marques of Excester, & erle of Deuōshire and sir Henry Pole knight, the Lorde Mountague, and sir Edward Neuell, brother to ŷ lord of Bargauēny sent to the tower. The two lordes were arreigned the last daye of December, before the lorde Chancellor, the third day after, was arreigned sir Edward Neuel, sir Geffreye Poole, and two priestes called Crofts and Collyns, and one Hollande a mariner, and all attainted, and the.ix. daye of January next folowynge, wer the sayd two lordes, and syr Edward Neuell beheaded at the tower hyll, the two priestes and Holland were drawen to Tyborne, and there hanged and quartered, and syr Geffrey Poole was pardoned.

Execution

Th

The .xxii. day of December, a priest, Henry Daunce a bricklayer, and an organ maker, bare fagots at Pauls cros.

On Ash wednesday, wer John Jones John Potter, & William Manering, hanged in the princes liueries, on the southsyde of Paules churcheyarde, for killyng of Roger Cholmeley Esquier in the same place of malice pretended. Execution

The third day of Marche, was syr Nicolas Carew of Bedingtō in Surrey, beheaded at tower hyll. Execution

The .xxviii. daye of Aprill, began a parliament at westminster: in the which the Margaret Countesse of Salisbury Gertrude, wyfe to the Marques of Excester, Reinolde Poole, syr Adrian Foskewe, & Thomas Dingley knight of saint Johns, and diuers other, were attainted of treason. Foskew & Dingley were beheaded the .x. day of July. An. reg. 31. Execution

This yere the .viii. day of Maye, the Citizens of London mustered at the Myles end, al in bryght harneis, with coates of white sylke and cloath, and chaines of gold in thre greate battailes the number was .xv. thousande, beside wyflers and other wayters: who in goodly order passed through Lōdon to Westminster then throughe the sanc- The great Muster at London.

 tuary

tuary, and round about the parke of S. James: and so by the fielde, home through Holborne.

Execution

The. viii. day of July, the Vicar of Wandsworth, with his chaplayne, his seruaunt, and fryer Wayre were drawē vnto saint Thomas a Waterings, and there hanged and quartered.

The. xvi. daye of September, Duke Frederik of Bauarie, the Paulsgraue of Rhine, the Marshall of duke John, Frederick electour of Saxonye, wyth other, came to London, by whome the mariage was concluded betwene king Henry & the lady Anne, sister to William the Duke of Cleue.

Anno. 31.

1539 Sir William Hollis Mercer } M { Tho. Heyre Tho. Huntlowe } S

Charitable deedes of Huntlowe

This Thomas Huntlow sheriffe before named, gaue to the company of the Haberdashers certain tenements, for which they be bound to geue. to. x. poore almes people of the same company euery one of them viii. d. euery friday, for euer. And also at euery quarter dyner to be kept by the maisters of the same companye, to be geuen to euery one of those. x. poore people before named, a

pe

peny lofe of bread, a potle of ale, a pece of biefe worth. iiii. d. in a platter, wyth porage, and. iiii. d. in money.

The. 14. day of Nouēber, Hugh Fecingdon, abbot of Reding, & .ii. priests the one called Rug, & the other named Onion, for denyeinge the king to be supreme hed of the church, were drawen, hanged, and quartered at Readynge. The same day was Richarde Whityng abbot of Glastenbury, lykewyse, hanged and quartered on Tower hyll besyde his monastery for the same cause. The first day of December, was John Beche, abbot of Colchester, put to execution for the lyke offence. Execution Execution

In Decēber wer appointed to waite on the kynges highnes person. 50. gentilmen, called Pencioners or speares. Pēcioners

The third day of January, was the lady Anne of Cleue, receiued at Blackheath, and brought to Grenewich with great triūph: & the syxt day of the same moneth, she was maried to king Hēry. K. Henry maried. 4.

The knyghtes of the Rhodes, was dissolued in England, wherof beynge syr William Weston knight, priour of S. Johnes. for thought dyed the fifthe day of May. Rhodes put downe

In May was sent to the tower, do-

An.reg.32.

ctor Wylson and doctor Sampson bishop of Chichester, for releuynge certain prisoners, which denied the kynges supremacie: and for the same offēce was one Richarde Farmer Grocer of Londō, a welthy man, and of good estimation, cōmitted to the Marshalsey, & after in Westminster hall was arraigned and attainted in the Premunire, and lost all his goodes.

Tho. Crōwel beheaded.

The .ix. day of July, Thomas lord Cromwel, Erle of Essex, beinge in the counsaile chaumber, was sodeinly apprehended, and cōmitted to the Tower of London. The .xix. daye of the same moneth he was attainted by parliamēt and neuer came to his answer: which lawe, he was the authour of, he was there attainted of heresy and hygh treson. And the .xxviii. day of Julye, beheaded at the tower hyll, with the lord Hungerforde.

Quene Anne deuorced.

King Henry by auctoritie of parliamēt was deuourced frō the lady Anne of Cleue: and it was enacted, that she shold be taken no more as Quene, but called the lady Anne of Cleue.

Execution

The .xxx. day of July, Robert Barnes, Thomas Gerrarde, William Jerome priestes, wer burned in Smyth-

field

field. The same daye Thomas Abell, Edward Powel, and Richard Fetherstone, were drawen, hanged and quartered, for denyenge the kynge to be supreme head of the church of England.

The fourth day of August, were drawen from the tower to tyborn, six persons, & one led betwene two sergeāts, and there hanged and quartered: one was the Priour of Dancaster, an other a Monke of the Charter house of London: maister Giles Horne, a Monk of Westminster, one Philpot, and one Carow, and a fryer. Execution

The. viii. daye of August, was the lady Katherine Haward shewed openly as Quene, at Hampton court: whiche dignitie she enioyed not long. K. Henry. maried. 5.

This yere was great death of hotte burnyng agues and fluxes, and suche a drought, that welles and small riuers were dryed vp, and many cattell died for lacke of water: the salte water flowed aboue London bridge. A great drouthe.

Anno. 32.

Syr wil. Roche Draper	}	M	{	William Laxton Mart Bowes	}	S	1540

The. xxii. daye of December, was Egerton and Harman put to death for counter- Execution An. reg. 33.

counterfaiting the kynges great seale.

Cōmotion in yorkeshire. In Aprill began a newe rebellion in yorkshire, the beginners wherof were shortely taken, and put to execution in dyuers places: of whiche Leigh Tatorsale, and Thorneton, were put to death at Lōdō, the .xxvii. day of May and syr John Neuell knight, was executed at yorke. The same day the countesse of Salisburye, was beheaded in the tower of London.

Execution.

Execution

The .ix. day of June were Dampott and Chapman, two of ye kynges gard, hanged at Grenewich, for robberies.

Execution

The .xxviii. daye of June, the lorde Leonard Gray, which before was deputie generall of Irelande, was beheaded at the tower hyll.

Execution

The .28. day of June, wer hāged at S. Thomas a Waterings, Mantell, Roiden & Froudes, gentilmē, for a spoile & murder that they had don in one of the kynges parkes vpon May Mornyng, the lorde Dacres of the South, beinge in company with them: and on the morrow which was saint Peters day, the Lord Dacres was led frō the tower a foote betwene ye two sherifes, through the city to tyborne, & ther put to death.

Execution

The kings progresse. This sommer the kyng toke his progresse

gresse to Yorke.

The fyrst day of July, was a welsh men drawen, hanged, & quartered, for prophecying the kyngs maiesties deth. Execution

Anno. 33.

Sir michel Dormer Mercer	W	Syr Roulād Hyll. Hē. Suckley	S	1541

The lady Katherine Haward, whom the kynge had maried, for her vnchaste liuyng committed with Thomas Culpeper & Francis Derehā, was by parliement attainted. Culpeper & Dereham, were put to death at tyborne, the x. day of Decēber. The. xiii. day of February, were beheaded within the tower, the lady Haward (otherwise called Q. Katherin, & the lady Rochefford And shortly after, kyng Henry maried the lady Katherin Parre, that had ben wife to the lord Latimer. Execution Execution K. Henry maried his 6. wyfe.

At this parliamēt the kyng was proclaimed kyng of Ireland, which name his predecessours neuer had, but were called lord of Irelande. K. Henrye named kīg of Ireland

The. x. daye of March, a mayd was boyled in Smithfield, for poysonynge many persons. A maid boiled in Smythfyeld.

In May, kyng Henry toke a loane of money of all such as were aboue the Anno reg. 34.

value

value of 50. pounde and upwarde.

The duke of Norfolk with an army royall was sente into Scotlād, where he bourned and wasted al the marches, and there taried without any battayle, proffered by the king of scottes, untyll the middest of Nouember followinge.

Anno. 34.

1542	John Cotes Salter	M	Henry Hoblethorne Henry Hancotes	S

After the departure of our army frō Scotland, the king of Scottes made a roade into Englād, & did much harm: but at the laste, sir Thomas Wharton, and syr William Musgraue, with a fewe of the borderers, mette with the Scottes on saint Katherins eue, where (by the greate power of God) they beyng in number. 15000. were ouerthrowen, in which conflicte was taken the lord Maxwell, the erles of Glencarne and Cassilles, with all the capitaynes of the army. And on saint Thomas euen ÿ Apostle, they were brought to the tower of Lōdon, where they lay that night: the nexte daye folowynge, they were by the kynges charge apparailed al in sylke, and rode through the city to Westminster, where they were

sworn

sworne to bee true prisoners, and then were deliuered to the custody of diuers noble men, whiche honorablye entertayned them.

In this season, an Harolde of England, rydynge on the borders syde, to do a message, was mette by certaine rebels, which cruelly against all lawe of armes, slewe him in his cote armor, but they for this dede, were sent to the king the yere folowinge, who executed them for that offence.

At newyeres tyde, the Scottes that were taken by Carlile. were by the kinge sente home agayne wyth greate giftes, vpon condition to agree to certayne articles.

The thyrd day of June the Abrine a lorde in Irelande, with diuers of the wild Irish submitted thẽ to king Henry, and in July, the sayde Abrine was created Earle of Clawricarde. An, reg. 35.

This yere in July king Henry sent ouer, 6000. men to Lãdersey, whether also came the Emperour in proper person with a greate army, and shortly after came downe the french Kyng wyth a great army, and offred to geue battell to the Emperour, by reason wherof the siege was raysed. Goynge to Laundersey.

The

The pestilence The .xxviii. day of July, were brent at Wyndsor, Anthony Person, Robert Testwood, and Henry Filmer.

This yere was a great death in Londō of the pestilence, & therfore Michelmas terme was adiourned to saint Albons, and there kept.

Anno. 35.

1543 Syr Wil. Bowyer Draper } M { John Toules Richarde Dobbes } S

Syr William Bowier deceased the .xiii. day of Aprill, about Easter, and sir Raufe Warren, serued out the residue of that yere.

A roade was made into Scotlande by the garryson there, who burned. 60 villages, and tooke great prayes bothe of men and beastes

In Nouember, the Englishmen that were sente to Lanndersey, came hom agayn.

Foure eclipses. This yere beyng leape yeare chaunsed foure Eclipses, one of the Sonne the .xxiii. day of January, and three of the Moone.

Execution The beginning of March Germaine Gardiner, Lacke parson of Chelsey beside London, and Singleton, wer executed at tyborne, for denying the kinge to be supreme head of the churche: and shortly one Ashbee was likewise executed for the same.

The .xxii. day of Marche, the Lord Admirall with a great nauy, departed from London towardes Scotland.

The fourth day of Aprill, a goune pouder house called the black swanne, standing vpon the east smithfield, was blowen vp with other houses nighe adioynyng, and therin were burned fyue men, a boye, and a woman.

Houses blowen vp

Vpon May day died the Lord Thomas Audeley highe Chancellor of England: After whom succeded lord Thomas Writhesley.

Anno. 36.

The nauie sent by the lord admirall with whō was the lord Edward Seymor Earle of Hertforde, the kynges lieuetenaunt, and generall of the army the fourth day of May arriued at Lith: the hauen of Edenboroughe, and toke the towne of Lith, and spoyled it: after which they made toward Edēborough where at a certaine bridge the Scottes had layde theyr ordinance: but by the policicie of our Captaynes and souldiors, the Scottes ordinãce was won, and discharged against them selues after this the town of Edenborough sent

Lith and Edenborough take

vnto the armye, pretendyng to deliuer the Towne vpon certaine conditions, to the behofe of our kinge: But when the army entred, they were inuaded by them: for which cause the towne was destroied and wasted.

Kynge Henry and the Emperour agreed ioyntlye to inuade the realme of France with two great powers.

Coynes in haunced. A proclamation made, enhaunsynge the value of Gold to the rate of xlviii. s and siluer to. iiii. shillings the ounce. It is to be noted, that at this time the kinge caused to be coyned the base moneys, which was called down the fifth yere of Edward the syxt, and called in the second yere of Quene Elizabeth.

Base moneys coyned.

After the whitson holye dayes, the Duke of Norfolke, and the Lorde priuie seale, with a great army tooke their voyage into Fraunce, and besieged Mottercl, where they laye vntyll the kinge hadde wonne Bologne: Not lõge after, the Duke of Suffolk with many other noble men passed the seas, and encamped before Bologne on the East syde.

King Henry went to Bologne. The xiiii. day of July kynge Henry with a goodlye companye passed from Douer to Calaice, and the 26. day encamped

camped on the north syde of Bologne, after whose comming the town was so sore battered with gonneshot, and certayne of their Towers beynge undermined so shaken, that after a monethes siege the capitayne sente worde to the king, that he would yelde the towne to his behofe, upon condition that al whiche were with in, mighte departe with bagge and baggage: which conditions king Hēry granted, & the Bologners departed to the number of. 4454. and the xxv. daye of September the Kinge entred into highe Bologne, with the nobilitie of this realme, and the trompettes blowyng: The fyrst of October king Henry departed from Bologne towarde Douer. Bologne wonne.

The nynthe day of October in the nighte the Frenchmen came unwares uppon the Englishemen in base Bologne, and slewe of them a great number. Howe beit they were shortely chased from thence.

Anno. 36.

William Larton Grocer	M	John Wilfordes Andrewe Judde.	S	1544

This yere was taken by the kinges shippes of the west countrey, and of the

En-

Englishe coast, the number of .300. sayle the shippes, and more.

Anno.37. The .vii. day of June a great army of Frenchmen came nere to the hauen of Bologne, and skirmished with the englishmen: & before they departed, they ther buylded a fort.

Worde was brought that the Frenchmenne entended to lande in the Ile of Wighte. Wherfore the kinge wente to Porthsmouthe. At whiche tyme of the kinges abode there, a goodly shippe of Englande called the Mary Rose, with syr George Carowe the capitaine, and many other gentilmen, were drowned in the middest of the hauen, by great negligence and foly.

Mary rose drouned

Certayne frenchemen landed in the Ile of Wighte, but they were dryuen awaye with the losse of their captayne and many souldiours.

Frenchmē landed at the Ile of Wight.

In August the lorde Edward Seymor Earle of Herford was sent by the king into Scotland, with an army of .xii. thousand men, where he destroyed diuers townes, and greately endomaged the Scottes.

S. Giles church.

The .xii. daye of September the Churche of saint Gyles without Creplegate was brent.

An

Anno. 37.

Syr Martyn Bowes Goldsmith	M	George Barnes Rafe Alleyn	S	1545

The. xxiiii. day of Nouember a parliament begon at Westminster, where was graunted to the king a Subsedye of. ii. s. viii. d. of the pounde of mouable good, and. iiii. shelings the pound in landes to be payd in two yere, and all colledges, Chauntreys, and hospitalles were committed to the kinges order durying his lyfe, to alter and transpose, whiche he promised to do to the glory of God, and the common profite of the realme. Chantries giuen to the kyng.

About this time the Lorde admirall landed in Normandy, and brente the suburbes of Treport, and diuers villages along the Sea coast, and destroyed and tooke almoste all the ships in the hauen.

The stewes & other like brothel houses wer by the kinges commandement put downe in all partes of the realme. The stewes put downe

In February should a woman haue ben burned in Smithfeld, for clipping of golde, but the kinges pardon came, she being at the stake.

This yere the citizens of Lōdon le- An. reg. 38.

The Conduit at Algate & Louthbury builded.

ated in the citie two Fenes for the conueyance of more water to thee citie: and then was the condites at Algate and at Lothbury begon, to be bulded.

A generall procession.

The xiii. day of June, beyng Whitsonday, a continual peace was proclamed in the citie of London betwene the kyng of England and the Frenche kynge with a solempne procession, at the tyme of the proclamation geuyng laude and prayse to God: and at night throughout the citie greate bonfyers were made.

The xxvii. day of June doctor Crome recanted at Paules crosse.

Execution

The. xvi. day. of July were burned in Smithfelde, Anne Askewe gentilwoman, John Lassels gentilman, Nicolas Otterden Priest, and John Hadland Taylour: And Doctor Sharton sometime byshop of Salisbury preached at the same fyre, recantyng his opinions perswading them to do the lyke but they would not

The Admiral of France.

The. xxi. daye of August, came into Englande from the French kynge, Mounsyre Deneuall highe Admirall of Fraunce, who brought with hym the Sacre of Diepe, and xii. galeis well besene in diuers pointes, and landed

at Lon

at London at the tower wharfe, where he was honourably receyued with many nobles and piers of this Realme and so broughte to the Byshoppe of Londons Palaice, and laye there two nightes. On Monday the. xxiii. daye of August, he rode to Hampton Court, where the Kynge laye: and before he came there, Prince Edward receaued him with a companye of fyue hundred coates of veluet: and the princes liuerie were with sleues of cloath of gold, and halfe the coate embroudered with Golde. There were to the number of eyghte hundred horses royally apparailed, whiche broughte him to the manour of Hampton court to his father.

Anno. 38.

Hen. Noblethorne merchant tailour	M	Rich. Jaruis Th. Curtise	S		1546

In January Thomas duke of Norfolke was sent to the tower of London and condempned to perpetuall prison. And shortely after his sonne the Earle of Surrey was condemned, and beheaded the. xix. day of January.

These thinges beynge doone, about the ende of Januarie, King Henry de- Execution parted out of his life, appointing his first heyre to be his yong son prince Edwarde, the seconde Ladye Mary his daughter by his first wife Quene Katherine, and the thirde, lady Elizabeth by his second wife Quene Anne Bolleyne.

Edward the sixt.

Anno regni. 1.

Dward the syxte, be-
ganne his reygne the
1546 xxviii. daye of Januarie in the yere. 1546.
when he was but. ix.
yeres olde. He decea-
sed in the yere. 1553.
the vi. daye of July,
so he reigned. vi. yeres v. monethes and viii, dayes. By his fathers will were appointed. xvi. gouernours and ouerseers of this yonge prince, the chiefe wherof was his vncle erle of Herford who shortly after was made Duke of Sommersette, and Protectour of the kinge and realme: the. xix. daye of Fe-

bruary

bruary he rode solemnely with the nobilitie of the Realme, from the tower to Westminster, throughe the Citie. And on the Southesyde of Paules churchyard, an Argosie came from the Battilment of Paules churche, upon a Cable, beinge made faste to an anker, at the Deanes gate, lying upon his breast, aydinge him selfe neyther with hande nor foote, and after ascended to the middest of the same Cable, tombling & playing manie pretie toyes, whereat the kynge with the nobles of the Realme laughed hartilye: the. xx. of Februarie he was crowned king at Westminster with great solempnitie.

S. Paule church la at ancre

The Lord Protectour with other of the Counsayle, sente Commissioners into all partes of the Realme, willing them to take all Images out of theyr Churches, with them were sent diuers preachers, to perswade the people frō theyr beades and suche lyke: also procession was commanded to be no more used: And shortelye after was a Parliament, wherein beside other thinges, Chauntries were geuen into the kings handes, to be used at his pleasure. And also an order taken for the use of the Lordes Supper, that it shoulde be

Images t ken dow

Processio forbidden

Chauntries geuen to king

in bothe kyndes of bread and wine.

In August the Duke of Somerset and the Earle of Warwicke with a noble army were sent into Scotland, and nere to Edenborowghe at a place called Muskelborowghe, the Englishmen and Scottes mett, where betwene them was foughten a cruel battayle. The victorie fell to the Englishmen, and the Scottes were slayne above .xiiii. thousande, and taken prisoners of Lordes, knightes, and gentilmen .xv. hundred.

Muskelborow field.

Anno. 1.

1547

Syr John Gresham mercer	M.	Tho. White	Robert Chertsey	S

Anno. 2.

This second yere of kyng Edward the syxt, the watche which in London had ben used at midsomer, and of long tyme layde downe, was now againe used, both on the even of saint John, & on the even of sainte Peter, in as beautiful maner, and as good order, as it had ben accustomed before tyme, which watche was greatlie beutified with a nomber of demilances & light horsemen which wer prepared to send into Scotland for the reascue of the town of Hadyngton.

The

The laste daye of Julye, Stephen Gardiner byshop of Winchester, was for a sermon made before king Edward and the Counsell sent to the Tower of London, where he remayned all thys kinges reigne.

This yeare in London was greate mortalitie by the pestilence. Wherfore a commaundement was geuen to all Curates, and other hauing to do therwith, that no corps shoulde be buried before syxe of the clock in the morning nor after sixe of the clock at night, and that there shoulde at the buryinge of euerye corps be rongue one belle at the leaste, the space of three quarters of an howre. A great pestilence.

Anno. 2.

syr Henry Aincottes fishmōger } W { William Locke John Olife } S. 1548

Syr Thomas Seimer high Admirall of Englande brother to the Lorde Protectour, and the kynges vncle, had maried Quene Katherine late wife to Kinge Henry, she conceiuyng a stomacke againste the Lorde protectors wife. Where vpon also in the behalfe of their wyues, displeasure and grudge began betwene the two brothers

thers, which at the length brake out to the confusion of theym both: For the twenty day of March was the lord admiral beheaded at tower hill.

An. reg. 3. Execution

Cōmotion in Cornewal & Deuonshyre.

This yere about Whitsontide: and so forthe untill September, the commons in most part of this realm, made sundry insurrections and commotions Amongest whom, diuers of the commons of Cornewall and Deuonshyre, rose against the nobles and gentilmen: and in sundrye Campes besieged the towne of Exceter, whiche was valiantly defended.

ōmotion in Norfolk

Also they of Norfolke and Suffolk encamped them selues, nere unto Norwich, declaryng them selues to be grieued with parkes, pastures, and inclosures made by the gentilmē, who required the same to be disparked and set among the commons. Into Deuonshyre againste Humfrey Arundell and his rebels, was sent the lord Russel, lorde preuy seale, with a number of souldiors. The Lord Gray was also sente with a number of strāgers, which wer horsemen, wher in diuers conflictes they slewe many people, and spoyled that countrey.

In Norfolke againe captain Kite a Tanner

Tanner, and his company, syr John Dudley erle of Warwicke, went with an army: where both he him selfe and a great number of gentilmen that wer with him, metynge with the rebelles, were in suche daunger, as they hadde thoughte all to haue dyed in the place: but God brought it so to passe, that as weal there as in all other places, they were partely by power constrayned, partely by promes of theyr pardon perswaded to submit them selues, and delyuered theyr chiefe capitaines to punishment, but yet after the losse of many thousandes of Englishmen.

The king of Fraunce perceauynge such sedition and trouble in England, did not omitte the occasion, but in the meane time assaulted certain holdes about the town of Bologne builded of the Englishmen for the defence of the same, and namely tooke the forte called newe hauen, and thereby muche indamaged the Englishe garrison that lay at Bologne. The losse of this was layd to the lorde Protectour because he hauyng the chiefe gouernement of the Realme, dyd not see those partes better furnished: in conclusion the erle of Warwicke, with the consente of other

no-

nobles of the Realme, by open proclamation accused him of misgouernemēt as well in this as in diuers other matters. Wherfore when he fled wyth the yong kyng to Wyndsour castell, they caused hym to be fette from thens, and brought as a traitoure to the tower of London, the.xiiii.day of October.

Duke of Somerset.

Anno. 3.

1549	Syr Rouland Hyll Mercer	M	John Yorke Richarde Turke	S

This syr Roulande Hylle, to the great prayse of his vocation, and to the syngular comfort of the weale publike of his countrey, erected many notable monumentes and good dedes, which were to long here to write. Wherfore I referre them to my Summarie.

Charitable dedes.

A murder.

Upon a Sondaye beynge the nyntene daye of Januarye, were murthered in London, betwene Newgate, and Smythfyelde, twoo Capitaynes which hadde serued the kynge in his warres at Bologne, and other where: the one was called Gambo, the other Filicirga, bothe Spanyardes: this murder was committed by Charles Gauaro a Flemmyng, whom came in

posse

poste from Warwicke to London to do that acte. And beynge hanged for the same with his thre men in Smithfield sayd at his death, he would neuer repēt it: they were all foure hanged on the fryday next after, whych was the. xxv. day of January. Execution

The. xxvii. daye of January, Humfrey Arundell capitaine of the rebelles in Deuonshere, was hanged, drawen, and quartered at Tyborn, with diuers other, as Wynslade, Holmes Bery, &c. About the same tyme, Robert Kite, capitain of them that rose in Norfolke with his brother William, was condemned and sente to Norwich, where the sayde Robert was hanged in chaynes vpon the top of Norwiche castell. Execution

About the begynnyng of Februarye, the Embassadoures of Englande and Fraunce, consulted of a peace to be had betwene both Realmes, whiche after was concluded. An. reg. 4

The. vi. day of February, the Duke of Somerset was deliuered out of the tower, and the same night he supped with the earle of Warwike at the sheriffes house called maister Yorke.

The. x. day of February, one Bell a Suffolke man, was drawen from the Execution

tower

towet to Tyborne, and there hanged & quartered for mouyng a new rebellion in Suffolke and Essex.

On mondaye, beyng the laste daye of Marche, a generall peace was proclaimed betwene the kynges of Englande and Fraunce, & in the same peace were included the emperor & the Scottes.

Bologne yelded Frenche. The .xxv. day of Aprill, the towne of Bulleyn was yelded vp vnto the frenche Kyng.

Execution. The .ii. day of May, one Joane Knel otherwise called Joane Butcher, or Joane of Kent, was burned in Smithfield for heresy, that Christ tooke no Joane boucher. fleshe of the virgin Mary.

Certaine lewde persons attempted a newe rebellion in some parte of Kent, but they were sone repressed, & certain of the chief, as Richarde Lyon, Godvard Gorran, and Richarde Irelande, Execution. wer apprehended and put to death for the same, the .xiiii. day of May.

Anno. 4.

1550	Sir Andrew Judd skin.	M	August. Hind John Lyon	S

This syr Andrew Judde erected one notable schoole at Tunbridge in Kent wherin be brought vp and norished in good learnyng, great store of youth, as

wel

wel brought vp in ỹ shire, as brought from other countreys adioyning.

This yeare vpon a thursday, beynge the. xvii. daye of December, the Thames beneth the bridge dyd ebbe & flow thre tymes within. ix. houres: and the same daye & time, the byshop of Wynchester was brought vnto Lambeth by water, before the byshop of Cantorbury, and other the kynges cōmissioners where were obiected vnto him certaine articles on the kinges behalfe, and day assigned him to answer. Thre fluds

It was enacted, that priestes childred should be legitimate.

This yere on saint Valentines daye, at Feuersham in Kente, one Arden, a gentleman, was kylled by the consent of his owne wyfe. For this act, iust punishement was afterward taken vpon those that were the doers and consenters to the same. The wife her self was burned at Cantorbury the. xiiii. day of Marche, the same day two other were hanged in chaynes at Feuersham, and a woman brent: Mosby and his sister were hanged in Smithfield at Lōdon. And black Wyll the Ruffian that was hyred to do the acte, after his first scape An. reg. 5. Execution

was

was apprehended and burnt on a scaffold at Flysshyng in Sealande.

The.xiiii.daye of February, beyng saterday, D. Stephē Gardiner bysshop of Winchester, was depriued of his bishopricke, and so cōmitted to the tower againe. Into his place was translated doctor Poynet, who before was bishop of Rochester.

An Arrian executed.

The.xxiiij.day of April, beyng fr[illegible]day, a duchemā was burned in Smithfeld for heresy, who held the detestable opinion of the Arrians.

The.viii.daye of May a proclamation was made that from and after the laste day of August nexte folowyng our shilling beyng curraunt for.xii.d. shoulde be curraunt but for.ix.d.

An earthequake.

The.xxv.day of May, beyng Monday betwene the howers of eleuen and one of the clock at after noone, was an earthequake of halfe a quarter of an howre longe at Blechyngleye, at Godstone, at Croydon, at Albery, and at diuers other places in Southerye and Middlesex.

The.ix.day of July beeing thursday, the forsaid proclamatiō, which was appointed to take effect the last day of August

gust next cōming, was shortned unto this present day, and toke effect immediatly upon ÿ publishinge of the same, whiche was done betwene ix. and ten of the clocke before noone, so that immediatly, a shilling went for. ix. pens, and a grot for. iii. d. and no word spoken of the smalle money, as pence and half grotes, by reason whereof, there was no smalle money to be gotten to geue the poore people.

The firste falle of the money.

The sweating sicknes began in London the. viii. day of July: and the. x. day of July it was most vehement: whiche was so terrible, that people beynge in best health was sodeynely taken, and dead in. xxiiii. howers, or. xii. or lesse, for lacke of skill in guydinge them in their sweate. And it is to be noted, that this mortalitie felle chiefly or rather onelye on men, and those also of the best age, as betwene. xxx. and. xl. yeares of age: wherefore this nation was muche afeard of it. And for the tyme began to repent, and remember God. But as the disease relented, so our deuotion decaied: the firste weke died in London, 800. persones, and then it ceassed.

Sweting syckness.

The

The secōde fall of the money

The.xvii.day of August, beyng mōday, was proclamation made, that the shilling, which of late was called downe to.ix.d. shold be currant for.vi.d.ÿ grot ii.d.ÿ half grote.i.d.a peny a ob.

The.xi.daye of October, beyng sondaye, the Lorde Marques Dorset was created Duke of Suffolk, the lord erle of Warwicke, was created Duke of Northumberland, and the erle of Wilshire, was created Marques of Winchester, and syr William Herberte, the master of the horse, was created erle of Penbroke, & diuers mē made knights

Duke of Somerset to ÿ tower.

The.xvi.day of October, being fryday, the duke of Somerset was broght againe to the tower of London, and in the next morning the duchesse his wife was brought thither also: ther wente also with the Duke the lorde Greye of Wylton, syr Rafe Vane, and syr Thomas Palmer, and diuers other gentlemen of his familiars.

Anno.3.

1551 Richarde Dobbes Skinner } M { John Lamberte John Couper } S

A newe coyne.

The,xxx.day of October, was proclaymed a newe coyne of money, bothe silver & gold: soueraines of fyne golde

at.xxx

at xxx. s. Angels of fine golde at x s. and diuers other pieces of golde of lesse value: a piece of syluer of v. s. and a piece of ii. s. vi. d. the sterlynge shillyng. xii. d. and sundrye other smaller pieces of money

The vi. daye of Nouember, beynge fryday, the olde Quene of Scots, rode through London and Cheape, wyth a great cōpany of englyshmen waytinge on her, after she had layne 4. days in ye bishops place besides Paules church. The quene of Scottes

The first day of December, the duke of Somerset was arreigned at Westmynster halle, and was there acquited of treason, but condemned of felonye. The Duke of Somerset araigned

The vii. daye of December, was a generall Muster of the horsemenne, whiche were in the wages of the nobles of the Realme: and for the whiche the kynges maiestie allowed yearelye for euery man. xx. pounde, the whiche muster was made vpon the caussey ouer agaynst the kynges palaice at saint James, the number of horse was esteemed to be a thousand. Execution

The. xxii day of Janury, beynge friday, Edward duke of Somerset, kyng Edwards vncle before mentioned was

was beheaded a the tower hill.

An, reg. 6. On the xx. day of February, the marchantes of the Styllarde att London, were put frome theyr priuiledge of occupyinge whyche they of longe tyme before had vsed.

Execution The xxvi. daye of Februarye, Sir Rafe a Vane, and sir Myles Partrige were hanged vppon the gallowes at tower hyll: and sir Michaell Stanhope, wyth syr Thomas Arundel, were beheaded vpon the scaffolde, whyche foure were condempned as accessarye in that whyche the Duke was condemned for.

A howse blowen vp The last daye of Aprill, through negligence of the gonne pouder makers, a certayn house with thre laste of poudar, was blowē vp, and burnt the said gonpouder makers being xv. in number, were all slayn at the tower hyll, a little from the Minories besyde Lōdon on the backe syde of New abbey.

A monster The iii. daye of Auguste was borne a meruailous strange monster at a place called Myddleton. xi miles from Oxenford, a woman brought forth a child which had ii. perfecte bodies frome the nauel vpward, and were so ioyned together at the nauell, that whenne they

were

were layde in length, the one head and body was eastward, and the other west the legges for bothe the bodies grewe out at the myddes, where the bodies ioyned, and had but one issue for the excrement of both the bodies: they lyued xviii. dayes, and when they were opened, it appered they wer womē childrē

Great fyshes taken

The viii. daye of August, there were taken about Quinborough thre greate fyshes called Dolphines, or by some called Rigs: and the weke folowinge at Blackwall, wer vi. more taken and brought to London, & there solde: the least of thē was greater then any horse

The same moneth of August, began the great prouision for the poore in Lōdon, towardes the whiche euerye man was contributorie, and gaue certayne money in hande, promisynge to geue a certain wekely. The first house whyche was begon was the Graye friers in Newgate market.

Great fyshes.

The vii. day of October were two great fyshes takē at Grauesend, which were called whirlepoles, they wer after ward drawen vp aboue the bridge.

The xiiii. day of October, ÿ bishop of Durhā Cuthbert Tunstall was depriued from his byshopricke

1552 George Barnes haberdasher } M { Wil. Garret John Maynarde } S

This sir George Barnes haberdasher gaue ye windmil which stãdeth toward the east in Finsbury fielde to the poore almose people of the same companye. And also he gaue to be distribute to ye poore people of the parishe of S. Bartholomew the little. xviii. d. in breade euery sondaye for euer.

The xxi. day of Nouember the children were taken into the Hospitall at the gray friers to the number of iiii C

In the sommer past kyng Edwarde went en progresse into the weste countrey, where he had so muche exercise of hauking and hunting, as was thought by some to bee daungerous vnto his healthe. Towarde wynter hee returned to London and frome thence to Grenewiche where all the Christmas season was passed with muche pleasantnesse and myrthe, vntyl at length

An. reg. 7 in Januarye hee fell sycke of a coughe, whiche ended in consumption of the lyghtes.

The xx day of May. iii. great shippes

pes well furnyshed wer set foorthe for the aduenture of the vnknowen voyage to Muscouia. And .ii other shyps were sente forthe to seke aduentures southwardes

Voyage to Moscouie.

In May Lorde Gylforde the Duke of Northumberlandes fourthe sonne, maried lady Jane the Duke of Suffolkes daughter, whose mother beyng then a lyue, was daughter to Marye, kyng Henries syster.

The xxi daye of June was a verye great & terrible clap of thunder aboute xii. of the clocke at noone, which bet open one of the doores of sainte Denyse church in London, & tore of both locke and lynyng of the same.

Great thunder.

Kyng Edwarde beyng about the age of xvi yeres, as is sayd before, was lõg sick of a consumption of the lightes, & the vi day of July the deathe of kynge Edwarde was published. The same daye at the after noone about, foure of the clocke the Ladye Jane doughter of the lady Francis, the duchesse of Suffolke, whiche Ladye Jane was maried vnto the Lorde Gylforde Dudleye the fourthe sonne vnto the Duke of Northumberland, was cunueyed by water to the tower of London, and betwene

Kyng Edwarde deceased

vii.

vii. and viii of the clocke in the euening, proclamatiō was made throughout the citie, wherby was declarede, that kyng Edward beyng deceased, by his wyll had assigned the sayde Ladye Jane to be quene, and therupon so proclaymed Quene of Englande.

Lady Jane proclaimed

But when it was heard that the Ladye Mary was fled to Framingham castel in Suffolke, the people of the countrey almoste wholly resorted vnto her, and in Oxenford syr John Wyllyams, in Buckynghamshire, syr Edmunde Peckham, and in dyuers other places many men of worshyppe, gathered great powers, and with al spede made toward Suffolke, where lady Marye was. The xiii day of July by appointmente of the councell the Duke of Northumberland, the Earle of Huntingdon, the lord Grey of Wilton, and dyuers other with a great numbre of men of armes, wente to fetche her by force, and was on theyr waye as ferre as Bury. But the xix daye of Julye, the counsell, partly moued wyth the right of her cause, partly considering that the most of the Realm was wholly bente on her syde chaunged theyr

mindes

myndes, and immediatelye came into Cheapesyde wyth the kynge of Heraldes where they proclaymed the ladye Mary, Quene of Englande, kepynge as prisoners in the Tower lady Jane lately proclaimed, and lorde Gylforde her husband: and the duke, returnyng to Cambridge, on the twentye daye at nyght, beyng apprehended of the gard he wyth other, was brought to the tower of London, the fiue and twentye of Julye Thus was the matter ended without bloudshed, whiche men feared, woulde haue brought the deth of many thousandes

Lady Mary proclaymed quene

Quene Mary
Anno. Regni. i

1553

Ary the eldest daughter of king Henrye the viii. began her reigne ouer this realme of Englande the vi. day of Julye in the yeare of oure Lord 1553 and deceased

ceased in the yere of our Lorde .1558. the 17 day of Nouember, so shee reigned v yeares iiii. monethes & xi. dayes: she was proclaimed Quene at London the xix day of July, and the xx. daye at the castel of Framyngham: and afterward being accompanied with a goodly band of noble men, gentylmen, and commoners gathered out of all partes of the Realme came to London, and entred the tower the iii. day of August In her fathers and brothers tyme dyuers noble men were caste into the tower: some for treason layde to theyr charge as the Duke of Norffolke, and the lorde Courtneye, some for matters of Religion, as doctour gardener byshope of winchester doctour Tõstal, byshoppe of Durham and other: whyche continued there prisoners at the Quenes commyng: to all these and manye other, she granted pardon, and restored them to theyr former dignities. Doctor Gardiner byshop of Wynchester, made hygh chancellor of England, the lorde Courtney erle of deuonshire.

A wherrye ouerturned

The xx day of August certayne gentylmen mending to passe through London bridge in a wherrye were there ouerturned and seuē of them drowned.

The

The .xiii. daye of August one maister Bourne a Canon of Paules, preached at Poules Crosse, whose talke myslyked the audience, that some cryed, Pul hym oute and one threwe a dagger at hym, which hyttyng one of the syde postes, rebounded backe agayne : & then maister Bradforde and John Rogers two preachers of kyng Edwards time with muche laboure conueyed the sayd maister Bourne out of the audience into Paules schole.

Execution

The .xxii. day of August the duke of Northũberlãd was beheaded, and with him wer put to death sir John Gates & syr Thomas Palmer called Buskyn Palmer knyghts.

The greate Mary

The .xxvi. day of August in the euenynge a ship was burnt at Wolwiche, called the greate Mary, by the negligence of mariners, she was of burthen a thousand tunne.

A man stoode on ẏ wethercok of Poules

The last daye of September the quenes hyghnes rode through the citie to Westminster in moste goodlye maner, and pagentes in all places accustomed beyng moste gorgeously trimmed: And as her grace passed by Pauls a certain duche man stode vpon the wethercock

with

wyth an enseigne in his hande, flourshyng wyth the same, very strange to the beholders. And ye morow her grace was crowned at Westminster by doctor Gardener bishop of Winchester.

The fyfth day of October began the parliament at Westminster, and masse of the holy ghoste was songe.

Grauesend barge.

The xxv. daye of October the barge of Grauesend by great misfortune of a catch running vpon her, was ouerthrowen and xiiii. persons drowned, and xvi. saued by swimming.

The xxiii. the xxv. the xxvii. dayes of October were certayn disputations in the long chapell at the north dore of Paules concerning Transubstantiation, but nothing throughly determined.

Anno. 1

1553 Tho. White marchant taylour } M { Thomas Ofley, Wil. Hewet } S

S. Johns colledge in Oxforde erected.

This syr Thomas White renewed or rather erected a colledge in Oxford that was in gret ruine and decay, now called S. Johns college, and before Bernard college, indowinge the same with landes & reuenues, to the great preferment of lerning and comfort of poore mennes children.

T

The lyke Colledge. also now called trinitie colledge syr Thomas Pope knight to his great praise and cõmendation erected, whiche sointime was called Durham colledge, appointynge for the maintenance of the fellowes and scholars lyke possession

Trinitie colleg erected.

Cardinall Poole, beyng sente for by the quene returned into this realme.

The xiii day of Nouēber D Cranmer Archbishop of Cantorbury, lady Jane that was before proclaimed quene, and the lord Gilford her husband wer openly arraigned & condemned for treason.

The v. daye of December the parliament was dissolued, in the whiche all statutes made eyther of Premunire in tyme of kyng Henry the viii. or concernynge religion and administration of the sacraments vnder king Edward the syxt, were repealed, and the latten seruice restored as it was in þ last yere of king Henry the eyght: and communication was had of the Quenes marriage wyth kynge Phillip the Emperours sonne &c

The beginning of January the emperor sent a noble man called Ecmondane and certayne other ambassadours into England to make a perfect conclusion

ssion of the mariage betwen kyng Philip and Quene Mary.
The xx day of January the lord Chancellor wyth other of the counsel, declared openly to the Quenes houshoulde
that ther was a mariage concluded, be
twyn her grace & the king of Spayne
whyche should bee a greate strengthe,
honour, and enriching to the realme of
England.

This mariage was so greuously taken of diuers that for this, and religiō
they in such sort conspired agaynst the
Quene, that if God hadde not wonderfully preuented them, it woulde haue
brought muche more trouble and danger. For syr Thomas wyat in Kente,
beyng one of the chiefe, aboute the xx.
daye of January, gathered a certayne
company, & much incensed the people
of those parts agaynst ẏ quene, saying
That she & the counsel intended not on
ly by alteration of religion to bring in
the pope but also by mariage of a strā-
ger to bring the realme into miserable
seruitude. The Quene sent the duke of
Norfolk with a cōpany of souldiors in
to Kent against Wiat, wher ẏ duke me
ting wyth Wiat, not farre from Roche

Cōmotion in Kent

ster

ster bridge was forsaken of his souldi=
ours, and returned to London. Also
Henry duke of Suffolke flyinge into
Leicestershire, & Warwikeshyre, in di=
uers places as he went agayn proclay
med his daughter queue, but the peo=
ple not inclining to him he was by the
earle of Huntington brought prisoner
to London and the same day beynge the
fyrst of February, the Quene came frō
Westminster to the Guelde hall in Lon
don: and there after vehement woordes
agaynst Weat, declared that shee mente
not other wyse to marry, then the coun
cell shold thynke bothe honorable and
commodious to the realme: and ther=
fore willed them truly to assiste her in
represslyng suche as con trarye to theyr
dueties rebelled. Moreouer, she ap=
poynted lord William Haward lieue=
tenaunte of the citie, and the Earle of
Pembroke generall of ỹ fyelde, which
bothe prepared all thinges necessarye
for theyr purposes

The duke of Suffolk proclaimed his daughter quene

Duke of Suffolk taken

The quene caine to the Guild hall in London

Wyat came neare vnto the Citye and entred into Southwarke, the third day of February, wherefore the drawe bridge was broken dowen, ordi nance bent to that parte, generall par=
don

don proclaymed to al them that would geue ouer and forsake the rebelles.

After Wiat had layne ii. dais in Southwarke, he turned his iourney to Kingstone on Shrouetuesday in yͤ morning beyng the syxt of February, wher hee passed ouer the Thames and purposed to haue come to London in the nighte: but by meanes that the cariage of his chiefe ordenaunce brake he coulde not come before it was farre daye. At that tyme the erle of Pembroke, and diuers other were in sainte James field wyth a great power & theyr ordenance so bēt that Wiat was fayne to leaue the common way, and wyth a small company came vnder saint James wal from the danger of the ordinance, and so wente by Charinge crosse vnto Ludgate without resistance, and ther thought to haue be let in. But perceauing that he was

Wiat taken

disapoynted of his purpose he returned & about tēple barre was taken prisoner

Proclamation was made in Londō that no man should keepe in his house any of Wiates faction. And shortly after aboute the nomber of fyfty were hanged on xx paire of gallouses made for that purpose in diuers places in and

about

about the citie.

The xii. day of February Lady Jane the duke Suffolkes daughter and her husbande lord Gylford were beheaded for feare leaste any other shoulde make like trouble for her title, as her father had attempted

Execution

The xvii. day of February was proclamation made that al strangers shold voyde the Realme within xxiiii. days next ensuinge, vpon payne of confiscation of theyr goods all free denisens marchantes, embassadours and theyr seruantes except.

Proclamatiō against strangers

The xvii. daye of February Henrye Duke of Suffolk was condempned of treason, & the fourth day after beheaded at the tower hill.

The 23. of February, about. 240 prisoners of Wiats faction went with halters about theyr neckes toward Westminster, who had theyr pardō in chepe

The x of April D. Cranmer archbishop of Cantorbury, D. Ridley of London, and Hugh Latimer ones byshop of Worcester, were conueyed as prisoners from the tower of London to Oxford, there to dispute with the diuines and lerned men.

The xi. day of Aprill syr Thomas

Wiat

Wiat was beheaded at tower hill, and after quartered his quarters were, set up in divers places, and his heade on the gallowes at Hay hill, wher it was soone after stolne away
Execution

The 27. of Aprill the lord Thomas Gray, brother to the late duke of Suffolke, was beheaded.

William Thomas a gentylman, and certayne other persons wer apprehended for conspiring quene Maries deth the same William Thomas the xviij. day of May was drawen hanged and quartered at tyborne.
Execution

The xxiiij. day of Maye beynge the feast of Corpus Christi, a ioyner called John Strete wold haue takē the sacrament out of the priest hands in Smithfield, in the time of procession, but he was resisted, taken & put to Newgate

The fourth day of June was taken down all the gallowes that wer about Londō. The same day began the crosse of Cheape to be new gylded
Crosse in Cheape

The x. day of June beyng sonday doctoure pendilton preching at Paules crosse a gonne was shotte at hym but mysfed & the shuter not taken

In. reg. a The .xv. day of July Elizabeth

wench did opē penance at Paules crosse where she confessed, that she beyng in- ticed by lewde councell, had vpon the xiii. daye of Marche laste passed coun- terfait certain speches, in an house, nere vnto Aldersgate in London, about the which, ÿ people of the whole citie wer wonderfully molested

The sprit in ÿ wall

The xix. day of July kyng Philip the emperours sonne, arriued at South- hampton, the. iii. day after he came to Winchester, and there was honorably, receiued of the bishop, and a greet num ber of nobles, the next day he met with the quene with whom after he had lōg and familiar talke. The second day be yng saint James day, the mariage was in honorable maner solemnised betwen him and Quene Marye. Shortly after king Philip and quene Mary depar- ted from Winchester, and with a good- ly company were brought to London, and there with great prouision wer re- ceaued of the Citizens the. xviii. day of August. At that tyme a man came as it were flying vpon a rope from Paules steaple to the deanes wall.

King Philip.

Paules steple laye at Anker

In October the emperor sent ambas- sadours into England to yeld vnto his sonne king Phillip the Dukedome of

Anno. M.2.P.1

1554	John Lyon grocer	M	Dauid Woodrosse Wil. Chester	S

Cardinall Poole

The xxiii. of Nouember Cardinall Poole came into Englande, and was receyued with honoure in all places as he passed. At the same tyme he was by parliamente restored to hys olde estate and dignitie that hee was putte from by king Henry the quenes father and shortly after came into the Parliamente house, where the king quene and other states were all present. Then he declaringe the cause of hys legasie, fyrst exhorted theim to returne thto cōmunion of the church and restore to the most holy father the pope, his due aucthoritie, secondly he aduertised them to geue thanks to God that had sent them so blessed a kyng and quene: finally he signified, for so much as they had with great gentilnes restored him to his honour & dignitie, that he most earnestly desired to see them restored to the heauenly court & unitie of the church. The next day the whole courte of parliamēt drue out the forme of a supplication, the summe whereof was that they greatly

repented

repented them of that schisme that they had lyued in. And therfore desyred the Quene and the Cardinall that by theyr meanes they might be restored to the bosome of the holy church & obedience of the sea of Rome. The next day, the king, quene, and cardinal beynge presente, the Lorde Chancellour declared what the parliament hadde determined concerning the Cardinals request, and offered vnto the kinge and quene, the supplication before mentioned, which beynge reade, the Cardinal in a large oration, declared how acceptable repentaunce was in the sighte of God. &c. Immediately hee makinge prayer vnto God, by authoritie to hym committed absolued them, and restored theim to the church of Rome. When all thys was done, they wente all vnto the chapell, and there synging Tedeum with greate solempnitie declared the ioye and gladnesse, that for this reconciliation was pretended.

The ii. day of December beyng sonday, the kinges maiestie the lorde Cardinal, and diuers other of the nobilitie repaired to saidt Paules church in London, and so vnto a windowe of the same directly against the crosse, wher, the by

shop of Winchester beinge lord Chaũce-
lor of England made a sermon, declaryng how this realme was agayne restored to the church of Rome.

The prince of Piamõt

The 27. of Decẽber the prince of Pia-
mont duke of Sauoy, with other lords
wer receiued at Grauesend by the lord
priuie seale & other, & so cõueyed along
the riuer of Thames to westminster.
In the beginning of Januarye the parliament was dissolued. Wherin it was
enacted, that the statutes before tyme
made for the punishment of heretikes,
and the confirmation of the popes power should be reuiued, and in so good
force as euer they had ben before kinge
Henries reigne: and that such actes as
wer made against the supremacie of the
Pope should be cleane abrogated.

The prince of Orenge.

The ix. day of January the prince of
Orenge beyng receiued at Grauesend,
was conueyed along the riuer of Thames and landed at Suffolke place.

Execution

The viii. of February John Rogers
was burned in Smithfield. The vii. of
February the lord Strange being ma-

Juga cana.

ried at the court, the same day at nighte
was a goodly pastyme of Juga cana by
cresset lyght, there were lxx. cressete
lightes

The

The xviii. of February the bishop of Ely, with ye lord Mountacute & diuers other, wel apparelled rode forthe of the citie of Lōdon towards Rome ambassadours frō the kyng quene & counsel.

The xvi. day of March a weauer of Shorditch was burned in Smithfild

On Easter day one William Flower with a wodknif, woūded a priest, as he was ministrynge the sacrament to the people in S. Margeretttes churche at Westminster: for the which offence, the sayd William had his right hand smitten of, and for opinions in matters of religion was burned in ye sanctuarie of westminster nyghe saincte Margarets churchyarde the. xxiiii daye of Aprill.

Execution

In Maye the Lorde Cardinall the Lorde Chauncellour the earle of Arundell, and the lorde Paget wente ouer sea to Calice, and nere vnto Marke, treated with the Emperors and french kynges Commissioners for a peace to be had betwene the sayd princes, who returned agayne into England, about the myddeste of June, without any agreement makynge.

The tenthe day of May a ladde called

led Wyllyam Fetherstone, aboute the age of eightene yeres, who named him selfe to be kyng Edwarde, the .vi. was taken about Eltham in Kent, & sent to ye marshalsey & ye xxviii. day he was had out in a carte, through London to west minster, with a paper on his heade: And so round about westmynster hall before all the Judges and then whipped aboute the sayde Hall, and sette at libertie.

A mylners sonne counterfeated to be K. Edward the 6

Execution

The fyrst of Julye John Bradforde was burned in smithfielde.

An. reg. 3

The xii. day of August was a terrible fight on the sea, betwene Dutchmen and Frenchmen, nere vnto Romney marshe, where as .xi. shippes were brente and sonke, that is, vi. frenche shyppes, and fyue great hulkes, and certayne hulkes taken by the Frenchemenne

The fourth day of September kyng Phillip passyng out of England arriued at Calice, and wente to Brussels in brabant to visite the emperour his father.

The beginning of October fel such rayn, that for the space of vi. daies men mought row with boates in saint Georges field, the water came into west min

ye waters.

ter hall, and there stoode halfe a yarde deepe. Also into the palaice of Westmynster, and into Lambeth churche, that men might row aboute the churche with a whirrie.

The.xvi.day of October doctour Ridley, and doctour Latimer were burned at Oxenford.

Anno, M.3 P.2

Wil.Garret, habberdasher } W { Thomas Lee, Jo.Macham } S 1555

In October and Nouember a parliament was holden in the which ye quene yelded vp vnto the spirituall men, the fyrst fruites and tenthes of all bishoprikes benefites, & ecclesiastical liuing before the end of this parliament dyed Stephen Gardiner Chancellor of England on the ix day of Nouember, and was buried at Winchester in his place was appoynted doctor Heath archbyshop of Yorke

Philpot was burned the.xviii.daye of Nouember. Executio

The iiii. day of Marche appered a blasing sterre, and continued the space of xii.dayes A blasin sterre

William Fetherston who before had named him selfe to be King Edwarde, now sayd, he had of late sene & spoken

with

with king Edward, for the whiche he
was drawen to tiborne, & ther hanged
ecution and quartered the xiii. day of Marche.

The xxi. day of March D. Cranmer archbishop of Canterbury was burned at Oxforde: and the same day the lorde Cardinal Poole song his fyrst masse at Grenewich in the fryers Churche: on sonday next folowyng hee was consecrated archbishop of Cantorburye, at the sam friers church with great solemnitie: and on the feast of the annunciation of our lady, he was stalled at Bow churcheyarde in Cheape.

On Palmesondaye euen beynge the 28. of Marche, part of the prison house of Newgate at London was burnt by casualtie of fyre.

A conspiracie was made by certaine
spiracie persons in Englande, whose purpose
was to haue robbed the quenes Eschequer, to the entent they might be hable to mainteyne war against the Quene This matter was vttred by one of the conspiracie: whereby Udall. Throgmorton, Peckham, Daniel, and Stan
ecution. ton wer apprehended for the same, and
diuers other fled into France

The xxviii. day of Aprill, Throgmorton, and Richard Udal wer drawen to

Tyborne

Tyborne, and there hanged and quartered. The xix. of May Stanton was likewise executed at tyborne. The viii daye of June one Rossy, Dedike, and Bedle were also drawen to Tiborne, and hanged and quartered.

The xxvii. daye of June were xiii. persons brent at Stratford the Bowe for matters of religion,

The vii daye of July Henry Peckhā and John Daniel were hanged and headed at the tower hill. An. reg.

Anno. M. 4. P. 3.

syr Tho. Ofley marchaunt taylour	M	William Harper John white	S	1556

About this tyme began the burning feuers and other strange deseases wherof died many olde persons, so that in London ther died from the last of Nouember in Anno. 1555. unto the last of December in Anno. 1556 vii. Aldermē whose names wer Henry Herdson, syr Richard Dobbes late maior, syr willīā Laxon late maior, syr Henrye Hüblethorn late maior, syr John Champneis blynde late maior. syr John Oliffe late sheriffe, and syr John Gresham late Maior. Seuen aldermand ceased in London

The 16. of December a smith beinge

arrai

arraigned at Newgate thruste a knife into the syde of his felowe prisoner, who gaue witnes agaynst him, so that he was in great peril of death thereby, for the which act his hand being strike of his body was hanged on a new gib=bet set vp for ye purpose: ye sametime the keper of Newgate was arraigned and endited for that the sayde prisoner had weapon aboute hym, and his handes loose whiche oughte to haue ben boūd

The iiii. of January a shyp passing before Grenewiche (the courte beynge ther) shotte of her ordinance, and one piece beyng charged with a pellette of stone was shot into the court but than=kes be vnto god it did no hurt: but pas=sed through the walles

n ambas=
ador from
ascouie.

The xxvii. day of February an am=bassador came to London from the em=peror of Cattay, Moscouie, and Russe=land: who was honorably met and re=ceiued at Totēham by the marchantes venturers of London, ridynge in vel=uet coates and chaynes of gold, and by them cōducted to the barres of Smith=fielde, and there receiued by the lorde Maior of London, with the aldermen and sheriffs: and so by them conueyde through the Citie, vnto mayster Di=mokes place in Fanchurche streete,

where

where he lodged untill the xii of May next folowyng, at the whiche tyme hee toke his iourney to Grauesend, & ther toke shippyng with the primrose, and iii other shippes to sayle to Moscouie

The lord Sturton murthered two men: and for the same was arraigned and condemned at Westminster: hee was conueyed through London to Salisbury, and there hanged with iiii. of his seruants, the vi. day of March.

A murder

Execution

Kyng Philip, who had ben in Flanders to take possession of the lowe countreys, in Marche retourned into England, and the. xxii daye he passed through London, beynge acompanyed with the Quene, and the nobles of the realm, But because great trouble was toward betwene him and the king of France, he taried not long here: but ỹ third of July next folowyng, passynge the seas agayne into Flaunders made great prouision for warre agaynst the Frenche kyng. The Quene in her husbands quarel sent ouer an army of one thousand horsemen. iiii. thousand footemē ii. M. pioners, to ayd king Philip wherof ỹ erle of Pēbroke was general

Saincte Quent in

The. xxiiii. daye of Aprill Thomas Stafford and other englishmen to the

Scarborough c[astel] taken

number of xxxii. persons comyng out of Fraunce, toke the castel of Scarborough, which they enioyed .ii. days and then were taken, and broughte to London where on the xxviii. daye of May the said Thomas Stafford was beheaded at the Tower hyl: and upon the morowe were thre of his company drawen to Tyborne, and there hanged and quartered.

This yere on ÿ .xv. day of July dyed the lady Anne of Cleue at Chelsey, & was buried at Westmin. ÿ 8 of August

The x. daye of Auguste were taken of Fraunce the cheefest capitaynes that the Frenche kynge had, as foloweth:

The duke of Montmorency Constable of Fraunce, and his sonne called Monsieur de Meru, the Duke of Monpencier, the Duke of Longueuile, the Mareshall of S. Andrewe, the Ringraue Coronal of the Almaines, Roche du Maine, the Conte of Roche foucault. The Vicount of Touraine, the Baron of Curton, the prince of Mantua besyde many gentylmen and capitaynes

The xvii day of Auguste was taken the towne of S. Quintin by king Phillip, with the help of englyshmen

This

This yeare before harueste, wheate was solde for iiii. marke the quarter. Malt at foure and forty shyllynges: Beanes at fortye shyllynges: Rye at forty shyllynges the quarter and pease at xlvi shillinges. viii. d. But after haruest, wheate was sold for v. s. the quarter: malt at vi. s. viii. d. rye at iii. s iiii. d. and in the countreye, wheate was solde for iiii. s the quarter: malte for iiii. s. viii. d. and in some place, a bushel of rye for a pound of candels whiche was iiii. d.

Dearthe & plentie of corne in one yeare.

Anno. M. 5. P. 4

Thomas Curteys fishmoger } M { Richarde Malarie James Altam } S 1557.

The fyrst of January the frenchmen came to Calaice with a great army, & layd seige therunto: and within iiii. or v days were maisters therof: and shortly after wan all the pieces on that syde the sea.

Calice lo

The Frenche Kynge also inuaded Flanders, and spoiled and brent Dunkirke, before king Phillip could come to the rescue: but before the Frenchemen returned out of Flaunders the Flemmynges and the englyshe ships meting with them vpon the sandes be

twene

twene Dunkirke and graueline slewe of them a great numbre.

John caius doctor of phisik aboute this tyme, for ye encrease of studentes in good litterature, & ye loue he bare to gonuell halle in cambridge in the whiche he was brought vp, became ye seconde founder & called it gonwell & caius colledge.

Gonwell caius colledge

This winter the quartene agues continued in like maner, or more vehemently then they had don the last yere wherthroughe dyed so many priestes that a great number of parishes in dyuers places of this realme were vnserued.

An reg. 6

Execution

This yere in June were vii burned at one stake in Smithfield, and in July were sixe burned at Braintforde.

Anno.M.D.L.5

1558	Sir Thomas Lee Mercer	M	John Halse Rich. Champion	S

Kyng Phillippe being absente out of this realme, Quene Mary beyng dangerously syche ended her lyfe, the xvii. day of Nouember, when she had reigned v yeres.iiii.monethes and xi days

The

¶ The same day dyed Cardinall Poole, and a lyttell before two of her physitions, and dyuers byshops and noble men, whom the quene estemed greatly.

Quene Elizabeth.

Anno regni.1.

Lizabeth oure moste
gracious & soueraigne 1558
lady to the great com-
fort of Englande, was
with full consent pro-
claymed Quene the
xvii. daye of Nouem-
ber, in the yere 1558. Not longe after
she came from Hatfielde in Hertford-
shire, vnto the Charterhouse in London: and went from thens to ÿ tower
where she remained vntil the xiiii. day
of January folowing at which tyme
the Londoners hauinge made sumpteous prouision she passed throughe ÿ
citie to her palaice at Westminster, shewyng very comfortable & gentil coun
tenance vnto ÿ people the next day folowynge, her grace was crowned in
Saint Peters church at Westminster

by

by doctor Oglethorpe bysh. of Carlile.

The report of this was very ioyfull to suche as in Quene Maries tyme for religiō sake fled into Germany, and other countreys wherupon they nowe shortly returned home agayne.

Parliamēt

The twenty daye of Januarye, beganne a Parliamente at Westmynster: And in this Parliamente, the Fyrste fruites and Tenthes were restored to the Crowne, and also the supreme gouernemente ouer the state Ecclesiasticall: lykewise the booke of common prayer and administration of the sacramentes in our vulgare tonge was restored.

Shortely after the quenes maiestie appointed a conference or disputation to be had at westminster churche, concerninge matters of religion but the matter came to none effect.

The vii. of Aprill was a ioyfull peace proclaymed betwixt our souerain lady Elisabeth quene of England and Henry the Frenche kyng.

At the feast of John Baptist, the seruice in the mother tongue was fully established throughout this realme, and the Masse with other Latine Seruice was cleane abolyshed.

Aboute

About Bartholomewtide the wardens of churches in Lōdon with their persons and ministers, broughte forth the Roodes and other images of their churches, and brent them before their churche doores.

Images burned.

Anno reg. 1.

Sir Wil. Hewet, clothworker	M	Tho. Lodge Roger Martin	S	1559

Many men of warre were conueyde out of Fraunce into Scotland: wherby it was suspected, that they woulde sodeinly inuade this realme, wherupon the Quenes maiestie sent the Duke of Norffolke towardes Scotlande, as generall, and the lorde Grey of Wylton beynge lieutenaunt, entred Scotlande with a sufficient power to ioyne with the Scottes and Frenchemen. And in the ende her grace sente sir Williā Cicill knyght, her maiesties principal secretarie with maister doctour wotton to treate with the Frenchmen, who by their wisedomes enforced the Frenchmen to depart, to the greate quietnesse bothe of Englande and Scotland.

An. reg. 2. The maior of London begynneth his yeare the 18. daye of October, whiche is in the firste yere of the quenes maiesties reigne. And the quenes second yeare beginneth on the. 17. day. of Nouember folowyng.

The. v. day of July through shoting of a gonne, whiche brake in the house of one Adrian Arten a Duchman in

ouses blo- crooked lane, and settyng fire on a fir-
en vp in kyn & a barell of gounpouder. xiiii. hou-
ñes lane ses were cleane blowen downe, there
were slaine. xx. persons men & wemen,
and diuers other sore hurt and bruised.

ase mo- This yere on Michelmas euen be-
es called fore noone, it was published by proclamation, that the teston of the best sorte
beynge marked with the porteculeys
should then forthwith be taken for. iiii.
d. ob. and the second sorte beynge marked with the greyhound for. ii. d. q. the
third and worst sort not beyng marked
with one of those markes afore named
not to be taken for any value: the three
ew coy- peny pece whiche was coyned for. iiii.
s. pence shoulde be but. i. d. ob. the. ii. d.
pece for. i d. &c. And shortly after, her
grace restored vnto al her subiects fine
and pure sterlyng money, both of gold
and syluer, for their corrupte and base
coyn, callyng in the same to her maiesties myntes, accordynge to the rates
before mencioned.

Anno. 2.

Sir Wil. Chester draper. } M { Thomas Roe Christoph. Draper. } S

1560

n. reg. 3. The. xxi. daye of Marche, a notable
grammer schoole was founded by the
maister

maister, wardeyns, and assistentes of the right worshypfull company of the marchant taylours of the citie of London in the parishe of Saint Laurence Pounteney.

A gramer schole by marchaunt taylers.

The .x. day of April was one Willi. Geffrey whipped from the Marshalsey in Southwarke to Bedlem withoute byshops gate of Lōdon, for that he professed one John Moore to bee Christe: and on his head, and aboute the carte were set papers, wherein was written as foloweth: William Geffrey, a most blasphemous heretike, denying Christ our Sauior in heauen. The sayd Geffrey beyng stayde at Bedlem gate, the Marshals officers caused John More to be brought foorthe, who was after tyed to the cart, and whypt an arowes shote from Bedlem where at the last he confessed Christ to be in heauen, & himselfe to be a synful man.

One saynyng him selfe to be Christ.

More was sent again in to Bedlem & William Geffrey to the Marshalseye, wher they had layne prisoners neghe a yere & a halfe before that tyme, the one for professyng himselfe to be Christ, the other a desciple of the same Christ.

The .iiii. daye of June beynge wednesday betwene .iiii. and .v. of ye clocke in

Poules stiple a fyre.

in the after noon e, the steple of Paules in London, being fiered by lightnynge brast foorth as it dyd seme to the beholders. ii. or thre yardes beneth the crosse and so brent rounde about in the same place, that the top with the crosse fell of, & lighted on the south syde of Poules church, the spire brent downwarde so terreblye and vehementlye, that within lesse space then. iiii. howers, the same steple and all the roofes of the same churche were consumed to ashes: which was a lamentable sight, and pitifull remembrance to the beholders therof.

Anno. 3.

1561	Sir Wil. Harper mar. tai.	M	Humf. Baskeuile Alexā. Auenon	S

The. xv. day of Nouember, a proclamacion was made for the restoryng diuers small peces of siluer money, as the pece of. vi. d. iiii. d. iii. d. ii. d. & i. d. thre halfpeny, & thre farthynges. And all forain coynes forbyden to be currant within this realme: as well gold as syluer, except two sortes of crownes of golde, the one was the Frenche crowne, & the other a Flemish crowne.

i. reg. 4. This fourthe yeare in England were many

many monstrous byrths, as in March a mare brought foorth a foale with one body being in good proportion, & two heads, hauing as it were a longe tayle growing out right like a horn betwene the same two heades. Also a sow farrowed a pig with .4. legs like vnto ẏ armes of a mã child with handes & fingers diffigured. &c. In April a sow farrowed a pig ẏ had 2. bodies. 8. fete, but one head, many calues & lambes were monstrous, and one calf had a coller of skinne growing about the necke, lyke to a double ruffe, whiche to the beholders semed strange and wonderfull. Mõstrou birthes.

The. 20. day. of May a chyld was born at Chichester in Sussex. The head armes and legs like vnto anotomy, the breast, and belye very monstrous byg, from the nauill, as it were a longe string hanging: about the necke a great coller of fleshe and skyn growyng like the ruffes of a shirt or neckerchief comming vp about the eares pleytinge or folding. &c.

In September the Quenes Maiestie addressed a band of her subiectes to the towne of Newhauen in Normandye: who were embarked at Portesmouth, because that hauen is moste apte for poꝛtation to that place. Upon whose arriuall the townes men and inhabitantes ioyfully surrendꝛed them selues and the towne into the possession of the Quenes Maiestie, whiche was kepte by Englyshmen frō September.1562. to the.29.daye of July then nexte folowyng, which was in the yeare.1563. the gouernour of whiche bande was the righte honoꝛable the Earle of Warwike, who with the capitaynes seruyng there (which were of great experience) and souldiours trayned by the to knowledge of seruice, together with parte of the olde appꝛoued garrison of Barwike, dyd at that time both manfullye defende the piece, and valiauntly encountered by sundꝛy skyrmishes, and conflictes with the countie Ringraue and hys bande, the moste parte wherof, were happelye atchieued, to the greate ouerthrowe of the aduersaries parte, and singuler commendations of ours.

Anno.4.

1562. syr Tho. Lodge grocer } M { William Alleyn Richard Chamberlaine. } S

Anno.5. When the Frenchmen with huge armies assēbled out of al parts of France

to re

to recouer the place of passage: the stop
ping wherof, by our power, was the
double wo of theyr common wealthe,
there bred through the heate of time, &
putrifactiō of the ayre: a miserable and
infortunate plague emonge our men,
which maruelously increased with the
death of diuers of the best captains and
souldiors, wher withall there folowed
a cruel & quicke siege, wherat was pre
sent the Constable, and the beste tried
number of warlike souldiors within
the whole countrey of France. The ma
rishes were made passable and firme
ground: which by men of great experience was thought impossible And with
common help the Canons wer placed,
the castel and wals wer battered, & sun
dry breaches made beyond expectation
How be it they were rewarded by our
gonners to their great terror and anoyance. The erle of Warwike with ye rem
nant of our captaines and souldiors in
couragious order, standing at the seuerall breaches ready to defend theyr as-
saultes: which perceiued by the enemy
they caused theyr trompets to sound the
blast of emparle, that composition of ei
ther part might be made to auoyde the
imminent slaughter & effusiō of blood.

This offer semed not unmete, both parties concluded, the towne was deliuered the. 29. day of July, and all the english licensed to depart.

This yere as ye haue hard, the plage of pestilence being in the toun of New hauen, & many souldiors infected with the same returnyng into England, the infection therof increased, being before that begonne in diuers partes of this realme, but especially the citie of Lōdō was so infected therewith, that in the same whol yere, that is to say, from the first of January. 1562. untill the last of December. 1563. there dyed in the Citie and liberties therof (conteinyng 108. parishes) of all diseases. xx. M. iii. C. lxxii. so that there dyed of the plague (beyng part of the number before named) xvii. M. iiii. C. and. iiii. persons. And in the out parishes adioynyng to the same citie, beyng. xi. parishes died of all diseases in the whole yeare aforesaid. iii. M. ii. C. lxxx. and viii. persons, and of them of the plage beyng a part of the said numbre last before named. ii. M. vii. C. xxxii. so that the whole totall summe of those that died of al diseases in the holle yere, as well within the citie of London and liber-

108. parys- es in London.

liberties of the same, as in the out parishes adioynyng was.xxiii.M.vi.C.lx.& of them of the plage died in all.xx.M.i.C.xxxvi.

The.viii.daye of July in the mornyng through tempest of lightenynge and thunder, a woman with.3.kyne were slayne in the couent garden nere to charyng crosse, many other such like hurts wer don in England by the same tempest.

This yere proclamation was made at Anwarpe and other places that no no Englishe shype, with any clothes shoulde come into any place of those lowe contryes, this restraint was (as they sayde) for daunger of the plague whiche was that time in London and other places of England e, as for oure woles they made no restreynt therof, but woulde receyue them gladlye, but the Quenes Maiestie through the sute of our marchant aduenturers wold not suffer anye wolle to passe towardes, Bruges in flanders, but caused ẏ woll flete to be discharged, and oure clothes flete to be sent to Emden in East Frieslande, about Easter next folowynge in Anno.1564.

This yere for so muche as the pesti-

stilence

lence was so hote in the citie of London there was no term kept at Michelmas. To be short, the pore citisens of London were this yere plagued with a treble plague, as with the pestilence, scarsitie of money, & derth of vitaels: the myserie wherof, were to long here to write, no doubt the pore remēber it.

The tolde plague.

In September was an earth quake in Lincolne and Northamptonshiere.

Anno. 5.

1563

Sir John White grocer	M	Edward Bāks Rouland Haiwarde	S

No Maiors feast.

By reason of the plage before sayde: this Maior kept no feaste at the Guildhall: Also he toke his othe at the uttermost gate of the tower of London.

In December from the first to the .xij dave was suche great lightnyng: thunder, & especially on the day of the epyphany at night from .viii. of the clocke tel it was past .ix. that the like had not bene sene in many yeres.

In this moneth of December was driuen on the shore at Grymsby in Lincolneshire, a greate and monstrous fyshe, beyng in length .xix. yardes, his tayle .xv. fote brode,

This yeare thankes be geuen to god was

was a peaceable yere, and the plague of pestilence well ceassed in London: neuerthelesse for feare therof, Hillarye terme was kept at Hertford castel, beside Ware.

The. xxiii. daye of Aprill was a ioyful peace poclaimed with the sounde of trompettes betwene Englande and Fraunce. An. reg. 6

This yeare through the earnest suite of the armorers, there was on the Vigile of Sainct Peter, a watche in the Citie of London, whiche dyd onelye stand in the hyghest stretes of Cheape, Cornhill, and so foorth towardes Algate: whiche was to the commons of the same citie (for the moste parte) as chargeable as when in times paste, it was most commendably done, wheras this being to very small purpose, was of as small a number wel liked. Watche o S. Peter euen.

The. v. daye of August the Quenes Maiestie in her progresse came to the vniuersitie of Cambridge, and was of all the studentes (beynge inuested according to þ degrees which they had taken in the schooles) honorably & ioyfullye receyued in the Kyngs college, wher she did lye durynge her continuaunce in Cambridge: The dayes of her abode were paste in scolasticall exercises of Philosophie, Phisike, and diuinitie the nights in comedies and tragedies set foorth partly by the whole vniuersitie, & partely by the studentes of the kings colledge. At the breaking vp of the diuinitie act, beynge on wednesdaye, the ix. of August on the whiche day she rode through the towne, and viewed the colledges, those goodly (auncient Monumentes of Kyngs of Englande her noble predecessours) she made within Saint Maries churche a notable oration in Latin, in the presence of the hole learned vniuersitie, to the studentes great comfort. The next daye she went forward on her progresse to Fynchinbroke by Huntyngton.

The. xx. daye of September arose so great a fludde in the ryuer of Thames, that many marysys and medowes were drowned, to the greate lose of manye throughe drownynge of their cattayle, and other wyse.

The second day of October in the after noone was a solempne obsequie kept at saint Paules churche in London, for Fardinando the Emperor, late beyng departed out of this mortal life, and

and lykewyse the morowe next after in the forenone.

In October many fyerie impressions were sene in the ayre and especially on the .vii. daye at night, from .viij. of the clocke tyll some what past .ix. All the North partes of the Element semed to be couered with flames of fyre procedyng from the Northeast and Northwest, towardes the mids of the firmament, where for the moste parte of an hower it stayed, and desendyd Westward: and all the same nyght (beynge the next after the change of the Mone) semed nyghe as light as it had ben day.

Anno. 6.

Richard Malary mercer	M	Edwarde Jackman / Lyonell Ducket	S	1564 An. reg. 7.

The .xx. daye of Nouember in the mornyng about vi. of the clock through negligence of a mayden with a candell, the snuffe fallynge in an hundred pound weight of gunpouder, three houses in Bucklers bury, were sore shaken, the maiden was so burnt, that she died therof within .ij. dayes after. It is to be noted, that if this pouder had layne in a lower part of the house, as it lay in a garret, it had done muche more harm: Wher-

Houses shaken with gunpowder

Wherfore I aduise men to loke warely to suche ware.

The.xxi.day of December being S. Thomas day began a frost, which continued tyll the.iii. day of January: on new yeres euen, people went ouer the Thames on the yce, & along the Thames from London bridge to Westminster, and great numbers of people, plaid at the footeball, on newe yeres daye, beyng monday, on tuesday and wednesday diuers gentlemen & others, set vp prikes on the Thames, and shotte at the same. And the people both men and women went on the Thames, in greater numbres then in any strete in London: On wednesday at night it began to thawe but men went ouer and along the Thames on thursday at night: but on frydaye beyng the fyfth daye of January at night, was no Ice on the Thames to be sene: but that al men mought rowe ouer and along the same, it was so sodenly consumed: which soden thaw caused such great fluddes and hye waters, that it bare downe many bridges and houses, and drowned many people.

On newe yeres daye Proclamation was made in London by the Quenes commaundement, that the restraint, before

before sayd betwene England & Flanders and other thinges done synce the first yere of her Maiesties reigne touchyng the premisses shold be suspended for a tyme: and therupon a diette, by cōsent of both realmes was appointed to be kept in Bruges for these matters and diuers other greefes of the subiectes on both parties

The. 26. day of January beyng Fryday at night wer two tides in the space of. iii. houres at London, on the morow was likewise. ii. in the mornyng, & . ij. at night, on sonday being the. 18. day of January were likewise. ij. tides in the morning, and at night but one.

eyght tides in. ii. nightes & a day

The. iij. daye of Februarye, Henry Stuert Lord Dernley, a yonge man aboue the age of. xix. yeres, eldest sonne of Mathew Erle of Lyneux, hauynge obteyned licence of the Quenes Maiestie, toke his iourney toward Scotlād, accōpanied with. v. of his fathers men: wher whē he came, was honorably receiued, & lodged in ẏ kings lodgings: & in the somer folowing maried Mary Quene of Scotland.

About this time, for the Quenes Maiestie were chosen & sent in commission to Bruges, ẏ honorable Lorde Montague, knyght of the order of the garter, master Doctor Wotton one of the Quenes Maiesties honorable Counsaile, master Doctor Haddon, one of the maisters of Requestes to her hyghnes with other in commission for the same, master Doctor Awbrey was chosen for the Marchants aduenturars of Englande, they came to Bruges in Lēt the yere. 1565. And there continued tyl Michaelmas, and then was the dyet prolonged tyll Marche. Anno. 1566. & all the commissioners aboue sayd came home into Englande.

The. xxii. daye of Aprill the Ladye Margaret Countesse of Lineux was commaunded to kepe her chamber at the White hall, & the. xxii. daye of June she was conuaide prisoner to the tower of London.

This yere on Saint Peters euen at night was the lyke standyng watche in London as was the same nighte. xii. monethes.

Great tempest.

The. xvi. daye of July about. vi. of the clocke at night, began a terrible tēpest of lightnynge and thunder, with shoures of hayle, which lightning and thūder continued vntil. iii. of the clock on the next mornyng In the which tempest much harme was doone in and about,

about Chelmsford in Essex, as by destroyng of fiue hundred acres of corne, the beatinge downe of all the glasse windowes on the East syde of the sayd towne, and of the West and south sides of the churche, the beating of the tyles of their houses, throwing downe diuers barnes and chymneys with the batilmentes of theyr church. &c. The hayle stones being measured, were found to be vi. ynches about. At the same time was much harme done in many other places of this realme, as at Ledes, at Cranbroke, at Douer in Kent. &c.

This yere Cristopher prince and margraue of Baden, with the Lady Cicily his wife syster to the Kinge of Swethland arriued at Douer and the xi. day of September, they came to Lōdō, and wer lodged at the erle of Bedfordes place, nere vnto Iuie bridge, where within .iiii. dayes after, shee was deliuered of a mannechylde: whiche the laste of September was baptised in the Quenes maiesties chapel of Whitehall The Quenes maiestie in her owne person beyng Gods mother gaue the name Edwardus fortunatus.

The marques of Baden.

1565. Sir Rich. Champion Draper } W { John Riuers Jam. Hawes } S

The .xi. of Nouember, the right honorable, Ambrose Earle of Warwike, maryed Anne eldest daughter to the Earle of Bedforde: for the honour and celebration of whiche noble mariage a goodlye chalenge was done at the tylt and barriers at Westminster. And at x. of the clocke at nighte the same day, a valiant seruisable man, called Robert Thomas Master gonner of England, desirous also to honour the feast and mariage day, in consideration the sayd erle of Warwike was general of thordinance within her Maiesties realme & dominions, made three great traines of chembres, which terriblye yelded forth the nature of their worke to the greate astonishment of diuers, who at the fyrynge of the second was vnhapely slayne by a pece of one of the chambers to the greate sorowe and lamentation of all those that loue theyr country and defence of the same.

Anno regni.8. The .xxviii. day of December there rose a greate storme & tempest of winde,

Great wind. by whose rage the Thames and Seas

ouerwhelmed manye persons, and the gret gates at the west end of S. Pauls churche in London (betwene whiche standeth the brasenpylor) were through the force of the winde then in the Western part of the world blowen open.

In January Mounsieur Rambuley a knight of thorder in Fraunce was sent ouer into England by the French king Charles the.ix. of that name, with the order of saint Mighell, who at Windsor was stalled in the behalf of the said Frenche king with the knighthoode of the most honorable order of the Garter and the.xxiiii. of January in the chapel of her maiesties pallace of Whitehall. the sayd Monsieur Rambuley inuested Thomas duke of Norfolk & Robert erle of Leicester, with the sayd order of saint Mighell. Knightes of thorder.

The Marquis of Baden and the Lady Cicylie his wife sister to ẏ king of Swethen, who came into this lāde in the moneth of September last paste as before is declared, being thē by the Quenes speciall appointment at their arriual honorably receiued by the lord Cobham an honorable Baron of this Realme, and the Lady his wife one of the Quenes Maiesties priuie Cham- The marques of Baden.

ber, now in the moneth of Aprill Anno 1566. departed the same againe the Marques a fewe dayes before his wife being both conducted by a lyke personage ye lord of Aburgauenny to Douer. The houses in Cornhil which were boughte at the Citizens charges and in Februarye by Abell manne cried to be solde, were in Aprill and Maye next following by such as had bought them taken downe and carried awaye. After the ground being made plane at ye chargs also of ye citie, possessiō therof by certē Aldermē was geuen to ye right worshipful sir Thomas Greshā knig Agent to the Quenes highnes in tha place to buylde a Burse or place for Marchauntes to assemble in, at his owne proper charges, who on the vii daye of June in the after noone Layd the fyrst stone of the foundation (being Bricke) and forthwith the workemen folowed vpon the same with suche di ligence that by the moneth of Nouember in anno 1567 the same Burse was couered with slate.

The burs in Cornhil

The Commissioners before nam appointed for the matters of Flanders keping their diet at Bruges agreed to referre the whole matter to the Prin res on both sides. And yf they can not agree, then the Marchaunts to haue xl dayes to repaire home with their marchaundise. And in the meane tyme all thinges to stande as they be nowe.

Our Commissioners departed from Bruges about the xxvi. daye of June, thensse toward the spawe.

The xxxi. of August the Quenes Maiestie in her progresse cam to thuniuersitie of Oxforde, and was of al the studentes, whiche had loked for her comming thither ij yeares, so honorably & ioyfully receaued, as eyther theyr loyalties towards ÿ Quenes Maiestie or therpectation of their frendes did require. Concerning orders in disputations, and other Academicall exercises they agreed muche with those whiche thuniuersitie of Cambridge had vsed ij. yeares before. Comedies also and tragedies were sett fourth by the vniuersitie, and played in Christes Churche, where the Quenes highnes lodged. Amongest the whiche, the Comedie intituled Palemon and Arcet, made by maister Edwards of the Q. Chappell, had such tragicall successe, as was very lamentable. For at that tyme by the fall of the syde wall of a

The Quenes progresse to Oxforde.

payre of stayres, and great presse of the multitude iij. men were slaine. the. v. of September after disputations, the Quenes maiesties, at the humble suite of certeyne her nobilitie, and the King of Spaynes Embassadour, made a brief oration in Latin to the vniuersitye, but so wise and pithie, as England maye reioyce, that it hath so learned a Prince, thuniuersities maye triumphe that they haue so noble a patronesse, and forrein Countryes maye wonder to behould such excellence in that sexe. The vj. of September after dinner her grace comming frõ Christs Churche ouer Carfox, and so to Saint Maries (the scholers standing in order according to their degrees euen to the Easte gate) certaine doctours of the vniuersitie did ride before her in their scarlet gownes and hoods, and masters of Arte in blacke gownes and hoods. The Maior also with certein of his bretherne did ride before her in scarlet to thend of Magdalene Bridge, where their liberties ended: but the doctours and Masters went forward stil to Shotouer a myle and more out of Oxforde, because their liberties extended so farre, and there after orations

made

made her highnes with thanckes to the whole universitie, bad them farewell, and rode that night to Rycot.

Anno. 8.

Sir Christo. Draper Ironmong.	M	Rich. Lāb. Ambr. Ni. John lāgley	S	1566.

The mightie and valiant Capitaine Edward Randolffe Esquier, Lewetenaunt of the ordinaunce, and Colonell of M. footemen, in September laste past, was with his band imbarked at Bristoll, and with in fewe dayes after landed at Knockferyus in the North parts of Irelande, and from thence by water to a place called Derry, by which passeth the River of Loughefoile, ther the sayde Colonel in shorte space fortified to the greate anoyance of John Onell: and by great foresyght and experiēce guarded himself & his charge, tyll the sayd Onell (to hinder and disturbe his abode there) the xij. of November arrived with a greate army of Kerne galowglasses and horsemen, with whome the saide Capitaine Randolfe incountred, and him there so discomfited as after that conflict he durste never approche the Quenes power, & to his perpetuall fame, the saide Capitaine

Souldiours transported int Ireland.

layne by reason of his bolde and hardy onset, that daye lost his lyfe.

Solempne christeninge in Scotland.

Charles Jamys the sixte of that name, sonne to Henry Stuert Lord of Darnley and Mary, Kinge and Quene of Scottes was borne in Edeburgh Castell the xix. of June last past, and the xvii. daye of December this saide yere solempnelye christened at Sterlinge, whose godfathers at the Christeninge were Charles Kinge of Fraunce, and Philibert Duke of Sauoye, and oure soueraigne Ladye Quene Elizabeth was the godmother, who gaue a fount of gold curiouslye wrought and enameled, wayenge 333. ounces amounting in valewe to the somme of M. xlviii. li. xix.s.

Kynge of Scottes murdred.

On shrouemondaye nexte followinge beinge the x. of Februarie in the morninge Henry stuart Lorde of Darneley before named kinge of Scottes by Scots in Scotland was shamfully murthered, the reuenge wherof remaineth in the mightie hand of God.

The xxii. of Febuarye the Ladye Margaret douglesse Countesse of Lyneaux, mother to the sayde Kynge of Scottes was discharged oute of the Tower of London.

With

With in the space of x. monethes last passed died vii. Aldermen of London the first Edwarde Bancks, who deceassed ye ix. of July an. 1566. Richard Chamberlayne late shriue, Syr Martin Bowes, Syr Richard Malorie, Syr William Hewett, and Syr Thomas Whyte late Maiors, & then Richard Lambert one of the Shriues for that yere the iiii. of April Anno. 1567. For him succeded John Langley goldsmith who served fourth til Mighelmas nexte followinge that the newe Shriues entred.

7. Aldermen deseased.

The. xxii of April. by greate misfortune of fyre in the towne of Osestry in Wales xvi. miles from Shrewesbury to the nomber of ii. C. houses that is to saye vii. skore within the walles & iii. score withoute in the Suburbes, besides clothe, corne, cattel, and many both men and women were consumed, whiche fyre continewing two houres began at ij. of the clocke in the after noone, and ended at iiii, to the greate merualynge of many, that so greate a spoyle and distruction in so short time should happen.

Osestry brent.

The xxiiii daye of Aprill beinge thursdaye the Sarieauntes feaste was kepte

Seriaunts feaste.

Kepte

kepte at Greys Inne neare vnto Holborne and there were at that tyme made vij. newe sergeants of the lawe.

Wilnall in Suffolke brent.

The .xvii. daye of mey by casualtie of fyre in the town of Wilnal in Suffolke viii. mil from newe market, to the nomber of xxxvii houses besides barnes, stables and suche lyke were consumed in the space of ij. houres, these things be here noted for thy warning gentle reader.

Watche at midsomer.

This yere on Saint Johns euen at night being the lyke standyng watche in the Cite of London as on saint Peter euen in the yere last before passed, certen Constables of euery warde who were very well appointed with the handsomest of theyr watchmen cleane armed in Corselets and also diuerse pretye showes done at the charges of yong mē in certen parishes awaighted on the Lorde Maior, he ryding from the Guildhall throughe Cheape to Algate and back againe, whiche beinge like to make a very handsome syght, was for lake of good order in kepinge their arraye muche defaced.

Coronatiō in Scotland.

The xix of July Charles Jamys the yoūg prince of Scotlād, after a sermō made by John Knokes, was crowned

kynge

King of Scottes at sterling churche, where was redde certen commissions with the Quenes priuie Seale at them for thestablishing of the same, the firste for her resignation of the crowne, and gouernement of the yong Prince her sonne, the seconde to authorise therle of Murry to be regent during his minoritie, the thirde to geue authoritie and power to dei other ioynyng with the saide Earle of Morrey in case he should refuse to exercise the same alone, that is to saye the Duke Chatilerays, therles of of Lenox, Argyle, Atheil, Morton, Glencarne, and Marr, these commissiones beinge ended the byshop of Akelley with ij. superintendents proceded to the Coronation, the earle Morton and Lorde Haime toke othe for the Kyng that he should rule in the faith feare and loue of GOD, to maintaine the religion nowe preached in Scotland, & persecute all aduersaries to the same &c. The whole ceremonie of the Coronation was done in theyr mother tongue, and at that tyme the Quene of Scottes was prisoner at lōghleuen.

Anno

Quone Elizabeth.
Anno. 9.

1567	Roger Martin. Mercer	} M {	Thomas Ramsey William Bond.	{ S

Thus (good reader) I haue brought as thou seest this abridged Summary to these our present dayes, meaning as tyme shall encrease to augment the same, desyringe thee to take these my trauayles in good part, lyke as I haue mente them towardes the.

FINIS.

THe fyrst age from the creation 1.
of Adam, to the floud of Noe,
which continued, yers. 1656.
The seconde from Noe to 2.
Abraham. 292
The thyrd from the byrth of A- 3.
braham, tyll the departyng of Israell
out of Egept, 503
The fourth from the departinge 4.
of Israel out of Egipt, til the building
of the temple, yeres 481
The fyfth from the buildynge of 5.
the temple, til the captiuetye of Babi-
lon. 414
The sixt from the captiuitie of 6.
Babylon tyll the birth of our sauiour
Iesus Christ yeres. 614
The vii. beginnyng at the birth of our 7.
sauiour Iesus Christ, hath continued
til thys presēt yere of our Lord 1567.
and shal last tyl the worldes ende.

The age of the world at the birth of Christe was 3962. The age of the world thys present yere of our Lorde. 1567. is 5529.

FINIS.

Howe a man may iourney from any notable town in England, to the Citie of London: or from London to any notable towne in the same realme.

The way from Walsyngham to London.

Rom Walsingham to Pikna xii. miles
From Picknam to Brādōfery x. mile,
From brandonfery to Newmarket x myle.
From Newmarket to Babram. x. myle.
From Babram to Barkway. xx myle
From Barkway to puchrich vii mile
From Puchriche to Ware v myle.
From Ware to Waltham viii myle.
From Waltham to London. xii. myle.

The way from Barwike to Yorke and so to London.

From

FRō Barwik to belforth xii mile
Frō Belforth to Anwik xii mile
Frō Anwike to Morpit xii mile
Frō morpit to Newcastel xii mi.
Frō Newcastel to Durham. xii mile,
Frō Durhā to Darington xiiii myle.
Frō darengtū to northalertō xiiii mi.
Frō Northalertō to Toplif vii mile.
From Toplife to Yorke xvi. mile.
From Yorke to Tadcaster viii mile
Frō Tadcaster to Wentbridge mile.
Frō Wentbridge to Dācaster viii mi.
Frō Dancaster to Tutford xviii mile.
From Tutford to Newarke x mile.
From Newarke to Grantham x mile
From Granthā to Stanford xvi mile
From Stanford to Stilton xii mile
Frō Stylton to huntington ix. myle.
From hūtington to Roiston xv: mile:
From Royston to Ware xii myle.
From Ware to Waltham viii. myle
From Waltham to London xii. myle

The way from Carnaruan to Chester, and so to London.

Frō Carnaruan to Cōway xxiiij mile
From Cōway to Denbigh xii mile
From Denbigh to Flynt xii myle.
From Flynt to Chester x. myle.

From

Hovve a man may iour-ney from any notable town in England, to the Citie of London: or from London to any notable towne in the same realme.

The way from Walsyngham to London.

Rom Walsingham to Pikuā xii. miles
From Picknam to Brādōfery x. mile.
From brandonfery to Newmarket x myle.
From Newmarket to Babram. x. myle.
From Babram to Barkway. xx myle
From Barkway to puchrich vii mile
From Puchriche to Ware v myle.
From Ware to Waltham viii myle.
From Waltham to London. xii. myle.

The way from Barwicke to Yorke and so to London.

From

FRõ Barwik to belforth xii mile
Frõ Belforth to Anwik xii mile
Frõ Anwike to Worpit xii mile
Frõ morpit to Newcastel xii mi.
Frõ Newcastel to Durham. xii mile,
Frõ Durhã to Darington xiiii myle.
Frõ daringtũ to northalertõ xiiii mi.
Frõ Northalertõ to Toplife vii mile.
From Toplife to Yorke xvi. mile.
From Yorke to Tadcaster viii mile
Frõ Tadcaster to Wentbridge mile.
Frõ Wentbridge to Dãcaster viii mi.
Frõ Dancaster to Tutford xviii mile.
From Tutford to Newarke x mile.
From Newarke to Grantham x mile
From Granthã to Stanford xvi mile
From Stanford to Stilton xii mile
Frõ Stylton to huntington ix. myle.
From hũtington to Roiston xv: mile:
From Royston to Ware xii myle.
From Ware to Waltham viii. myle
From Waltham to London xii. myle

The way from Carnaruan to Chester, and so to London.

Frõ Carnaruan to Cõway xxiiij mile
From Cõway to Denbigh xii mile
From Denbigh to Flynt xii myle.
From Flynt to Chester x. myle.
From

From Chester to Wyche xiiii. mil
From Wyche to Stone xv. mile
From Stone to Lechefield xvi. myle
From Lichfeeld to Colsil. xii myle
From Colsyll to Couentree viii. mile
And so from Couentre to London, as hereafter foloweth.

The waye from Cokermouth to Lancaster, and so to Lōdon.

FRō Cokermouth to Kiswik vi. mi.
Frō Kiswik to Grocener viii mile
From Grocener to Kendale xiiii. mile
From Kendale to Burton vii mile
From burtō to Lancaster viii myles.
From Lancaster to Preston xx. mile
From Preston to Wygam. xiiii myle
From Wygam to Warington. xii. mile
Frō warington to Newcastel xx. mile
From Newcastle to Lichfield xx. mile
from Lichfield to Couentre xx. mile
from Couentre to Dauetre. xiiii. mile
from Dauetre to Tocester. x. mile
frō Tocester to Stony Stratforde. vi. myle.
frō Stony stratford to Brichyl vii mi
from Brichel to Dunstable vii mile
from Dunstable to S albans x mile.
from S Albans to Barnet x. myle.

From Barnet to London x myle

The way from Yermouth to Colchester, and so to London

FRom Yermouth to Beccles viii mi.
from Beccles to Blybour vi. myle
frõ Blybour to Snapbridg viii. mile
frõ Snapbridge to wodbridge viii mi
from Wodbridge to Ipswich v. myle
from Ipswiche to Colchester xii mile
from Colchester to Eastford viii myle
from Eastford to Chelmesford x myle
frõ Chelmesford to Brentwod x myle
from Brentwod to London xii myle,

The way from Douer to London,

FRõ Douer to Cantorbury xii myle
frõ Cãterbury to Siting born xii mi
frõ Sitingborn to Rochester viii mi.
from Rochester to Grauesend v, mile
from Granesend to Datford vi myle
from Datford to London xii myle,

The way from S Buriene in Cornwal to London.

FRõ S Burien to the mount xx mi.
from the mõunt to Thury xii myle
From S, Thury to Bodnam xx mile

from Bodnam to Launston xx myle.
from Launston to Ocomton xv. myle
frō Ocomton to Crokehornwel x mi.
frō Crokehornwel to Exceter x myle
from Excester to Honiton xii myle
from Honiton to charde x myle
from Charde to Crokehorne. vii. mile
frō Crokehorne to Shirborne x mile
frō Shirborn to Shaftesbury x myle
frō Shaftesbury to Salisbury xviii mi.
from Salisbury to Andeuor xv mile.
frō Andeuor to Basingstocke xviii mi
frō Basingstock to Hartford viii. mile
from Hatforde to Bagshot viii myle
from Bagshot to Stanes, viii myles.
from Stanes to London, xv miles

The way from Brystow to London.

FRō Bristow to Marsfelde x myle.
from Marsfeld to Chipnam x mile
frō Chipnā to Marleborow xv. mile
frō Marleborow to Hūgerford x myle
frō Hūgerford to Newberye vii myle
from Newbery to Readyng xv myle
from Readyng to Maidenhead x myle
frō Maidenhead to Colbroke vii mi.
from colbroke to London xv myle.

The

The way from Saynt Dauyd to London

FRom S Dauids to Arford xx myl.
from Arford to Carmerden x myle
from Carmarden to Newton x myle
from Newton to Lanbury x myle.
from Lanbury to Brecknock. xvi myl.
from Brecknocke to Hay x myle.
from Hay to Harford xiiii myle.
from Harford to Roso. c[illegible] myle.
from Roso to Glocester xii myle
from Glocester to Cicester. xv myl
from Cicester to Faryngton xvi myle
from Faringtō to Habington, vii mile
frō Habington to Dorchester vii mil
from Dorcester to Henley xii myle,
from Henley to Maidenhed vii myle
frō Maydenhed to Colbroke vii myle
from Colbroke to London xv myle

The Summarie of Englishe Chronicles.

(Latelye collected and published) abridged and continued til this present moneth of Nouember in the yeare of our Lord GOD.

1567.

By J. S.

Imprinted at London in Fletestrete nere to S. Dunstones church, by Thomas Marshe.

this booke, as foloweth.

KL. [illegible]

iii			
	b	Octa. of Saincte Stephen	1
xi	c	Octa. of Sainct John	2
	d	Octa. of Innocentes	3
xix	e	Deposition of saincte Edward	4
viii	f		5
	g	Transla. Wilhelmi	6
xvi		Lucian priest.	7
v	b	Lewes confessor	8
	c	Paule the first Heremite	9
xiii	d		10
ii	e	Richardus martir	11
	f	Hillarius	12
x	g	Felicis	13
xviii		Archadius martir	14
vii	b	S. Mauritius	15
	c	Saincte Anthonie.	16
xv	d	Prisce virgin	17
iiii	e	Wolstan byshoppe	18
	f	Fabian and Sebastian.	19
xii	g	Agnes virgin.	20
		Vincent martir.	21
i	b	Emerentie	22
	c	Timothe bishop	23
ix	d	Conuersion of S. Paule.	24
	e	Policarpe bishop	25
xvii	f	Julian confessor	26
vi	g	Valerii bishop	27
		Theodore priest	28
xiiii	b	Basileus bishop	29
iii	c	Saturne & victor.	30
			31

KL.

	d	Brigide virgin. Fast.	1
i	e		2
ix	f	Blase bishop	3
viii	g	Gilbert confessor.	4
		Agathe virgin	5
xvi	b	Amandus bishop & confes	6
v	c	Augull bishop	7
	d	Paule bish.	8
xiii	e	Appolline virgin	9
ii	f	Scholastice vir	10
	g	Desiderius bish.	11
x		Dorothe virgin.	12
	b	Wolstane bishop	13
xviii	c	Valentin martir	14
vii	d	Faustine Jouine	15
	e	Julian virgin	16
xv	f	Policronius bishop	17
iiii	g	Symon bishop	18
		Sabin and Julian mar.	19
xii	b	Mildred virgin	20
i	c	[illegible] martyrs.	21
	d	Cathedra Petri	22
ix	e	Fast. Locus bisexti	23
	f		24
xvii	g	Alexander bishop	25
vi		[illegible] priest	26
	b	[illegible]	27
xiiii	c	[illegible] bishop	28

KL,

iii	d	David bishop
	e	Chadde confessor
xi	f	Maurice confessor
	g	Adrian bishop
xix		Foce & Eusebii
viii	b	Victor & victoris
	c	Perpetue & felix
xvi	d	Deposit of Felix.
v	e	Quadraginta mar.
	f	Aggeus prophete
	g	Gorgonius mar.
xiii		Gregorius bishop
ii	b	Theodore martir
x	c	Longius mar.
	d	Cyriace martir
xviii	e	Hilarius bishop.
vii	f	Patrick & Gertrudis
	g	Edward king and confessor
xv		Joseph the husbãd of Mary.
iiii	b	Cuthbert bishop
	c	Benedict abotte
xii	d	Aphrodosius bishop
i	e	Theodore virgin
	f	Pigmeni. Fast,
ix	g	
		Castor martir
xvii	b	Eulalie virgin
vi	c	Victor martir
	d	Augustin mar.
xiiii	e	Quintin mar.
iii	f	[illegible] bishop.

kynge a greuous displeasure. John the brother of kyng Richarde toke on him the kingdome of Englande in his brothers absence.

King Richard restored to the Christians the citie of Joppa, and in many battels put the Turke to great sorow.

Anno. 4.

1192 Nicolas Duke }
Peter Newlay } Balliffes

Kyng Richard [illegible] Cypres with Guye of Lesyngham for the kingdom of Jerusalem, Wherfore the king of England a long time after was called king of Jerusalem.

1193 Roger Duke } An. reg.
Richard Fitz Alyn } Balliffes

King Richarde hauinge knowledge that Philip of Fraunce inuaded Normandy, and that John his brother [illegible]

ma[illegible]

William Fitz Arnold.

John the kinges brother by the setting on of the Frenche king made gret warre [illegible] gthe the castelles of Wendlore, of Notingham, & others. And the Frenche king made strong warre in Normandy.

Robert Beysant } Anno. reg. 7. 1195
Johe le Josue } Bailiffes.

Hubert bishop of Salisbury was by king Richard [illegible] into Englād to haue the guiding therof, and also to treate with the lords & cōmons for the kings deliuerance. The sayd Hubert was by the monkes of Christs church in Cantorbury chosen archebishop.

Gerard de Antelochel } Anno reg. 8 1196
Robert durant. } Bailiffes.

This yere king Richarde was deliuered out of prison for the summe of

one

Founteuerard, his bowels at Carlile, his hart at Roan.

Kyng John.

Anno Regni. i.

IOhn, brother to Richarde afore named, began his
1199 reigne ouer this realm of England the .vi. day of Apryll, in the yeare of our lord. 1199. and deceased in the yere. 1216. the .xix. day of October. He reigned .xvii. yeres. vi. monethes, and .xiii. dais. Of person he was indifferent. But of melancolye and angry complection.

1199 Arnold Fitz Arnold } An. reg. i.
Richard Fits bartilmewe } bailiffes.

Philip king of Fraunce (in the quarell of Arthur duke of Britain, whom certayn of the Lordes had named king of England) made warre vpon kyng John, inuaded Normandy, and tooke from him deuers castels and townes.

iii. s. of euery ploughland.

Kyng John hearyng therof, assembled a counsayle, wherein was graunted to him iii s. of euery plough land through England, beside the subsidy of

fif

the spirituall landes: he sayled into Normandy, where he spent the tyme to his losse and dishonour. But aboute Michelmas a truce was concluded.

This yere was a deuorce betwene king John & his wife, the erle of Glocesters daughter, because of nerenesse of bloude: and after he was maried to Isabel, the daughter of the Erle of Engolesym in Fraunce: by whom he had .ii. sonnes, Henry and Richard, and .iii. daughters, Isabel, Elianor, and Jane. — King John deuorced.

Roger Dorset } An.re.2. 1200
James bartelmew alderma͂ } bailiefes.

This yeare Raynulphe Earle of Chester, by thexample afore shewed by kynge John, lefte his owne wife named Constance, which he before had maried, & wedded one Clemens some saith, he did so to haue issue: but he therwith displesed God so muche, that he would suffer him to haue none issue. 1201

Walter Fitz Ales } An.re.3
Simon de Alderma͂bury. } bailiffs.

This yere in Yorkshyre were sene .v. Moones, one in the east, an other in the Weste, the thirde in the northe, the fourth in the southe, and the fyfthe in the myddes of the other: and went compassing the other .v. times, as it were — Fiue mones in the firmamente

the

the space of an houre, and banished a-
waye.

xxv. gouer-
nours of
the citie.

In this yere were chosen. xxv. of the most substantial and wysest men of the Citie of Londō, to maintayn and kepe the assises of the same Citie, of the whi-che yerely the bailiffs were chosen: and after the Maior and Sheriffes were taken of the same number.

1202 Norman Blundell An. reg. 4.
John de Ely Bailiffes.

Great tem-
pest.

This yere fel excedyng lightnynge, thunders, & other stormes of wynd and rayn with hayl of ye bignes of hen-nes egges: which perished fruit & corn houses, and yong cattell. Also spirites were sene in the ayre, in likenes of fou-les bearyng fire in their bylles, which set fyre on dyuers houses.

Philip of France cōtinually made warre vpon the Duchy of Normandy, tyl at the last he subdued the same with the prouinces of Guyen, Poytiers, and Britaine, whiche before pertayned to the crowne of Englande.

Kyng John saylyng into Normandy warred on the borders of France, but of his victories is litle written.

Anno. 5.

Walter Brown } Bailiffes. 1203
Willia̅ Chā̄berlain }

This yere by meanes of euyll wea-ther, in the yeare passed, wheate was solde for xx.s.a quarter, Dearth of wheate

Kyng John maried his bastarde dau-ghter to Lewlyn prince of wales, and gaue with her the castel and lordshyppe of Elyngsmore, being in the marches of Southwales.

The byshop of Rome wrate to kynge John, gentilly requirynge hym to ad-mytte Stephen Langton into the by-shopryke of Cantorbury, and the mon-kes by hym expelled frome theyr owne abbeye, to restore theym agayne to the same: but the more hys lordes aduised hym so to do, the more was hee bente to to the contrary. So that they retourned wythout obteynynge their request.

Thomas Haueril } { Anno Reg. 6 1204
Hamond Bronde } { Baylyffes.

The bishop of Rome denoūced king John with hys whole realme acursed because he woulde not admet Stephen Langton to thee bishopryke of Cantor-bury: but he litle regarded hys threat-nynges, and would not obbey hym Englonde interdited

At this time in Suffolke a fish was takē like to a man, & was kept lyuynge vi. monethes vpon the lande wyth rawe A mon-streus fi fleshe and fyshe: and after when they sawe they could haue no speche thereof they cast it agayne into the sea.

1205. John Walgraue } Anno re.7.
Richard Winchester } Bayliffes.

Kynge Philip of France subdued the countrey of Normādy, whych sens the tyme of Charles the simple (that is to say) the space of 300. yeres (was not in the possession of the kinges of France.

Normādye loste.

1206. John Holylande Anno re.8
Edmond fitz Gerrard Baliffs.

About this tyme the Irishemen and shortly after the Walshemen rebelled, for that he leuied on theym suche greuous taxes so that the kyng was faine to rayse a great taxe throughout Englande to wythstonde theyr force.

Wales and Ireland rebelled

He required of the white monkes sixe thousande marke: but they refused the payment of so greate a summe, so that the kyng toke great displeasure agaynst them: by reason whereof after hys return out of Ireland he exacted of them more then before he had desyred, whereby hee caused some abbottes to forsake theyr houses.

1207. Roger Winchester Anno Reg.9
Edmond Hardell Bailiffes

King

kyng John sayled into Normandye: wher after certayn skirmishes, he made peace wyth kynge Phylyp of Fraunce for ii. yeares.

This yere was graunted to the Citisens of London by the kynges Letters patentes, that they shoulde yearly chose to them selues, a Mayre and .ii. Sheriffes, on S. Mathewes or Mychelmas day, whose names were as foloweth

Fyrst maire of London

Anno Reg. 10

Hēry Fitz Alwyn	Maire	Peter duke Tho. Nele	S	1208

This yeare London bridge was begon to be buylded of stone: The origi-nall wherof, was as foloweth. Fyrste beyng no bridge but a ferry, the Ferry man and his wife deceasynge, lefte the same to theyr daughter, a mayden named Mary Audery: who wyth the goodes left to her by her parentes, buylded an house of systers, whiche is the vppermost end of S. Mary Auderis churche vnto the whiche house she gaue the ouersyght and profite of the same ferry but afterward the same house of sisters was conuerted vnto a colledge of priestes: who builded the bridge of tymber, and frome tyme to tyme kepte the

London bridge builded

 same

same in reparations: but consyderynge the great charges in repairyng ye same, in the yeare of oure Lorde .1209. by the great ayde of the citesens of Londen and other, they began to build the same of stone, and then the abouesaid college of priestes was conuerted unto a priorie of chanons, bearynge styll the name of the mayden, whiche kept the ferry: & so called S. Mary Auderie.

Anno. 11

1209 Henry fitz Alwyne } M { Peter le Iosue / Willm̃ Eloũd } S

The Englishemen whiche were sente by kyng John to ayde the erle of Flanders chased the frenchemen: and in the hauen of Sluce compassed and tooke theire whole nauy of ships, which was in number .1020, saile. Anno. 12

1210. Henry fitz Alwine } M { Adam Whetley / Stephẽ le grase } S

This yere Pandolphe legat cam fro the byshop of Rome mouyshyng ye king in sharpe maner yt he shold restore maister Stephen Langton to hys see of Cantorbury, and the monkis unto their abbey. The kinge swoin to ye sea of Rom The king callyng to mynde the daungers he was wrapped in, bothe in his owne realme, and also in Normandy

by

ly, made promise by othe, to be obedi=ent to the court of Rome,

Anno Reg. 13

Hēry fitz Alwyn	M	John fitz Pet John Garlonde	S	1213

STephen Langton archebyshoppe of Cantorburye wyth the other exiles landed in England: the kyng receyuing them ioyously, & was there assoyled of the sayd byshop: and after that, the king makyng restitution to the byshopp and other, accordyng to the thirde article of his othe, the lande was released of the interdiction: the kyng beyng bounden, that as well he as his heires shoulde euer after be feodars to the sea of Rome paying yerely tribute a thousand markes, and to holde the Title of the Crowne by the bishop of Rome.

Anno. 14.

Hēry fitz Alwyn	M	Radolph Eilād Constātin Iosue	S	1214

This yeare fell greate discention betwene the kyng and his lordes, partly for that he would not meynteyne the lawes of king Edward, partli for that he would haue exiled the Erle of Chester, who oftentimes had aduised the kynge to leaue his crueltes, and his accusto= Discentiō betwene ŷ kyng and his Lordes accustomed aduoutrye, whyche hee exercised with his brothers wife and others. But by meanes of the Archebyshop of Cantorbury, and other prelates, a peace was taken for a whyle.

The xi day of July, a great part of Southwarke and London was brente

Great fyre in Southwarke and London.

The kyng and his lordes mett wyth great strength on eyther partye vppon Baramdowne: where a charter or wrytyng was made and sealed by the kyng so that the barony was wyth it contented, and departed in peace euerye man to hys countrey

A Charter to the Barons.

Anno. 15

1215.

Roger fitz Aluyne	M	Martin fitz alis Peter Bate	S

The peace whyche in the laste yeare was agreed betwene kyng John & hys barons was thys yeare by the Kynge violated and broken. Wherfore the lordes assembled to theim great powers, and made cruell warre upon the kyng so that he was constrayned to sende intoo Normandye for ayde. Thenne camme into Englande, a Normane knight named Foukes de brente, whyche broughte wyth hym a companye of Normans, Flemmyngs and Picards. He and his cōpany were so cruell, that they destroyed as wel religious houses as other, and dyd muche harme to the lande, puttyng the lordes to the worse, the kynge made Foukes and other of his companye wardens of castels and stronge holdes in Englande. The lordes seynge the kynge, perseuer in his wronge, and that he woulde in no wyse be induced to hold his own grantes, but to do all thynges after ỹ pleasur and nothyng after lawe or iustice cast in their myndes how they myght bryng the realme in a better rule, and by one consent wrote to Philip kyng of Frãce that he would send som noble man into Englande, and they would yeld the land vnto hym.

Piers of Pomfret

This yere kynge John caused to be drawen and hanged att Warham, one Piers of Pomfrete, and his sonne, for speakyng of dyuers thynges agaynste the kyng

Anno. reg. 16.

Roger Fitz Alwyn	W	Salomõ basing Hugh basyng	S		1214.

Kyng John layinge siege to the castell of Rochester, wanne the same, and toke therin certayn gentylmẽ, and sent them to dyuers prysons, placinge strangers in the same Castell. The barons held them together at London, abiding the

K. John beseged ỹ castel of Rochester.

the commynge of Lewes sonne to the Frenche kyng, whiche landed in England wyth a great armye, and so came to Rochester, and wanne it with small payne: he caused all the straungers therein to be hanged: and after came to London, where certein alliances and couenants were established and concluded betwene the lordes and hym, and receiued of them homage. Then he with the Lordes departed frome London, and gatte the castell of Rigate, of Gilforde, and of Fernham, and frome thens to Winchester, wher the Citie was yelded wyth all other holdes in these parties: and thenne hee wyth the lordes came againe to London. At whose commyng the tower of London was delyuered they slewe all straungers that hadde ben placed by the kynge in any place. The kyng beynge thus ouerset wyth his lordes sent messengers to ye bishop of Rome, shewyng to hym the rebellion of his lordes, and how they labored his destruction. Wherfore the bishop of Rome wyth all haste sent a Legate into England, called Swalo: The whyche after his commyng, commaunded Lewes to returne into Fraunce, and la-

A legate frō Rome

[e]ndeuoured to the vttermoste of his power: [t]o appease the Kynge and hys baronye, [b]ut all his labour was in vayne

Anno regni.17

Williã Hardel } M { John Trauers Andrew Newlã } S 1215

This yeare Kyng John dyed of the Flixe at Newarke: hee was bowelled in the abbey of Croxton, and buried at Worceiter. in other writers it is said he was poisoned by a monke

He buylded the abbey of Bewley, in the new Forest, in recompence of the parysh Churches, which he there ouerturned, to enlarge the Forest, and an abbey of Blacke monkes in the citie of Winchester. He deceassed in the yere of our Lorde.1216. the xix. of October, when he had reigned.17.yeares.vi. moneths and 13 dayes.

Bewlaye abbey builded

Henry the thirde

Anno Regni.i

HEnrye the sonne of John, of thee age of nyne yeares, was proclaymed Kynge of Englande, who began hys reigne the.xix. day of October, in the yeare of 1216

our

oure Lorde. 1216. and deceased in the
yeare. 1272. the vi. day of Nouember.
So he reigned. lvi. yeres, and. xxviii.
days. The noble men wyth their retinue kept sharpe warre with Lewes the
Frenche kynges sonne, who by the couenants made before. wyth the English
men, claymed the crowne. But after
Crouned at Glocester. certayne skirmishes and batailes, Lewys began to desyre peace, whych was
concluded, and Henry was crowned
at Gloucester. Anno, 1

1216. Jacob Aldermā } M { Benet Couētrie / Wil. Blūtivers } S

Swale ye Legat accursed Lewis ye frē-
che kings sonne. He accursed Lewlyn
prince of wales, & interdicted hys lād.
At the last, Lewis toke a. M. marks
(or as som authors affirm. xv. M. markes) of money, & departed this realme.

Anno. 2.

Serle mercer } M { Tho. Bokerell / Rafe Holyland } S

1217. WHen the land was delyuered frō
straungers, enquisicions were
made to know what psons assisted Lewes against the kyng: of whych ye king
pardoned manye of the laye men: But
the spirituall men were put to such hei-
nes, that they were compelled to laye

al

that they had to pledg. And also to sue Rome to be assoyled

Raynolffe Erle of Chester, toke hys arney to the holy land,

Anno. 3.

erle Mercer } M { John Wayle Josenus Spicer } S 1218.

A parliamente was holden at London, by vertu wherof was graunted to the kyng. ii. s. of euery ploughe lande through England. ii. s. of euery ploughe lande.

And thys yere king Henry beganne to bylde the newe worke of the church of westmynster Westminster abbey,

Anno. 4.

erle Mercer } M { Rich. Wimbeldey John Wayle } S 1219.

Alexander kinge of Scottes maried lady Jane syster of kyng Henry.

This yeare was great harme doone in England by violence of whirlewinds and fiery dragons and spirits were sene flying in the ayre. Spirites & fiery dragōs

Proclamation was made that all straungers shoulde auoyde the realm excepte suche as camme wyth merchandise, and to make sale of them vnder the kynges saufe conduite, whyche was done to aduoyde Faukes de Brēt, and his complices, who kepte the castell

Hery crouned the secōnd tyme

The castls of Chartley Bestan, & the abbeye of Delacresse built

stell of Bedford agaynst the kyng.

This yere was kyng Henry secondly crowned at Westminster.

This yeare Rainolphe earle of Chester came out of the holy land into England, and began to buylde the castels of Chartley and of Beston, and after builde the abbey of Delacresse

Anno. 5

Serle } M { Richarde Renger } S
1220. mercer } { Josence le Josue }

This yeare was a counsell holden at Oxenford of the byshops of Englād wherein one was condemned, which taught that he was Jesus Christ, and to confirme the same: he shewed the tokēs or woundes in hys handes bodye and fete: Hee was therfore crucified on a Crosse at Alburbury, tyll he dyed

Anno. 6.

Serle } M { [illegible] d Ren } S
1221. mercer } { [illegible]osens Josue }

Execution

A conspiracy was made against king Henry by one Constantine in the citie of London: for the whiche hee was drawen hanged and quartered, the morow after our Lady day assumption. Whiche conspiracie so moued the kyng, that he was in mynde to haue cast downe the walles of the citie

Anno

Anno. 7.

Serle mercer } M { Richard Renger / Tho. Laubert } S — 1222

This yere John kynge of Hierusalem came into Englande, and required ayde of kyng Henry to wynne againe Hierusalem, but hee returned wyth small comfort

Anno. 8.

Rychard Renger } M { Williā Joyner / Tho. Lābert } S — 1223

Thys yeare the Lordes and gentylemen of Englande fyrste graunted too kyng Henry and his heires, the warde and mariage of theyr heyres, whyche was then by learned men, called the begynnyng of euyls

The fyrste graunt of wardes to the king

Anno. 9.

Richard Renger } M { John Trauers / Andrew Bokerel } S — 1224.

Richard the brother of kyng Henry ouercame thee Frenchemen, recouered Poytiers, and kepte the Gascoynes in due obedience.

Anno. 10

Rychard Runger } M { Roger duke / Martin fitz William } S — 1225

This

This yeare the pleas of the crowne were pleaded in the Tower of Lōdon.

Lewis kyng of Fraunce wan certain castels in the countrey of Poytiers: & shortely after spoyled the citie of Ancowe. Anno.11.

1226 Rychard Renger } M { Stephen Bokerell / Henry Cobhame } S

Shiriffewike of Lōdon & Middlesex

In this yere was graunted by king Henry to the Sheriffes of the Citie of London, the shiriffe weke of London & Midlesex for the sum of .CCC. pound by the yeare.

Free warreyn.

It was also granted to the citie free warren, that is to saye, free libertie to hunt a certain circuite about the citie.

Toll free.

It was also granted, that the citisens of Lōdon shold passe tole free throughout all England: and also graunted by the kyng, that all weeres in ye Thames shoulde bee plucked vp, and destroyed for euer,

Anno.12.

1227 Roger Duke } M { Stephē Bokerell / Henry Cobham } S

The cities liberties ratified.

The liberties of the Citie were this yeare confirmed, and to eche of the sheriffes was graunted to haue .ii. clerks and two officers, with oute any more.

Anno

Anno.13

Roger Duke } M { Walter Winchester / Robert fitz John } S 1228.

Kyng Henry sailed with an army in to Britayne agaynste Lewes kynge of France: where after spoyling the countreye, a peace was concluded betwene them

Anno.14

Roger Duke } M { Richard. Fitz William / John Wodborne } S 1229

This yere was ordeined by ye Maior and rulers of the Citie of London, that no sheriffe of the citie should continue lenger in office then one yere, because they shoulde not by longe continuance of office become couetous bribers.

No sheriffe in London past one yere

Anno.15

Roger Duke } M { Michael of Sainct Cleue / Walter Bufelde } S 1230.

This yere was muche harme doon in London by fyre whych began in the house of a wydowe named dame Jane Lambert

Great fire in London

Anno,16

Andrewe Bokerell } M { Henry Edmonson / Gerrarde Bate } S 1227

Variance grewe betwen kyng Henrye

Warre betwene the king & his lordes, — ry and his lordes, because he put from hys seruice Englishemen, and trusted straungers as wel in hys counsayle as other officers nere aboute hym.

Anno.17

1232	Andrew Bockerel	M	Symon Fitzmarer Roger Blunt.	S

S. Johns without Oxenford, begon — IN this yere the kyng began the foundation of the hospitall of sainte John wythout the east gate of Oxenforde. In whyche yeare also fell wonderfull foule wether wyth such thunder & lightning that the lyke had not ben sene. And ther folowed an earthquake, to the gret feare of the inhabitantes of Huntingdon, and there about.

Gret tempestes,

Anno.18

1233	Andrew Bokercell	M	Rafe Ashelwy John Norman	S

THis yere the kyng put from hym ye strangers, and restored the English men to their officers

The Jewes dwelling in Norwiche were accused for stealyng of a chylde, whom they purposed to haue crucified.

Fredrike the Emperour maried Isabel sister of the kyng of England

Anno.19

Anno.19.

Andrew Bokerel } M { Gerrard Batte / Robert Ardell } S. 1234

King Hēry maried Elianor daughter to the Earle of Prouance.

There appeared as it were hostes of men fyghtyng in the ayre.

The statute of Merton was fyrst enacted at the parliament of Merton. The statute of Merton

Anno.20.

Andrew Bokerel } M { Henry Cobbam / Jorden Couētry } S 1235

Quene Elianor founded the hospital of Saint Katherins besydes the tower of London for the reliefe of poore women. S. Katherines by the Tower built.

Anno.21.

Andrew Bokerel } M { John Thesalan / Gerard cordwaner } S 1236

Octobonea, a legat came into Englande takynge order for the churche But not all to the pleasure of the yong clergy. Wherfore as he one day passed thorow Oxeforde, the scholers sought occasion againste his seruantes, and fought with them, and slue one of the same, and put the legate in suche feare, that he for his safegard tooke the belfray of Osney, and there helde him tyll the kings officers commynge from Abingdon, deliuered hym, and conueied him to Wallingford.

Syr Symon Mountford maried the kinges syster, named Elianor, countesse of Pembroke. Anno.22.

1237 Richard Renger } M { John Withall / John Goodresse } S

King Henry like to haue bene slayne.

A clerk of Oxenford (or more verely a foule) counterfeting himselfe mad, enterprysed to haue slain king Henry in his chamber at Wodstocke: but he was taken and put to death at Couentry.

This yere was borne Edward the kinges sonne called Long shankes.

Anno.23.

1238 William Joynce } M { Reimund Bingley / Rafe Ashewy } S

This yeare on Candelmas daye the king created syr Simō de Mountford Erle of Leycester. Anno. 24.

1239 Gerard Batte } M { John Gysors / Michel Tony } S

The kinge subdued the Welshemen which oftentimes rebelled. An.25.

1140 Reymond Byngley. } M { Jhon Woile / Tho. Duresyne } S

The fyrste aldermen in London

This yere were aldermen fyrst chosen in London, which thē had the rule of the wardes o. the citie, but were euery yere chaunged, as ÿ sherifs are now.

Anno.26.

Reymond Bingley } M { John Fitz John / Rafe Ashewy } S 1242

KIng Henry sayled into Normandy with a faire cōpany, purposing to recouer Poyteirs, Guian, & other coūtreys: but after many bickerings, somwhat to the losse of Englishmen, he retreated a peace.

Anno. 27.

Rafe Ashewy } M { Hugh Blunt / Adam Basing } S [illegible]

THis yere the pleas of the crowne, were pleaded in the tower of Londō. And in this yere Griffeth whiche was sonne of Lewlyn, lately prince of Wales, entending to haue broken prison fel ouer the inner ward of the Tower of London, and brake his necke.

Griffith of wales brake his neck.

Anno. 28.

Michell Tony } M { Rafe Spicer / Nicolas Batte } S 124[illegible]

THis yere Michell Tony Maior, and Nicolas Batte Shiriffe were bothe conuict of periury, by the othe of all the Aldermen. Because Nicholas Batte had bene Shirife ouer one yere, and for the same they were both deposed, and other were in their places.

Anno. 29.

1244	John Gysors	W	Robert Cornhill / Adam Beawlay	S

Robert Grosthed bishop of Lincoln with other prelates cōplained to ẏ King, of the wast of the goods and patrimony of ẏ church, which daily was wasted by the aliant bishops, ⁊ clerks who shortly were auoided.

Anno.30.

1245	John Gysors	W	Symon fitz mary / Laurēce Frowike	S

The abbey of Hayles builded. This yere Richarde the Kinges brother builded the abbey of Hayles.

Anno.31.

1246	Piers Alleyn	W	John Wolle / Nicolas Batte	S

An earthequake. In this yere was a mighty erthquake in Englande, that the lyke, was not sene many yeres before.

The kinge seised the fraunchises of the citie of Londō. The kynge seised the fraunchise of the citie of London for a iudgement that was geuen by the Maior and aldermen against a wydowe, named Margaret Viel: but shortly the Maior and sheriffes were again restored to their offices: and this yere was a new coine, and the olde called in. Coyn chaunged.

Anno.32.

1247	Michel Tony	W	Nicolas Joy / Geffrey winton	S

This

This yeare the wharfe of Quene-hiue in London was taken to ferme by the Communaltie of London, to paye yerely fifty pound for the same.

Anno 33.

Roger Fitz Roger } M { Rafe Hardell / John Tolason } S 1248

This yere dyed Robert Grosthed a famous clerk and byshop of Lincoln, who compiled many famous bokes, whiche remayne to this daye in the latin and the frenche tongue: the names wherof are partly declared by mayster Bale in his boke of English writers.

Anno. 34.

John Norman } M { Humfrey Basse / Williā Fitz Ric. } S 1249

This yere was a great winde vpon the day of Simō and Jude, whiche did muche harme in many places of Englande. A greate winde.

Anno. 35.

Adam Basyng } M { Laurēce Frowike / Nicolas Batte } S 1250

The frier Augustins began to build or inhabite in wales, at Woodhous.

Kinge Henry maried his daughter Mary to Alexander king of Scots, & receiued of him homage for the realme of Scotlande.

Anno. 36.

1251 John Toleson } M { Williā Durham / Tho. Wimborn } S

The maior of London is sworne in theches quer.

This yere was graūted by the king, that wher before this time the citizens of London, did present theyr Maior before the kyng wheresoeuer he were, and so to be admitted, now he should come onely before the Barons of the eschequer, and they shoulde admitt him, and geue him his othe.

Anno. 37.

1252 Nicolas Batte } M { John Northāptō / Richard Picard } S

Many diuers drowned.

This yere in the moneth of January the sea rose in such height that it drowned many vilages & houses nere vnto it in diuers places of Englande. Also the Thames sprange so highe, that it drowned many houses about the water side. And this yere was graunted of the kynge that no citizen of London should paye scauage or tolle for any beastes by them brought as they before time had vsed.

Anno. 38.

1253 Ri. Hardel Dra. } M { Ro. Belington / Rafe Ashewy } S

The liberties of London seased.

The liberties of London were agayne seased by the meane of Rycharde Earle

Earle of Cornwalle, because the Maior was charged, that he loked not to the bakers for their syses of bred: so that the citie was forced to please the Earle with. 600. markes or they were restored againe.

Alphonce king of Castel gaue Elinor his daughter in mariage to prince Edward the sonne of king Henry, to whō his father gaue the princedome of Wales, and gouernance of Guian and Ireland, wherof beganne that the kings of Englande ordeined their eldest sonnes princes of Wales. Anno. 39.

The kings eldest sonne prince of Wales.

Richard Hardel draper } M { Stephen Oeste rgate / Hen. Walmode. } S 1254

The king againe seased the liberties of the citie for certain mony which the Quene claymed for her right of the citizēs, so that they gaue vnto his grace 400. marke, and then were restored to their liberties againe.

The liberties of London seased.

The. 22. day of Nouēber, wer brought to Westminster. 102. Jewes from Lincolne, which were accused for crucifyinge of a chylde, they were sent to the tower of London: of these. 2. were hanged, and the other remayned long in prison.

Execution of the Jewes.

Anno. 40.

1255 Rich. Hardell draper } W { Mat. Bokerel / John Mynor } S

This yere a peace was made betwen the citizens of London & the abbot of Waltham, who had ben long in controuersie for tol, that he demaunded of the citizens that came to Walthã faire: but at the last the citizens were set free and bound to no toll. Anno. 41.

1256 Richarde Hardell Draper } W { Rich. Ewyll / William Ashewy. } S

Maior Aldermen, & sherifs depriued.

Great variance was betwen ye king & the Londoners, in so muche yt the Maior & diuers aldermen & sheriffes, were depriued of their offices, and the gouernance of the citie cõmitted to certeine persons of the kings appointing.

The mad parliamẽt.

The kinge for so much as he had oftentimes promised the restitution of certayne ancient lawes, but neuer performed the same, the lordes murmuryng against him, to appeace their malice, he held a parliament at Oxforde, whiche was called the madde parliament, because many things were there enacted, which proued after to the confusion of the Realme: and death of manye noble men. In confirmation of these actes were

er chosen.xii.piers, who altered and Twelue
anged many thinges, greatlye to the piers.
scontenting of the kinges minde.

Anno.42.

ich. Har= } M { Th. fitz Rich. } S 1257
ll draper } { Ro. Cathelion }

This yere Hugh Bigot Justice, and
oger Turkeley, kept theyr courts in
e Guildhal of London, and punished Bakers on
e Bakers vpon the tombrell, where the tūbrell.
times passed they were punished on
e pillorye, and they dyd manye other
inges against the lawes of the citie.
Richarde the kings brother retour=
d out of Almain into England.

Anno.43.

hn Gisors } M { John Adrian } S 1258
perer } { Ro. Cornhell }

King Henry fearing some rebellion
his nobles, went into Fraunce, and
re concluded a peace: After whiche
ace finished, the kyng retourned.
A Jewe at Tewkesbury fell into a A Jewe
iue vpon the saturday, & would not drouned in
reuerēce of his Saboth day be pluc a priuie.
out. Richard of Clare earle of Glo
ter, hearing that the Jew did so gret
erence to his Saboth day, thought
would do as much to his holy day,
ich is sonday, and so kept him there
tyll

tyll mondaye, at which season he was found deade.

Anno. 44.

1259 Williã Fitz Richard } M { Adam brawn, Ri. Couentry } S

a folk mote at Poules crosse.

In this yere the king commaunded a general assembly or meting at Poules crosse, wher the king in proper person commaunded the Maior that the nexte day after he shoulde cause to be sworne before his Aldermen euery striplynge of .ij. yeres of age and vpwarde, to be true vnto the king & his heires kings of Englande: and that the gates of the citie shold be kept with harnessed men.

Othe to the king.

Anno. 45.

1260 Wil. Fitz Richard } M { Io. Northãptõ, Rich Pickard } S

Kyng Hẽry published at Poules cros the bishops of Rome absolutiõ for him and al his, that wer sworn to mainteyn the articles made in the parliament at Oxforde: for which cause the barons of Englãd begon to vtter their malice which they had long before conceiued against the kyng, and caused an insurrection that continued thre yeres. Richard erle of Glocester deceised, & Gilbert de Clare was Erle after him.

Anno

Anno.46.

.. Fitz / ..omas	M	Phi. walbroke / Rich. Tayler	S	1263

..his yere was so gret a frost ẏ men rode on hors back ouer the thames: ..e barons of Englande armed them ..inst their king, and all this yere ho..ed about Lōdō & other places they ..bed and spoyled aliens and certain ..ee persons, whom they knew to be ..inst their purpose: speciallye they ..o the Jewes in all places.

A gret frost
The barōs against the king.

Anno.47.

..omas / ..tz / ..omas	M	Ro. Mountpeler / Osbern Buc-kerell.	S	1262

..00. Jewes were slain by the citezēs ..Londō, because one Jew wold haue ..ced a christen man to haue paid more ..ii.d. for ẏ vsury of.xx.s. for a weke ..ugh le Spencer with the citezēs of ..ndon, spoyled & brent the manors of ..chard the kinges brother, which hi..erto had ben a great stay of the warres ..wen the king and his nobles.

Jewes slaine

..ere to Lewis in Sussex, king Hēry ..is barons fought a cruell battel, in ..ich the king himselfe with Richard .. brother: syr Ed. his son & other no.. .. men to the nūber of 25. wer taken:

A battell at Lewis.

and

and of the commons were slaine about 20000.

Anno. 48.

1263 Tho. Fitz Thomas } M { Tho. Ramford, Edward blune } S

Debate and variance fel betwene Symon Mountford erle of Leicester, and Gilbert de clare erle of Glocester, chief capitains of ye barons: which torned to theyr great euil. For prince Ed. beyng nowe at libertie, allied hym with the erle of Glocester, & gathering to him a gret power, warred so freshly vpō Simon of Leicester, that at the end he and Hugh spencer with many others of the nobles, were slaine in the battel at Euisham in Worcestershyre.

The battel of Euishā

A Parliament at wynchester

The same yere was holden a parliament at Wynchester, where all the statutes made before at Oxforde, were dissanulled & abrogate. And all writinges made for the confirmation of the same, cancelled.

Lōdō like to haue ben spoyled.

The citie of London was in greate daunger to haue bene destroyed by the kyng for greate displeasure that he had conceiued againste it, because of the forenamed commotion: he gaue vnto prince Edward, the Maior of London and. iiii. of the beste Aldermen with

thal theyr goodes & lands, and put
uers other of the moste welthy into
ers prisons.

Anno .46.

ho. Fitz } W { Peter Armiger } S
homas } { Greg. Rockesle } 1264

he kinge came to Westminster, and
ortly after he gaue vnto diuers of his
ushold seruants, vpon .60. housholders
s & houses within the citie, with all
ch landes & tenementes, goods & cat
ls as the sayd citizens had in any o-
er places of Englande, and then he
ade one Custos or Gardein of the ci-
e, syr Othon Constable of the tower.
nd after this, the kinge toke pledges
f the best mens sons of the citie, that
e peace should be surely kepte in the
me, the whiche were put in the tower
f London, and there kepte at the coste
f their parentes. And shortly after, by
reate laboure and suite made, all the
oresayd persons whiche shoulde be in
e keping of the bailife of the castel of
Windsor, eyght onely excepte, and all
e other londoners .31. in nūber, were
eliuered and came to London. Daylie
ite was made vnto the kinge, to haue
is grace and knowe what fine he
would haue of the citye for theyr trans-
gres-

The kinge gaue diuers citizens of Lōdon with all theyr landes and goodes to his household seruātes.

gressions, for the which the kyng asked xl. M. poundes, and stucke at. l. M. markes, but suche continuall laboure was made to ye king, that lastly it was agreed for. xx. M. markis, to be paid by the citie, for all transgressions by them done: certaine persons excepted, which the kyng had geuen his son, beynge in the tower of Windsor. Then for the leuying of this fine, were taxed as wel seruantes, couenaunte men, as house-holders. And many refused the liber-ties of the citie for to be quite of the charge.

Kenel-worth ca-stel besie-ged.

King Henry besieged the castell of Kenelworth, which Henry Hastinges defended against hym the space of halfe a yere. Anno. 50.

1265. William Fitz Richard. } M { T. de la Fourd / Gre. Rokesly } S

A Parlia-ment at Northamp ton.

The olde franchises and liberties of London with a new graunt for the shyrs of Myddelsex, wer confirmed by a parliament at Northampton. When also many noble men yt had taken part with the Barons, were disherited of their landes, and therfore fled to Ely and strengthened it in suche wyse that they helde it long after.

Anno. 51.

lleyn } M { John Adrian } S 1266
owch } { Lucas Batecote }

About the .li. yere, was made the sta-
utes of weightes & measure, that is to
ay, that .32. graynes of Whete dry and
ound & take in the middes of the eare
hold way a sterlig peny, & .xx. of those
es shold make an ounce, & .xii. ounces
hold make a poũd troy, and .8. pound
roy shold wey a gallon of wine, and .8
allõs of wine, shold make a bushel of
London, which is the .8. part of a quar
er. Also that three barley cornes drie &
ound, should make an inche, and .xij.
nches to a foote, and three foote to a
arde, and fyue yardes and a halfe to a
erch or pole, & xl. pole in lẽgth, & .iiii
n bred to make an acre of lãd, & thes
tandards of weight and mesures, were
onfirmed in the .xv. yere of Edwarde
the thirde. And also in the time of Hẽry the sixte, and Edwarde the fourth,
and lastly confirmed in the .xi. yere of
Henry the seuenth. Howe be it in the
yme of kyng Henry the sixt, it was ordeined that the same ounce shold be deuided into .xxx. parts called .xxx. pẽce:
and in kynge Edwarde the fourth hys
ime into .xl. partes, called xl. pence.
And in kyng Henry the eight his days
into

The statute for weightes and measures.

Alteration of coynes.

into.xlviij.partes, called.iij.S. viij.d. but the weyght of the ounce troy, and the measure of the foote, was ordeined euer to be at due stint.

Anno.52.

Alleyn } Souch } M { Thomas Basing / Rob. Cornhyll } S

1267 Gylbert de Clare Earle of Glocester with the exiled gentilmen and other nobles of Englande, rose againste the kyng, and held the citie of Londō, buildyng therein bulwarkes, and cast ditches and trenches in diuers places of the citie and Southwarke, and fortified it wonderously. The kyng lying at the abbey of Stratford, also assaulted the same citie, more then a moneth: but by diligent labour vpon his partie, and by the Legate and the kynge of Romains on ye other partie, Agreement was made betwene the kyng and him: In this meane time many robberies were done, wherfore foure ye bare cognisance of the Erle of Darby, were put in sackes, & cast in the Thames.

The kyng besieged London.

Foure persons cast in ye Thames

Anno.53.

1268. Aleyn } Souch } M { Willia de Durhā / Walter Haruy } S

Variāce fel betwene goldesmithes & taylers

taylers of London, which caused great ruffelynge in the citie, and many men to be slayne, For whyche ryot. xiii of the chief capitains were arreigned, cast & hanged. Alein Souch was discharged of his maioraltie by the king, and Stephen Edworth made constable of thee tower, & custos of the citie.

A great ryot in London.

Execution

The disherited gentylmen were this yere reconciled to the kinges fauoure. And the fiue citesens which had remaine [illegible]rysoners in the towre of Wyndsor [illegible]he whych the Kynge had geuen to hi[illegible] sonne Edward, when they had made the[illegible]r end wyth great summes of money were deliuered. Anno. 54.

The maier & iiii. aldermé released out of Windsor castell.

Thomas Fitz Thomas	M	Will. Hadstock / Anketill de Aluerne	S

1269

The riuer of thames was soo harde frosen from the feast of S. Andrewe to Candelmas, that men and beasts passed ouer on foote from Lambeth to Westminster. The marchandises was caried from Sandwiche, [illegible]nd other hauens vnto London by land.

A greate frost.

The citie of Lōdon with þ reuenues therof was geuen to prince Edwarde.

London geuen to prince Edward

Anno. 55.

John

1270 John Adrian vintener } M { Walter Potter / John Tailour } S

This yere the liberties of London were newly confirmed. And thys yeare the steple of Bowe churche in Cheape fell downe, and slue many people both men and women.

The steple of Bowe Churche broken downe.

Anno. 56

1271. Io. Adrian vintener } M { Greg. Rokesle / Henrye waleis } S

This yere deceased Richard king of Almayn and earle of Cornwal brother to the kynge and was buried at Hailes.

A ryotte in Norwiche

In June began a great ryot in ye citie of Norwich, where through the monasterie of ye Trinitie, was burned. And for that fact the kyng rode downe, and made enquiry for the chiefe doers therof: whereof xxx. yonge men were condemned, drawen hanged and brent.

Execution

Thys yere were diuers prodigies & strange tokens seene in diuers places of Englande.

Anno. 57.

1272. Sir walter harui } M { Richard Paris / John Bedill } S

In the beginning of this yere kynge Henry sickened: and he called before hym syr Gilbert Clare earle, of Glocester & caused hym to be newly sworn to kepe the peace of the lande, to thee behofe of

Edwarde

Edwarde his sonne, and then dyed the xvi day of November, in the yeare of our Lorde.1272. when he had reigned lvi.yeares and. xviii. dayes. Hee was buried at westminster upon the southe syde of Sainct Edwarde. Hee builded a great part of the same Churche.

Kynge Edwarde the Firste surnamed Longshanke

Anno Regni.

Edward the firste, after the conqueste, surnamed Longeshanke, began his Reigne over this realme of Englād the xvi. day of Novēber, in the yeare 1272. and deceased the. vii. daye of Julye, in the yeare .1307. So he reigned. xxxiiii. yeares .vii. monethes, and, xx, dayes

Anno.1

Syr Walter Harvy knyght	M	John Horne Walter Porter	S	1273.

IN the ende of this yere, the kyng returned into England. Ther was yet busynes about chosynge of the Maior

Stryfe for chosing the

Maior of London — for dyuers woulde haue made suche a Maior as they had lyked. But for that tyme they were disappointed: whyche in the yeare folowynge vpon the same day toke further effecte.

Anno. 2

1274 Henry Walleys } M { Nicholas Wynchester, Henry Couentrie } S

The kyng of Scotts dyd homage to kyng Edwarde for the kyngedome of Scotland

The kynge ordeyned certayne newe lawes for the wealthe of the Realme, emong the which was one. that bakers making bread lackyng weighte, assigned after the price of Corne, shold firste be punished by losse of their bread, and the seconde by enprisonment: and thirdlye by the correction of the pillorye. Myllers for stealynge of corne to bee chastised by the tumberyll, and nighte walkers to be punished in the Tonne in Cornhyll. And this to be put in execution, he gaue auctoritie to all maiors, bailiffes, & other officers through England, & specially to ye maior of Lōdon.

Anno. 3.

Gregory Rockesle } M } Lucas Batecourt Henrye Frowyke } S 1275

Kyng Edwarde buylded the castell of Flynte, and strengthened the castell of Rutlād, & other agaynst the welshmē. The castell of Flynte buylded

Anno, 4.

Gregorye Rockeslye } M { John Horne Rafe Blunte } S 1276

The statute of Mortmayn was enacted by kyng Edward. Aleenynge in Mortmayn.

Michell Tony was hanged, drawē, and quarted for treason.

Anno. 5

Gregory Rockesle } M { Rob, de Bracy Rafe Fenour } S 1277

Kynge Edwarde gaue vnto Dauyd brother to Lewlyn prince of Wales, the lordshyp of Frodesham.

Anno. 6

Gregory Rockesle } M { John Adrien Walter Lāgley } S 1278

Michelmas terme was this yere kept at Shrewsburye. Term kept Shrewsb

Anno. 7

Gregory Rockesle } M { Robert Basinge Wil. Merser } S 1279.

Reformation was made for clipping of the kynges coyne: for which offence 297. Jewes were put to execution. Execution of Jewes.

Black friers in London builte.

In thys yeare began the foundation of the Church of the friers preachers or blacke Friers by Ludgate, and also Castell Baynard.

The towne of Boston was greatly empaired wyth fyre.

Anno. 8.

1280 Gregorye Rokesley } M. { Thomas Boxe, Rafe Moore } S.

Halfpenyes & farthings

This yeare was fyrst coyned halfepens and farthinges of syluer: where before, other coynes of other mettall ran amonge the people to theyr greate losse and noyance

Anno. 9.

1281 Gregory Rockesley } M { Wil. Farringdō, Nicolas Wynchester } S

Rebellion in Wales.

Dauid the brother of Lewlyn prince of Wales, vnkyndly and traiterouslye moued his brother againste kynge Edwarde.

Anno. 10.

1282 Henry Waleys } M { Williā Mazerer, Nicholas Wynchester } S

Kyng Edward sente a companye of souldiors into Wales, vnder guyding of the Earles of Northumberlande & Surrey: of whiche company manye

were

were slayn, and syr Roger Clifford taken prisoner. The Welshemen subdued certayne castelles and holdes, and of some townes threwe down the walles.

Anno. 11.

Henry Waleys	M	Rafe Blunte / Haukyn Betuel	S	1286

Lewlyn prince of wales was slayn by syr Roger Mortymer: and his heade set vpon the Tower of London. Execution

William Marton Chancellor of England about thys tyme builded Mertō colledge in ẏ vniuersitie of Oxenford. Martō colledge builded

Anno. 12.

Henry Waleys	M	Jorden goodchepe / Martin Boxe	S	1284.

David the brother of Lewlyn prince of Wales was taken & beheaded

Prince Edward was borne in Wales, at the castell of Carnaruan, and a parliament was held at Shrewsbury. A parliament at Shrewsbury,

Laurence Ducket a citisen of London was found dead, and hanged within saint Mary Bow church of Chepe: for the whiche were condemned. viii. men, which were drawen and hanged, and one woman brent. Laurence Ducket hanged.

This yere the greate conduite standyng againste sainte Thomas of Acres in Chepe was first begon to bee made. Condite in Chepe builded.

Anno

Anno.13

1285 Gregory Rockesleye } M { Stephē Cornhil, Roberte Rockesley } S

Liberties of London seased.

This yeare the liberties of the Citie of London was agayne seysed into the kynges handes, and Stephē Sandwiche admitted for Custos, and the Maior discharged, for takynge brybes of the Bakers.

Anno.14

1286 Rafe Sādwich } M { Walter blūt, John Wade } S

Parliamēt at Glocest.

This yeare was enacted by ye kynge the Statutes called Additamēta Glocestrie

Anno.15.

1287 syr John Byrton } M { Thomas Crosse, Williā Hautein } S

A hot somer & gret cheape of corne

This yere the sommer was so excedyng hot, that many men died through the extremitie thereof. And yet wheat was so plentuous, that it was solde at London for, iii.s.iiij.d.a quarter

Anno.16

1288 Rafe sandwyche } M { Williā Herford, Tho. Staines } S

Greate haile fel in England, & after ensued

ensued so continual rain, that the yeare folowing, wheate was sold for .xvj.d a bushel: and so encreased yerely þ reigne of this Kyng and hys sonne, tyll it was lastly solde for xl.s.a quarter. Tempest

Anno.17

Rafe Sandwiche } M { William Betain / John of Cantorbury } S 1289

Execution

Rice ap Meridoke, a welsheman, rebelling agaynst Payn Tiptoft, warden of the countreye, was by the Earle of Cornwall in the kyngs absence, taken, drawē, hanged, & quartered at Yorke.

Anno.18

Rafe Sandwiche } M { Fulke of S, Edmonde, / Salomō Langford } S 1290,

This yeare Kyng Edwarde returned out of Fraunce and was honorably receaued of the citisens of London.

Anno, 19.

Rafe sandwich } M { Tho. Romaine / Williā de Lyre } S 1291,

Wolstaple at sādwich

This yeare the staple of woll was ordeyned to be kept at Sandwiche. And this yeare the Jewes were banyshed the land: for the whyche cause þ cōmons gaue to the King a fyftene.

Jewes banished.

Anno, 20

Rafe

1292 Rafe sandwiche } M { Rafe Blunt / Hamond Boxe } S

This yere died quene Elianor ye kinges wife, & was buried at westminster. This yere also died Elinour wyfe unto Henry the thirde, & mother to thys Edwarde, whose hearte was buried at the graye friers in London: and her body at Ambresbury, in the house of Nunnes

Quene Elinor deceased

Anno. 21.

1293 Rafe Sādwich } M { Henry Balle / Elis Russell } S

This yere, iii men had theyr ryghte handes smitten of in the Westchep for rescuynge a prisoner: arested by an officer of the Citie of London

Anno. 22

1294 Rafe Sandwiche } M { Roberte Rokesleye / Martin Aubreye } S

The, xviii. daye of Maye fell a wondrous snow, and therwith an exceding wynde. By violence whereof greate harme was doone in sundrye places of Englande, as overthrowynge houses and trees. &c.

Great tempest.

Anno. 23.

1295 Sir John Britton } M { Henry Boxe / Richarde Glou cester } S

Madock

Madocke wyth the Welshemen rebelled against the kyng, wherefore he in all haste made agaynst them, and ouercame them:

Thys yeare the Frenchemen arriued at douer, and spoyled the towne, and brente a parte of it, in which skirmishe was slayne one Thomas of Douer.

Douer spoiled by Frenchemen.

Anno. 24.

Syr John Bryton	M	John Dunstable Adam Harlyngbury	S	1296

John Baylel was by kyng Edward admitted to be kynge of Scotts, & hee for the same dyd his homage, & sware vnto hym fealtie.

Thys yeare was taken Madocke of Meredoke capitayne of the rebelles in Wales: hee was drawen and hanged at London.

Rebellion in Wales.

Anno. 15

Sir John Bryton	M	Thomas Sulli Adā de Fullam	S	1297.

John Baylell kyng of Scots cōtrary to his allegeance, by the settinge on of the Frenchmē, rebelled agayn king Edward, Wherfore kyng Edward hasted him thyther. He wan from hym the castels of Barwicke and Dunbarre,

Barwike wonne.

Hee

he slewe of the Scottes. xxv. M, and toke prisoner syr William Douglas & other noble men. Hee conquered also Edenbrough, where he found the regal ensignes of Scotlande: that is to witt, the Crowne, the Scepter and clothe of estate. Anno. 26

1298. Syr John Britton } M { John de stortforde William de Stortforde. } S

Certain persons brake vp ye Tonne in Cornehyl, and toke oute prisoners, that thither were cōmitted by syr John Britton: for the whyche .ix. of theym were greuously punyshed by longe imprisonemente, and great fines. The tunne aboue named is nowe the cundit in Cornhill

Liberties of London graunted. The kyng cōmyng agayn into England, and so to Winchester: the citisēs of London made suche labour that they obteyned their liberties that had in som part be kept from theim by the terme of xii. yeares or more Anno 27

1299 Henrye Walleis } M { Richard Reshā Thomas Sely } S

This yere the kyng made cruel war vpon the Scots, & had of them a greate victorie, and then yelded theym selues agayne to his grace and mercy.

Thys

This yere also the king called in certayn coynes of money called pollardes Crocardes and rosaries:

Anno.28

Elis Russell	W	John Armenter / Hery Fringrith	S	1300

Kinge Edwarde hearinge of the untruth and rebelliō of the Scottes, made his third voyage agaynst them, wherin he subdued a greate part of the land, and toke the castell of Estriuelyn wyth other, and made the lords sweare to him fealtie and homage

Anno.29

Elis Russell	W	Luke Hauerynge / Rich. Champeis	S	1302

This yeare the kyng gaue unto Edward hys son, the princedom of Wales and ioyned thereunto the dukedome of Cornwall, and the erledom of Chester.

Anno.30

John Blunt	W	Roberte Caller / Peter Bosham	S	1302.

This yeare the kynge helde a greate parliament at Cantorburye. Parliamēt at Cātorb.

Anno 31

John Blunte	W	Hughe Pourte / Symon Parys	S	1303

Thys yeare kyng Edward made greate warres in Scotland, where hee had many ny greate victories,

Anno.32

1304 John Blunt } M { William Combmartein, John.de Burforde } S

This yere the kyng caused greate inquerie to be made of ÿ behauior of his Justices throughout his realme, which was called Troyly Baston.

Anno.33

1305 John Blunt } M { Roger Paris, John Lincolne } S

William Wales which had done so many displeasures to kynge Edwarde in Scotland, was taken, drawen, hanged and quartred at London on Saint Bartholomewes eue, and his head sette on London bridge:

Execution at London.

And the nobles of Scotland in a parliamente at Westmynster voluntarilie swore to be true to the kyng of Englād and kepe the land of Scotlande to hys vse agaynst all persons.

Anno.34

1306 John Blunt } M { Raynold Doderel, William Carson } S

Roberte le bruse contrarye to hys oth assembled ÿ lordes of Scotlande & caused hym selfe to be crowned. When kynge Edward hearde of this treasone, he went into Scotlande, where he chased syr Roberte le Bruse, and al the power of Scotlande, and toke manye of the noble men prisoners.

Anno.35

John Blunt	M	Symon Belet Godfrey de la conduite	S	1307

The warres continuinge in Scotlande, the noble kyng Edwarde ended his lyfe, the seuenth day of July, in the yeare. 1307. when hee had reigned.34, yeres.7 monethes, and 21.dayes. Hee lyeth buried at westminster in the chapell of saynct Edwarde vpon the south syde in a playne tombe of marble at the head of his father.

Kyng Edwarde deceased

King Edward the secōd

Anno Regni.i

Edwarde the second, sonn of the fyrste Edward, and prince of wales borne at Carnaruan, began his reigne ouer ŷ realme of England, the.vii daye of July in the yere 1307

yere of our lorde.1307. who was deposed the.25. day of Januarye: and in the
yere.1326.so that he reigned, .9. yeres
He was fayre of bodye, but vnstedfast
of maners, and disposed to lightnes: he
refused the company of his lordes, and
men of honour: haunting ye company of
vile persons. He gaue him selfe to ouermuch
drinkinge, and lyghtly would disclose
thinges of great councell: Piers of Gaueston, Hugh Spencer, and others,
whose wanton counsel he folowynge
gaue hym selfe whollye to the appetite
and pleasure of the body, not regarding
to gouerne his common weale, by sad-
nes discretion, and iustice.

Anno.1

1307. Syr John Blunt } M { Nicolas Pigot, Michell Drury } S

Kyng Edwarde toke to wyfe, Isabel the daughter of Phillip king of Fraunce he gaue Piers of Gaueston, the earle-dome of Cornwal, and the lordeshyp of wallingforde, and was ruled al by his counsel

Anno.2.

1081. Nicolas Faringdon Goldsmith } M { William Basyng, John Butler } S

The king callyng to mynd the disple-
sure done vnto hym and hys familiar,

Piers

Piers Gauestō, by ye bishop of Chester commaunded him to the tower of London, where he was straightlye kepte many dayes after. But the lordes perceauing the king geuen all to wantonnesse, and that he was much prouoked thereunto by ye meanes of Piers Gaueston, caused the kyng to banish him the realme, into Ireland, where the kynge notwithstandynge comforted him wyth many riche giftes and made him chiefe ruler of that countrey.

Anno. 3.

Thomas Romayn } M { James of S. Ed. Roger Palmer } S 1309

The kinge and his lordes were at great strife for the banishmēt of Piers of Gaueston, in so much that the kinge woulde not be pleased vntill he were again restored.

This yere was the Isle of Rhodes recouered from the Turke, by the knightes of the order of saint John Baptist. the Rhodes wonne

This yere the crouched friers came first into England. Crouched friers.

Anno. 4.

Ry. Reffā Wint. } M { Simō Croppe Pet. Blacknay } S 1310

Piers of Gaueston more and more encreased; in so much that he had the cu-

stody of all the kynges iewels and tre=
sure of the which he tooke a table and a
payre of tressels of golde, and conueig=
hed them with other iewels out of the
lād. He also brought the kyng to many
folde vices: as adultery & suche other.
Wherefore the lordes againe banished
him out of Englande into Flaunders,
to the kinges great displeasure.

Anno. 21.

1311 John Gysours Peperer } M { Symon Mer=wood, Rich. Welforde } S

Piers of Gaueston, was againe by the king called out of Flanders, wherfore the lordes being confederate, besie=ged him in the castel of Scarborough, where they toke him, and brought him to Gauersyde besyde Warwicke, and smote of his heade. This yeare the kynges fyrst sonne, named Edwarde, was borne at Windsore.

Execution in Gauersyde.

Anno. 6.

1312 John Gysours Grocer } M { John Lam=byn, Adam Lutekyn } S

This yere was manye good lawes made in the parliamente at London, wherunto the kyng and his lords were sworne.

Anno. 7.

Nicolas

Nicolas Faringdon goldsmith } M { Adam Burden Hugh Baytō } S 1313

The Englishe men encountered with Robert le Bruse and his scottes, at Estriualen, where was foughte a strong battel. In the ende whereof, the Englishe men were discomfited and so egerly pursued by the scottes, that many of the noble men were slayne: as Gilbert de Clare Earle of Glocester, syr Robert Clyfforde, syr Edmonde of Maule, with other lordes and barons, to the nūber of .xlij. knightes, & .xxvij. barons, beside .xxij. men of name, whiche were taken prisoners, and .x. M. common souldiours slayne. After this tyme Robert le Bruse reigned as Kyng of Scotland. The battel at Estriualen.

Anno. 8.

John Gysors Grocer } M { Stephen of Abingdon Hamōd Chikwel } S 1314

A villayn called John Poydras, a tanners son of Excester, in diuers places of England, named himselfe the son of Edward the first, & said that by a false nourse he was stolne out of his cradel, & Edward that was now king put in his place, which was but a carters son A barkers son made clayme to the crowne

 but

but shortly after, he was conuict of his untrueth, and confessed, that he dyd it by the motiō of a familiar spirit, which he had in his house in likenes of a cat, whom he had serued .iii. yere, & he for his seruice was drawen and hanged at Northampton. Anno. 9.

1315 Steph̄ } W { Hamōdgoodchep } S
abingdō } { Wil. Reading }

The castel of Barwike was yelded up to the Scottes by the treason of Peter Spaldyng.

Two cardinalles beyng sente from Rome to conclude a peace betwene the king of England & the Scots: as they went through Yorkshiere, were robbed by two knightes called Gilbert Midleton, & Walter Selby, with .600. men, which had don many robberies in those partes, or they were taken, the two knightes were drawen & hanged at Londō. And the kinge recompensed the Cardinalles double so muche as they lost.

Notable theues in Friers apparell.

Shortly after syr Gosslen Deinuile and his brother Robert, with two hundred in habite of Friers, goynge about as outlawes, did many notable roberies, they robbed and spoyled the byshop of Durhams palaces, leauyng no thing in them but bare, walles, & such lyke robberies, for the which they wer after hanged at Yorke. Execution

Anno. 10.

John Wengraue	M	Wil. Caston Rafe Palmer	S	1316

The Scottes entred the borders of Northũberland and most cruelly robbed and spoyled the countrey, sparynge neither man, woman nor child.

To this mischief was ioyned so exceding dearth and scarsitie that wheate was sold for. iiii. mark the quarter: the cōmō peopie did eat hors flesh, & other vile beastes, & many died for hunger. Great famine

Anno. 11.

John Wengraue	M	Jon Prior Wil. Furner	S	1317

Kinge Edward layde siege to Barwike. But in the meane time the scots by an other way inuaded the borders of England, & wasted the countrey euen to Yorke, & slew a great nūber, specially of religious people: Wherfore it was called the white battel. King Edward was constrained to break vp his siege, & returne againe into England. The white battell.

Syr Hugh the Spencers, the father and the sonne were, of great power in Englād, and by the fauour of the king practised suche crueltie, and bare them selfe hautie, that no lorde in this lande durst contrary them in any thynge that they thought good: whereby they were greatly hated of the nobles.

Anno.12.

18 John Mõgraue } M { John Pouñtney, John Dalling } S

The Lords and nobles of England, detestynge the outragious pryde of the Spencers, in suche wyse conspired against them, that they caused the kinge halfe against his mind, to banish them the Realme.

Anno.13.

Hamond
19 Chikwel peperer } M { Symon Abingdon, John Preston } S

This yere king Edward contrary to the mind of his lords reuoked the Spencers from banishment, and set them in like authoritie as they before had bene, to the greate disturbance of the realme. and not long after pursued the barons and chased them frõ place to place: as fyrst at Ledes castell in Kent: after in the marches of Wales, where he tooke the Mortimers, and sent them to the Tower of London.

Anno.14.

Nichos

Nicholas Faringdon goldsmithe	W	Reynolde at cundet / Wil. Prodham	S	1320

This yere kyng Edwarde ouercam the barons in many battels and tooke many of them, whome he put to death in diuers parts of this realme, to the numbre of two and twentye noble mē. Master John Baldocke, a man of euil fame was made Chancelor of Englād, who extreemely pilled the commons of this realme: for the which he was wel rewarded after.

Great execution.

Anno. 15.

Hamond Chikwel Grocer	W	Richard Constantine / Rich. Hakeney	S	1321

This yere the sonne appeared to mens sight as red as bloud, and so continued the space of vi houres. The Irishemen by the ayde they had out of Englande, droue the Scottes out of theyr lande. At whiche time many noble men of Scotlande were slayne. Among whiche was Edwarde le Bruze the kinges brother.

The sunne appeared as bloud

Anno. 16.

Hamond Chikwel Grocer	W	John Grantham / Rich. of Ely	S	1322

W. iiii. King

King Edward with a great army entred Scotland: but with sicknes and other misfortunes that chanced among the soldiors, he within short space was forced to returne: wherof syr James Douglas, & the Scots hauing knowledge, pursued him in such wise, that they slew many english men, and had welnere taken the kyng at an abey called Beighland, frō the whiche he was forced to flee, and leaue his treasure behinde him.

Anno reg. 17.

1323	Nicolas Faringdon Goldsmith	W	Adam Salisbury Jo. of Oxford	S

Charles of France warred vpon the lands of king Edward in Gascoyne to Guien, and tooke there many townes and castels. Wherfore king Edwarde sent his wyfe Isabell to entreate wyth her brother Charles for peace, or (as Froisard saith) the Quene her selfe fleyng the tyranny & mischief of the spencers, fled with her yong son Edwarde into France, and was gently receiued of her brother, which made greate promise to ayde her againste the tyranny & iniury of the Spencers.

Anno. 18.

Hamond Chikwel Grocer } M { Benet of Fulham John Causton } S 1324

Quene Isabel by the ayde and helpe of syr John of Haynold with a smal company of Henowayes returned into England: to whome the nobles and the commons gatheringe in great number pursued the kinge, the Spencers, and other enemies so egerly, that shortlye after they toke them, and kept the king in prison at Kenilworthe.

King Edward taken prisoner.

And after at Barkley they toke maister Robert Baldock, the Chauncellor both ẏ Spẽcers, the father, and the sonne, the earle of Arundel, with divers other, & brought them to the toun of Hereford.

Robert baldocke, the spencers taken prisoners.

Anno 19.

Richard Betain Goldsmith } M { Gilbert Mordon John Cotton } S 1325

The morow after Simon and Jude, syr Hugh Spencer ẏ father was put to death at Bristowe, & on saint Hughes day folowing was syr Hugh his sonne drawen hanged & quartered at Hereford, & his head sent to London, & sette emong other upon the bridge. After Robert Baldock the Chancellor was sent to London to Newgate, where he died

Great execution.

miʃera-

miserably. The earle of Arundell was put to deth at Hereford: and kinge Edward was by parliament deposed frō his kingdom, when he had reigned .xix. yeres. syxe monthes & .xviij. dais, and not longe after was murthered by syr Roger Mortimer, and was buried at Glocester.

King Edward deposed.

Edwarde the third.

Anno Regni. i.

1328 

Dwarde the thirde after the deposing of his father was crowned king of England, he began his reigne ouer this realm the .xxv. day of January: in the yere of our lord .1326. and deceased the .21 day of June in the yere .1377. so he reigned .50. yere, and .5. monethes lacking 3. daies. In feates of armes he was very expert, as the noble enterprises by him atchieued, do well declare. Of his liberalitie & clemencie, he shewed many great examples. Briefly, in al princely

y vertues he was so excellẽt, that fewe
noble men before his time were to be
compared to him. At the beginninge
of his reigne he was chiefly ordred by
n Roger Mortimer and his mother
Isabell.

In this fyrst yere of his reigne he cō-
firmed the liberties of the citie of London, and ordeined, that the maior of the
city of London should syt in all places
of iudgemẽt within the liberties of the
same for chiefe Justice, the kinges person only excepted, and that every alderman that had ben maior sh[o]uld be iustice
of peace of al London and Middlesex:
and every Alderman that had not bene
maior should be iustice of peace within his owne warde. Divers other privi-
leges be graunted to their citie.

The liberties of London cōfirmed.

The king went towarde Scotland
having understandinge that the scottes
were entred into England, as farre as
Stanhop parke. He beset them rounde
about, hopynge to have broughte them
under his subiection. But when he
thought to be most sure of them by reason of some of his host, the scottes escaped cleane, & returned back into Scotland. About the. xxi. day of September
Edward ye second was murdered in the
castell

Edward ye second murdered.

castell of Barkley by syr Roger Mortimer, and was buried at Glocester.

Anno. 1.

1326	Richard Britayn, Goldsmeth	M	Ric. Roting Roger Chãcellor	S

The King maried the lady Philip the earles doughter of Henaude in the citie of Yorke.

A Parliament at Northampton.

The kinge helde his parliament at Northampton, wher through the counsaile of syr Roger Mortimer, & the old Quene his mother, he made with the scots an unprofitable and dishonorable peace: For why he restored to them all theyr writings, charters, and patentes whereby the kynges of Scotlande had bounde them selues to be tributarye to the crowne of Englande, with other like unprofitable conditions.

Anno. 2.

1327	Hamonde Chikwell Grocer	M	Henry Darcy John Hawden.	S

Dauid the yong prince of Scotland maried Jane, the syster of Kynge Edwarde, whome the scottes in dirision called Jane make peace. The scottes made many rymes againste thenglishmen, for the fond disguised apparell by them

em at that tyme worne, amongest the
hich this was one.

Long beardes hartlesse,
Paynted hoodes witlesse, Scottishe tauntes
Gay Cotes gracelesse,
Makes England thriftlesse.

Anno.3.

ohn rantham rocer	M	Simō Fraūces Henry Combmarten	S	1328

Edward erle of Kent, uncle to king
dward of England, beynge falselye
cused of treason, was by syr Roger Execution.
Mortimer put to death at Winchester.
Prince Edward was borne at Wod-
ock. The.xvii.of October, syr Roger
Mortemer was taken in Notingham
astell, and sent to the Tower of Lon-
on.

Anno.4.

ymonde walond	M	Richard Lazar Henry Gysors	S	1329

yr Roger Mortimer was accused for
uers points of treason, as þe he mur-
ered king Edward the second, & that
rough him the scots escaped at Stan
ope parke, for receiuynge summes of
oney of the Scottes: for which accu-
tions he was shortly after drawen Execution
d hanged at London.
Edward Baylel, the sonne of John
Baylel

Baylel late kinge of Scottes by lycense purchased of king Edward, entred into Scotland, clayming the crowne by the right of his father, where he vanquished the Scottes, and was crouned at Stone. Anno.5.

John } { Robert Ely }
1330 Pountney } M { Thomas whorwod } S
Draper. } { wod. }

Barwike wonne.

The king with a great army wente into Scotland, and at Halidō hil gaue the Scottes battaile, wherein he obteined a triumphant victory, and slew of them .viii. erles 900. knightes & of barons, and esquires .400. & .33000. cōmen souldiors: he wan Edenborowe, Barwike, and many other castels, and gaue the gouernance of Scotlande to Edward Baylel. Anno.6.

John } { Jon Mocking }
1331 Pountney } M { Andrew Au- } S
Draper } { bery }

The king of France sent .x. shyps toward Scotland, which were so wether driuen into Flaunders, that they were little worth after that time.

Anno. 7.

John } { Nicolas Wike }
1332 Preston } M { John Hus- } S
Draper } { bande. }

Kyng

Kyng Edwarde wente agayne into Scotlande, and layd siege to the castel [o]f Kylbridge: he wan it by strength, [s]et the countrey in quietnes, and came [b]ack to the castell of Tyne where short[l]y after Edward Baylel kyng of Scot[t]es, came and dyd[e] hym homage, and [s]ware unto hym fealtie.

Anno. 8.

[I]ohn [P]ountney [D]raper	M	John Hamond William Hansarde.	S	1333

Embassadors wer sent from Philip [d]e Waloys King of Fraunce, for to conclude upon certein articles of variãce [b]etwene their lord and the kyng of En[g]land, but it toke none effecte.

Anno. 9.

Reignold [a]t Cõduit [V]intner.	M	John Hyngston Walter Turke	S	1334

This yere kyng Edward sent ambas[s]ado[r]s into Fraunce, to cõclude a peace [w]hich likewise toke none effect.

Anno. 10.

[I]ohn [P]oũtney [D]raper	M	Walter mordon Richard Uptõ	S	1335

[T]his yere kyng Edward made claime

to the

to the crowne of France, and therfore proclaimed open warre betwene England and France.

Anno.xi.

1336 John Pountney draper } M { William Hakelsworth John Northhal } S

This yere the kyng considering the charge he had with warres in Scotlād and also that he intēded to haue against the Frenchmen, gathered togither treasure by diuers and sundry ways, wherof the maner is not expressed: but suche greate plentie came to his handes, that money was very scant throughout the whole Realme: by reason of whiche scarsnes, vitaile and other merchandise were exceding good cheape: for at London a quarter of wheate was solde for.ij.s. A fat oxe for.vj.s.viij.d. A fatte shepe for vj.d.and.viij.d.six pigeons for one peny, a fat goose for ij.d.a pyg for a peny: and so all other victuals after the rate.

Cheape of vitailes.

This yere appered a blasing sterre,

Anno.xij.

1337 Henry Darcy } M { Walter Neale Nicolas Crane } S

King Edward sent Embassadors beyond

yond the sea, to allie with hym the earle of Heynault, and other lordes, whiche obeye not the french kynge: of whō by the meanes of Jaques Dartuel he hadd great comfort bothe of the Flemmings & diuers lords & princes of those parts This yeare the kyng granted, that the officers of the Maior and Sheriffs of London should beare maces of syluer.

Anno.13.

Henry Darcy } M { Williā of Pomfret / Huge Marble } S 1338

Kyng Edwarde for establishement of amitie betwene hym and the Hollanders, Selanders, and Brabanders, sayled to Andwarpe where he concluded the matter with his aleances, & by the consent of ŷ emperor Lewys was proclained vicar generall of the empire.

In this mean time certain frenchmē had entred the hauē of Southhamton and robbed the towne, & brent a greate part therof, and vpon the sea they toke ii great ships, called the Edward, and the christopher. — Southāpton robbe

Anno.14.

Andrew Aubery grocer } M { William Thorney / Roger Frosham } S 1339

The Kynge helde a perliamente at Westminster; he demaunded thee fythe — Great subsidye.

M. [parte

part of euery mans goods. The custo-mes of the wolles to be paid. ii. yeares before hand: and the nynthe sheafe of e-uery mans corne.. Which was granted hym. But before it were all payde, the loue of the people dyd turne into hatred and their prayer into cursing. &c.

Coyn chan ged

The kyng changed his coyn, & made the noble, and half noble. The noble at vi. s. viii. d.

Armes of Englande and France enterined = led.

king Edward entred the borders of France, and made clayme to the whole realme of France, as his rightefull in-heritance: and for more auctoritie na-med hym selfe kynge of France, and en termedled the armes of Fraunce, as it remayneth to this day.

Anno. 15.

1340 Andrew Aubery grocer } M < Adam Lucas Bartholomew marys. } S

The quene of England wife to kyng Edward beinge at Gaunt, was deliue-red of a sonne, which afterwarde was called John of Gaunt, which was first earle of Richmounte, and after Duke of Lancaster

John of Gaunt.

Battayl on the sea

Kyng Edward saylyng into Flaun ders nye to the towne of Sluce mett wyth the Frenche kyngs nauye, wher was

was foughten a cruell battaill, Wherof the kyng of England had the victorye, and the Frenche flete that was in number. 400. sayle was welnere distroyed and the souldiors taken slayne & drouned, so that of. 33000 four escaped alive

After this victory kyng Edward beseiged Turney, and the towne of saint Omers. At the ende of xi. wekes after the siege, a peace was concluded for xii monethes and the kyng returned.

Anno. 16

John Oxenford vintener } M { Rich. barkinge / John Rockesley } S 1342

This yeare came into Englande. ii. cardinals to treat a peace betwene the kynges of Englande and of Fraunce, who concluded it for iii. yeares, but it lasted not so longe.

This yere the quene was deliuerred of a man child at Langley, who was named Edmund of Langley

Anno. 17.

Symond Francys mercer } M { John Lukyn / Rich. Kyllingbury } S 1343

This yere died John duke of britayn by reason of whose deathe war & strife grewe, and parts takeng by yͤ French kyng and kyng Edwarde.

Anno.18

John Hamond } M { John Sewarde, John Aylesham } S

1343. This yere yͤ king made a coin of fine gold, and named it the Florentine, yͭ is to say, the peny of yͤ valu of .vi. s. viii. d. yͤ halfpeny of the valu of .iii s. .iiii. d. & the farthing of the valu of .xx. d. which coyn was ordeined for hys warres in France, for the gold therof was not so fyne as was the noble before named

A newe coyne.

Anno.19

1344 John Hamōd } M { Geff. Wichingham, Thomas Legget } S

Thys yere yͤ king held a solemn feast at his castel of Windsor: where he deuised the Order of the garter, and stablished it as it is at this day. And then hee sayled into Sluce, & so into little Britain with a strōg army. He sent yͤ earle of Derby with a strōg army into Guyē for to ayde the earle of Northampton.

The order of knights of the garter.

Anno 20,

1345 Richard Lacer Mercer } M { Edmonde Heuenall, John Gloucester } S

kyng

king Edward made a greate preparation for the warres of fraunce: and Phillipp de Waloys kynge of Fraunce made as great preparatiō to defend hys land agaynst him Anno.21

Geffrey Wichinghā } M { John Croydon Wil. Clopton } S 1346.

Kynge Edward sailed into Normādy with.1100. sayle, wyth his son Prince Edwarde, they ouer rode spoiled & destroyed ye cōutrey before them vnto Paris: & gathered wōderful riches of pray which he sēt into Englād. Shortly after, he encoūtred ye French kyng nye the forest of Cresse, when he had not in his hoste the eight man in comparison of ye Frenche army, and obteyned of theym a triumphant victorie. Wher was slain the kynge of Boheme wyth tenne other great princes.80.baners.1200.knighttes, and .3000.common souldiors After this victory kyng Edwarde wente toward Caleys, and besieged it. In the meane whyle Dauid of Scotlād made warre vpon the borders of Englande: but the bishop of Yorke with other lordes gathered a great companye aswell spirituall as temporal, and nere vnto Durham did byd the kyng of Scottes battaile, where was fought a cruel and fierce batttaile. But in the end the victorye fell vnto the quenes syde, & there was taken thee kyng of Scottes, wyth

K. of scots taken. many of his greatest lordes, and there was slayne one an other aboue, 15000. souldiours. Anno.22

1347 Thomas Legget Tainner } W { Adam Bramsõ Richa. Basingstoke, } S

Caleys yelded. This, yere after kyng Edward had lien afore Calais a yere & more, it was yelded vp to hym, as yee maye reade in John Frosarde.

Anno.23

1348 John Lukyn fishmõger } W { Henrye Pycarde Symõ Dolell } S

Great plage In the ende of this yeare about August the pestilẽce began in dyuers places of England, and specially at London, and so continued tyll that tyme twelue moneth Anno.24

1349 Walter Tucke fyshmonger } W { AdameBury Rafe Lynne } S

Alteration coyne The king caused to be he coyned grotes and halfe grotes, the whych lacked of the weyght of his former coyn.ii. & vi.dc. of a pound troy, And about ỹ end

of

of August ceased the death in London, whych was so vehement and sharp, that over thre bodyes buryed in churches and churchyardes: monasteries, and o- ther accustomed buryng places, was buried in the Charter house yarde of London. l, M. persons.

Great pesti- lence

Anno. 25

Richarde Kyllyng burye	M	John Notte Wylliam Wo- cester	S	1350

This yeare kyng Edwarde hadde goodly victory uppon the sea agaynste the Constable of France, where he toke xxii. of their ships. Anno 26

Andrew Aubery grocer	M	John Wroth Gibbon Stain- drope	S	1352

This yere the castel of Guynes was yelden unto þ englyshmen, dwellinge in Calice, by treason of a Frenche man,

Also the englishmen beinge in Bri- tayn had a goodly victory over þ Frēch men wher they toke manye noble men prisoners. Anno. 27

Adam Francis mercer	M	John Peache John Stode- ney	S	1353

This sommer was so long dry, that it was called after, the dry sommer: for

Kein

Dry Sommer — from March till the latter end of July fell litle rain or none: by which reason corne that yere folowyng was scant,

Anno.28

1353 Adam Frances mercer } maior { John Welde, John Lytle } S

The duke of Brunswike made an appeale agaynst Henry duke of Lancaster: for whiche was waged battaile in the frenche kynges courte, and beynge bothe ready with in the lystes to fyght, the french king staied the matter, and toke the quarell into his hands, so that either of them departed the field without any stroke striken. Anno.29

1354 Thomas Legget Skinner } M { Williã Totingham, Richar. Smelt } S

Woll staples at Westmin. Chichester Lincolne, Bristow & Cãtorbury — For so much as the townes in Flãders brake their promyse before tyme made by Jaques Dartuel, and now fauored the frenche partie, kyng Edward remoued the market and staple of wol out of Flanders into Englande: as to westminster, chichester, Lincolne, Bristow & Cantorbury.

Freer Augustines — Also this yeare was the house of the Freers Augustins in London finished which was reedified by syr Humfreye Bo-

...ohune Erle of Herforde and Esser, ...hose bodye lieth buried in the quere ...the said hous before the high aulter.

London builded churche in

Anno.30

...imond ...rancis ...Percer	M	Tho. Forster Thomas Bran=don	S	1355

...dwarde prince of Wales, nie to the ...y of poitiers ioined battel with king ...hn of Fráce: of whõ þ prince by hys ...artial policy wan a noble victory not ...ith stãding þ he had in his army but ...oo. souldiors: & on the Frẽchpart wer ...ooo. fightig mẽ. In this cõflict king ...hn was takẽ with his yong son Phi... ...,and many of his nobles, & brought ...o England.

Anno.31

...enry ...icard ...ntener	M	Rich. Noting=ham Thoma Dosell	S	1356

...reat and royal iustes were holdẽ in ...ithfeld before the king of Englande ...Frẽch king being prisoner the king ...Scotts, and diuers other nobles.

Iustes in Smithfield

Anno 32

...hn ...ody ...ntener	M	Stephẽ Cādish Barthol. Frost lyng	S	1357

This yere Dauid le Bruze kinge of ...ots was set at libertie, when he had

put

put kynge Edwarde suretie of. 10000, marke for his ransome.

Anno.33

1358 John Lukyn fyshmonger } M { Joh. Barnes John Burys } S

The Englishemen in Britain toke the towne of Ancore, and diuers other, and put them to great raunsome

Anno.34

1359 Symon Dolel grocer } M { Simon Bedington John Chechester } S

A fynall peace was concluded betwene the kynges of Englande and of Fraunce, on this condition, that kynge Edward should haue to his possession, the countreis of Gascoyn and Guyen, Poetiers, Lymosyn, Balcuile, Xantes Calice, Guines, and diuers other lordshyps, castels, townes, and al the landes to them belonging, without knowledge of any soueraigntie or subiection for the same: and the Kyng of Fraunce should pay for his raunsome. 30000 crownes: and so kyng John returned into Fraunce

Anno.35

1360 John Wrothe fishmonger } M { John Denis Walter Burney } S

Kinge

Kyng Edward returned frō Caleys
o England, and broughte wyth hym
ny noble mē of Frāce for hostages.
ys yeare men and beastes perished
England in diuers pla ces, wyth
nder and lightenynges: and fiendes
e sene in mans lykenes & spake vnto
as they trauailed by ẏ way Anno 36

m ch mmonger	M	Williā Holbeche James Tame	S

1362

Thys yeare was great death and pestilence in Englād, whiche was called seconde mortalitie: in whyche dyed nry duke of Lancaster: & then was n of Gaunt the kyngs sonne which maried the dukes daughter, made e of Lancaster

The secōd pestilence.

Also there were sene this yeare in the e Castelles, and hoostes of menne htynge,

Anno.37.

ephen adishe	M	Jo. of S. Albons James Andrewes	S

1363

is yeare was a greate wind in England, wherwith manye steples & towe were ouerthrowen,

Great wynde.

nge John of Fraunce came into England, & shortly after died at ẏ Sauoy London. Also this yere was a greate froste

Great frost

frost in England, whiche lasted frome the myddest of September, to the moneth of Aprill

Anno 38

1363 John Notte peperer } M { Rychard Croydon John Hiltofte } S

Prince Edward sayled into Burdeaux, & receiued the possession of Guyen that kyng Edwarde, had newly gyuen unto hym

Anno 39

1364. Adam Burye Skinner } M { Symon Mordant Jo. of Motford } S

S. stephēs chapell.

This yere the kyng began the foundation of Saint Stephens Chapell at Westmynster, which was fynished by Richarde the second, & sonne of prince Edward

Anno.40

1365 Adam of Burye Skinner } M { John Bukilsworthe John Orelande } S

Adam of Bury was maior one parte of the yere, & John Lukayn ye residue.

This yeare the kyng commanded that Peter pence should no more be gathered nor payd to Rome

Anno

Anno.41.

lm ouertyn shmõger } M { John warde William Ditt man } S 1366

This yere was borne the second son [o]f prince Edward, named Richarde.

Anno 42

James Andrewe Draper } M { Rich. Torgold William Dack=man } S 1367

This yere appered a blasing starre. And the Earles of Armenak, of Brett, and of Perygort, with other nobles of the Duchye, of Guyan, appealed the Prince of Wales in the Frenche kings courte, that he had broken the peace, & wronged them, as in exacting of theym ouer great summes of money. &c But the French kyng deferred it for certayn causes

Blasynge sterre.

Anno, 43

Syman Mordon fishmõger } M { Adã Wimbing ham Rob, Girdler } S 1368

This yeare the Frenche kynge proceded in iudgemente vpon the appellation before made by the earle of Armanak, the lord of Brett, and earle of Perygort agaynst prince Edward. Wherevpon, discorde and variance began to

take

take place betwene the two kynges: & those lordes whiche before was sworne to kyng Edward, dyd nowe yelde dyuers townes of the countrey of Portiers vnto the French kynge.

Anno.44

1369 John Chichester goldsmyth } M { John Pyell Hughe Holbitch } S

Quenes colledge in Oxforde

This yeare dyed Quene Phylyppe wyfe to Edward the thirde, she builded the colledge in Oxford, called quenes colledge.

In this yere was the third mortality or pestilence, wherof died much people

Anno.45.

1379 John Bernes mercer } M { William Walworth Roberte Gayton } S

John Barnes maior of London, gaue a cheste with three locks, and a .1000 markes, to be lent to yonge men vppon sufficient gage, so that it passed not one 100.marks: and for the occupying therof, if he were lerned, to say Deprofundis for the soule of John Barnes: if he were not lerned, to saye Pater noster. But how soeuer the money was lent, at this day the chest standeth in the chamber of Londō, with out eyther money or pledges

ges for the same. Anno. 46.

John Barnes mercer	M	Robert Hatfielde, Adam Staple	S	1378

The erle of Pembroke, as he passed the sea to reskue the castell of Rochell, was encoûtred with a flete of Spaniardes, which kynge Henry of Castell had sent to ayde the Frenche kynge. Of these Spanyardes after cruel fight, the Erle was taken, and syr Guystarde de Angle, and other, to the number of. 160. persons, and the more parte of his men slayne and drowned.

Anno. 47.

John Pyel marchant	M	John Philpot Nicolas Brember	S	1372

John Duke of Lancaster, entred by Calays into France, & passed throughe out the realme, by Vermendoys and Châpayn, nigh to Burdeaux in Aquitayne without battaile.

Anno. 48

Adam of Burye Skinner	M	John Aubery John Fyshyed	S	1373

Dyuers entreaties of peace were made betwene the kyng of England, & Fraunce, by meane of the byshoppe of

Rome

Rome, but none was concluded.

Anno.49

1374 William Walworth fishmõger } W { Richard Liõs William Wodhouse } S

The entreatie of peace cõtinued, but not concluded, but for foure monethes at the moste: in which time of entreatie the Frenche Kyng wan many holdes, & townes of the Englishmen, as wel in Guyen as in Britayn, and in other places:

Anno.50.

1375 John Warde grocer } W { John Hadleye William Newe-port } S

Many wonderfull sycknesses fell among the people, aswel in Italy as in England, whereof there died an exceadyng great number.

Anno.51.

1376 Adam Staple Mercer } W { John Northampton Roberte Launde } S

Prince Edward departed out of this life, who was in his time the flower of chiualrie. Hee was buried at Cantorbury, and then kyng Edwarde created Richard son of prince Edwarde prince of Wales: and because the Kyng wared feble and sicklye, he betoke the rule of the

the land to syr John of Gaunt duke of Lancaster, who so continued durynge his fathers lyfe, who deceased at Richemond, the. xxi. day of June, in the yeare of our Lord 1377. When he had reigned. 50. yeres fyue monethes lackyng foure dayes, and was buried at Westminster. He buylded a house for students in Cambridge called ẏ kings halle, the abbey of our lady by ẏ tower of London, the house of fryers at Langley, and the nunnery of Dertforde. The kings haull in Cambridge new abbey by ẏ tower of London buylded.

He lefte behynde hym foure sonnes: Lionel duke of Clarēce, John of Gaūt, duke of Lancaster, Edmonde of Langley, duke of Yorke, and Thomas of Wodstocke, Earle of Cambridge.

Richarde the seconde

Anno regni. 1.

Ichard the seconde, son of Prince Edward of Wales, was ordeyned kyng of England, beynge as yet but eleuen yeares of age. He began his reigne the. xxi. 1377.

O.j. day

day of June, in the yeare of our Lorde 1377. and left the same the .xxix. daye of September. in the yeare. 1399. so he reigned. xxii. yeres. iij. monethes and eight dayes. In bountie and liberalitie he farre passed all his progenitoures: but he was ouermuche geuen to rest & quietnes, and loued litle dedes of armes, & marciall prowesse, and for that he was yonge, he was moste ruled by yong counsayle, and regarded nothing the aduertisementes of the sage & wise men of his Realme: for the chiefe about hym were of no wisedome nor estimation. Whiche thing tourned thys lande to great trouble, and himselfe in fine to extreme miserie. Of hym John Gower writeth these verses folowing.

Vox clamantis.

When this king first began to reigne,
the lawes neglected were:
Wherfore good fortune him forsoke
and thearth dyd quake for feare.
The people also whom he poulde,
against him did rebell,
The tyme doth yet bewayle the woes,
That Chronicles do of tell:
The foolishe councell of the lewde
and yong, he dyd receyue:
And graue aduice of aged heds:

he did

he dyd reiect and leaue.
And then for gredy thirst of coyne,
some subiectes he accusde:
To gayne their goodes into his hande
thus he the Realme abusde.

Anno regni. i.

Nicolas Brember grocer } M { Andrew pickmã, Nicolas Twyforde } S 1377

By the enticement of the Frenchmẽ, the Scots began to rebel, and a squire of theyrs, called Alexander Ramsey, with.xl.persons, in a nyght toke the castell of Barwike, whiche was rescued and recouered by therle of Northumberladde.

Barwyke taken.

Anno. 2.

John Philpot grocer } M { John Boseham, Thomas Cornewalis. } S 1368

This John Philpot gaue to the citie of London certain tenementes, for the whiche the Chamberlayne of Londõ, payeth yerely for euer, to.xiij.poore people of the same citie, euery of thẽ viii pence the weke, which is payd to them at the. iiij. quarter feastes of the yere.

Charitable dedes of John Philpot.

Anno. 3.

1379 John Hadley grocer } M { John Heylisdom, Wyllyam Barret } S

The Frenche men entred into the Thames and burnt diuers townes, & at the last came to Grauesende, where they spoyled the towne, and set it on fyre, and returned into Fraunce wyth muche riches. This yere was suche a pestilence in Englande that most people dyed. Also a parliament at Westminster, where was graunted, that all men and women, beynge of the age of xiiij. yeares or vpwarde, should pay to the King. iiij. d. by reason wherof great grudge and murmure grew among the commons: and this was graunted towardes the warres in Fraunce.

Newe colledges in Oxforde, & Winchester

About this time William Wicham bishop of Winchester buylded the new colledge in Oxford, and the new colledge in Winchester.

Anno. 4.

1380 William Walworth fishmõger } M { Walter ducket, Will. Knightlode } S

Tis yeare the makynge of gunnes was fyrst found in Almayne

Gunnes inuented.

By the meane of the paimẽt aboue named, this yere ẏ cõmons of this lande, specially

specially of Kent & Essex, sodeinly rebelled & assembled together vpō black Heath, to the number of. 60000. and aboue, whiche had to their captaines, Watte Tyler, Jacke Strawe, Jacke Shepard, Tom Myller, Hobbe Carter, and suche other: whiche were animated to this rebellion, by one John Wall or bal, a seditious prcher. They caused muche trouble and busynes in the realme: and chiefly about the citie of London, where they practised muche villany, and destroying many goodly places of the nobles, as the Sauoye, Saint Johns in Smithfield, & other. They let foorth al prisoners, and sette them at libertie: they spoyled all the bookes of lawe in the Innes of court, the Recordes of the Counters, and other prisons. They set the king forth of the tower of London, cōpelling him to graunt al bondmen fredome, & that he shold neuer demande tribute or taxe of his commons: and also required Jacke Straw, & Wat Tyler to be made dukes of Essex, and Kent, and gouernours of the kynges person from thens foorth, both in peace & warre: which thinges he granted, for he durst in no point deny thē. But William Walworth fishemonger

The Sauoy burnte and Saint Johns spoyled.

monger Maior of London beynge in Smithfielde, nere unto the kinges person, seynge him stande hoodlesse afore Jack straw, rebuked the said Straw of his great leudenes, and with a dagger slew him, & brought the kyng into the citie: Wherupō the rude company was dispersed, & fled as shepe, som one way and some an other. In memory of this dede, the city geueth the dagger in their shield of armes.

Jack straw slayne.

Why ỹ city of London geueth the Dagger.

Anno. 5.

1381 John Northāpton Draper } M { John Rote, John Hynde } S

This yere was a terrible earthquake throughout all England, which threw downe many castels, steples, houses, and trees.

An earthquake.

Anno. 6.

1382 John Northāpton Draper } M { Adā Baume, John Sely. } S

This yeare was a combat foughten at Westminster, betwene one Carton appellant, and syr John Ansley knight defendant, the knight was Victor and Carton was from that place drawen to Tyborn, and there hanged for his false accusation.

A combat

Anno. 7.

Nicolos

Nicolas Brember grocer — M — Simon Winchcombe, John Moore — S 1383

This yere was one Wall, or Ball taken at Couentre, by Robert Treusilian, and hanged at saint Albons, for that he was the animator of the rebels spoken of in the fourth yere of this kyngs reigne. Execution at S. Albons

Anno. 8

Nicolas Brembre grocer — M — Nicholas Exton, John Frenche — S 1384

The kyng went toward Scotland with a great army, but when he drewe nere the borders, suche means was sought that a peace was concluded.

Anno. 9.

Nicolas Brembre grocer — M — John Organ, John Churcheman — S 1385

Kyng Richard maried the daughter of Wenceslaus, emperour of Almayn.

Anno. 10.

Nicolas Exton fishmo̅ger. — M — William Stonden, Willia̅ More — S 1386.

The Erle of Arundel went into the Duchy of Guyan, for to strengthen suche souldiors as the kyng at that tyme had in those parties, or to scoure the sea of Rouers. The erle Keping his coursh encountred with a mighty flete of Flemyngs laden with Rochell wyne, and tooke them, & brought theim to dyuers portes of England: wherby wyne was sold for. xiij. s. iiij. d. and xx. s. a tonne, of the very choyse.

Anno. 11.

1387	Nicolas Exton fishmõger	M	Wylliam Venour Hugh Fostalfe	S

¶ Thomas of Wodstocke duke of Glocester, the erles of Arundel, Warwike, Darby, and Notingham, consyderinge how this lande was misgouerned, by a few persons about the kinge entendyng reformatiõ of the same, assembled at Radecocke bridge, where they toke their counsell, and raising a strong power, cam to London, where they caused the kyng to cal a parliament wherof hearyng Alexander Neuyll, archbyshop of Yorke, syr Lionel Vere, marques of Deuelen, & syr Michael de la Poole, Chãcellor & Erle of Suffolke fearing punishment, fled the lande and died in strange countreis. The kynge by consaile of the aboue named lordes during the parliament, caused to be taken sir Robert Tresilian, chief Justice

of En-of Englande, sir Nicholas Brembire, late Maior of Lōdon, sir John Salisbury knight of housholde, sir John Beauchampe steward of the kings house, sir Symon Burley, sir James Barnes and syr Roberte Belknappe knightes and a sergeant of armes, named John Uske, the whiche by authoritie of the sayd parliament, were conuict of treason, and put to death at the tower hil, & at Tyborn. And John Holt, John Locton, Richard Graye, Williā Burgth, and Robert Fulthorpe iustice, with the other foresayd lordes, which before had voided the lande, were exiled for euer. Execution

Anno. 12.

Sir Nico. Twyforde goldsmith	M	Tho. Austen Adam Catehyll	S	1388

This yere the kyng kept a great iustes in Smithfeld, whiche continued xxiiij. days. This yere on ý fifth day of August, was the battayle of Otterborn where syr Henry Percy slewe the erle Douglas of Scotlande, and after was taken prisoner. Iustes in smithfielde Battaile at Otterborn.

Anno. 13.

William Venour grocer	M	John Walcot John Loueney	S	1389

An esquire of Nauarre accused an A combat.

englishe esquiere called John Welsh of treason: for the triall wherof, a daye of fyght was taken, to be in the kinges palais at Westminster: where John Welshe was victor, and cõstrained the

Execution the other to yelde. He was despoyled of his armour, and drawen to Tyborne, and hanged.

Anno. 14.

1390	Adam Bauldwine goldsmith	M	John Francis Thomas Vicent	S

The duke of Lãcaster uncle to king Richard sailed with a company of souldiors into Spayn, to claim the realme of Castile: for so much as he had taken to wife the eldest daughter of kyng Peter, that was expelled his kingdom by Henry his bastard brother: he conquered the countrey of Galice, and made league with the king of Portugal: but by great mortalitie, which fell among his people: he was fayn to dismisse his army and shortly after loste all that euer he had wonne. Anno. 15.

1391	John Hynde Draper	M	John Chadworth Henry Wamer	S

A fraye in Fletestrete A bakers man bearynge a basket of horsebread in Fletestreet, one of the bishop

bishop of Salisburies men toke out a lofe, yͤ baker requiring his lofe, yͤ byshops man brake yͤ bakers head: wherupō folowed such parties taking, yͭ the Maior and sheriffes and all the quiete people of the citie coulde not order the vnrulynes of the multitude, but yͭ they wold haue him deliuered to them, who brake the bakers head, or els to breake open the gates of the saide bishops palaice, who was the kings highe treasorer: for the which the kyng seased the liberties of the citie, and discharged the Maior and Sheriffes of the rule of the Citie, and committed the gouernement therof to a knyght of the courte called syr Edward Dalingrige.

Anno.16.

William Stonden Grocer	M	Gilb. Mãfield, Thomas Newenton	S	1392

This yere by the great sute & laboure of doctor Grauesend then bishop of Lōdon, the liberties were shortly restored to the citizens of London.

The liberties of Lōdō restored

Anno.17.

John Hadley grocer	M	Drew Barentin, Richarde Whittington	S	1393

A truce prolonged betwene Fraunce

and

and Englande for thre yeares.

This yeare died Quene Anne, wyfe to kyng Richarde.

Anno.18.

1394 Jonh Frenche Mercer } M { William Bramton, Tho. Knolles } S

John Wikliffe. Aboute this tyme was Wikliffe famous in England.

Kyng Richarde made a voyage into Ireland, whiche was more chargeable thē honorable. And this yere was great tempest of wynd in England.

Anno. 19.

1395 William More vintener } M { Roger Elys, William Sheringham } S

A truce for.xxx.yeres was made betwene England and France: and kyng Richard toke to wife Isabel the daughter of Charles the Frenche kyng.

Anno.20.

1396 Adam Bame goldsmith } M { Thomas Wilforde, Will. Packer } S

The duke of Glocester king Richardes uncle with the erle of Arundel and other was put to cruell death: for so muche as they rebuked the kyng in certain matters ouer liberally. Execution

Anno,

Anno.21.

Richard Whittingtõ Mercer } M { Wil. Askham, John Woodcocke } S. 1397

This yeare deceased John of Gaūt duke of Lancaster: He was buried in Poules Churche, on the north syde of the quier.

The Duke of Herefor d and also the Duke of Norffolke were bothe banyshed the lande.

the duke of Herefor de banished.

Anno.22.

Drewe Barentine goldsmith } M { John Wade, John Warner } S 1398

Kinge Richarde lette the realme of Englande to Ferme, to syr Willyam Scrope Erle of Wyltshyre, and to .iij. knygtes, Bushye, Bagot and Grene. And then in Aprill he wente with an army into Irelande, leauynge for hys Lieutenaunt in Englande, syr Edmund of Langley his vncle, Duke of Yorke.

Englande let to ferme

Kynge Richard beynge occupied in Irelande, Henry Bolyngbroke, Duke of Herefor de, and of Lancaster: whiche was banyshed into France, beynge sente for of the Londoners, came into Englande with a small power, and

landed

landed in Holdernesse in Yorkeshire, to whome the Commons gathered in greate number: whereof Kynge Rychardе hearyng, about September hee returned and landynge at Mylforde hauen, he went to the castell of Flynte in Wales, where he rested hym entendynge to gather more strengthe: In the whych tyme, Henry Duke of Lancaster came vnto Bristowe, where he tooke syr William Scrope, Erle of Wylteshire, and Treasourer of Englande, syr John Bushy, and syr Henry Grene Syr John Bagot was there taken but he escaped and fledde the other thre were put to Execution. king Richard beyng in the castell of Flynte was taken: and by Henrye Duke of Lancaster, sente to the Tower of London: where shortly after hee yelded vp and resygned to the sayde Henrye, all hys power and Kyngely tytle to the Crowne of Englande and Fraunce, knowledgynge, that he worthily was deposed for his demerites and misgouernyng of the common weale.

Kyng Rycharde takē prisoner.

Kyng

¶ Kynge Henry the fourth.

Anno regni. 1.

Henry the fourth was ordeined kinge of Englande more by force, then by lawful succession or election: which thinge tourned him to much vnquietnesse, & caused often rebellion in this realme, he began his reigne ouer this realme, the. xxx. of Septẽber, in the yere of our Lord. 1399. and lefte the same the. xx. daye of Marche, in the yeare. 1412. So he reigned thirtene yeres. vi. monethes, lackyng. ix. dayes. 1399

Henry the sonne of Kynge Henry was chosen prince of Wales, and duke of Cornewall, Earle of Chester, and heire apparant to the Crowne: he deposed thre Dukes, that is to saye, of Albumarle, Excester, and Surrey, and the marques of Dorset.

Anno. 1.

Thomas Knolles Grocer	M	William Walderne William Hyde	S	1399

Syr

A consperacie against King Henrye.

Syr John Hollande duke of Excester brother to Kinge Richarde, the duke of Albumarle, ye duke of Surrey with the Erles of Salisbury & Gloucester, and other that fauored Richard of Burdeux, conspired against Kynge Henry, and appointed priuely to murder him at a feaste, whiche shoulde be holden at Windsore: but theyr treason

Execution

was disclosed, and they al put to death with as many knightes & esquires as were of that aliance and confederacie.

King Rychard murdered

Kyng Richard was put to death in Pomfret castel, by a knight called syr Piers of Exton, and after brought to the tower of London, & so through the citie to Poules barefaced, & ther stode iij. dayes for all beholders: and from thence to Lãgley, and ther buried in a house of Friers: but he was since remoued by Henry the. v. and lieth at Westminster. Upon the deathe of this king Richard, John Gower doth write as foloweth.

Vox clamantis.

O myrrour for the worlde mete,
Which shouldest in gold be bette,
By whiche all wise men, by forsight,
Theyr prudent wittes may whette:
Lo God doth hate suche rulers as

there

Here viciously do lyue
And none ought rule, that by theyr lyfe
Doo yll example gyue.
As this King Richard witnesseth wel
His ende thus playne doeth showe,
For God allotted him such ende
and sente hym so greate woo,
As suche a lyfe deserude as by
The chronicles thou mayst knowe.

Anno 2.

John Fraunceis Goldsmith	M	John Wakel William E-bot	S

Whyle the kyng was yet in Wales, certayne persons enuying that he had so shortelye obtayned and possessed the Realme, blased a broade amongeste the vulgare people, that kynge Richarde was yet liuing, and desyred ayde of the common people to reposesse his royal dignitie. And to ye furtherance of their inuention, they sette vpon the poastes, and caste about the stretes raylyng rimes agaynst kyng Henry. He beynge netled with those vncurteous prickes searched out the auctores and amongest other were found culpable, syr Roger Claryngdon knyght wyth two of his seruauntes, the Priour of Launde, and eyghte Freyers Mynours, or graye

Folers who were drawen, hanged an quartered at Tyborne

Execution

Owen Glendour of Wales rebelled and kyng Henry went thither with a strong armye, but they fledde to theyr mountaynes.

Rebellion in Wales

This yeare was greate scarsitie of wheate and other graine, so that wheat was sold at Lōdō, for, xvi.s, a quarter

Dearthe of corne

Anno.3.

1401 John Chadworth Mercer } M { Wil. Wenour, John Fremingham } v= n

This yere the condite standyng [v]pon Cornehill in London was bego[n] to be made (wher as before tyme it was a pryson for preestes called the Tonne in Cornehill.

Condite in Cornhill builded

A great battaile at Shrewesbury, began by sir Thomas Percy, erle of worcester, and other agaynste the kynge, where syr Thomas Percie was taken and beheaded, and syr Henry Percye slayn, wyth many other noble men.

Batayle at Shrewesburye

Execution

Anno.4

1402 John Walcot Draper { M { Richarde Marlowe, Robert Chichley } S

The Lorde of Casteill in Britayne landed

landed within a mile of Plymmouthe, with a greate company, hee lodged all nyght in Plimmouthe, and on the mo= row robbed and spoyled the town, and returned agayne to their shyps. Plimmoth spoyled

Anno.5.

William Askham fishmonger } M { Thomas Fauconer Tho. Poole } S 1403

The Britaynes and Frenchemen, which the yere before had spoyled and robbed the town of Plimmouth, were discomfited and slayne by the englishe men, in a battayle on the sea nere thee towne of Dartmouth.

This yere one William Serle was ta ken in the marches of Scotland, and brought to London and there hanged drawen and quartered for murdrynge the duke of Gloucester at Calice. Executis

Anno.6

John Hind Draper } M { Wil Lowsche Ste. Spelinā } S 1404

Syr Rychard Scrope then archby shop of York, and the Lord Mowbray then marshall of England with other, gathered greate strengthe to haue put down the kyng, but they wer taken at York, where they were bothe behaded Execution

Anno.7.

1405 Jo. wodcock Mercer } M { Hẽry Bartõ Wil. Cromer } S

Rochester bridg builded. This yere was the bridge and Chapel of Rochester finished by sir Robert Knols, who also new reedified the body of ye church of white friers stãding in Fletestrete, and there was buried: That Church was first founded by the auncestores of the Lord Gray Cotner.

Anno. 8

1406 Richard Whittingtõ Mercer } M { Nicolas Wotton Geff. Broke } S

Whittington college. Thys Richarde Whittington aboue named, builded in London Whittingtons colledge, A great parte of the hospitall of sainct Bartholomewes in weste Smithfielde: the librarye at the gray friers and a great part of the east end of the guyld hall.

Execution. This yere syr Henry Erle of Northumberland, and the lord of Bardolfe comming out of scotland: with a strõg company, were met & foughten with, and discomfited, and theyr heades were stryken of, and sent to London.

Anno,

Anno. 9,

William Standen Grocer } M { Henry Pomfret, Henry Halton } S 1407.

This yere was a great frost which began in December, and lasted fyftene wekes. Gret frost

Edmond Hollande Erle of Kent and admirall of the sea, scouring the sea landed in Britayn, and besieged the Castell of Briake and wan it: but he was ther wounded with an arrow, wherof he dyed.

Anno. 10

Drewe Barentine Goldsmith } M { Thomas duke, William Norton } S 1408.

This yere in Smithfielde was held a great Justes betwene the Henowayes and Englishemen, in the whiche were many feats of armes done. Gret iustes in Smithfield

Anno. 11.

Richarde Marlowe Ironmonger } M { John Lawe, William Chichley } S 1409

John Badley Taylour was brent in Smithfield for the Sacramente of the Aulter. Execution in Smithfield

This yere the market house called the

Lightning Source UK Ltd.
Milton Keynes UK
UKOW06f1908040913

216561UK00004B/67/P

9 781240 406364